AF395812

QUEEN VICTORIA'S
FAVOURITE GRANDDAUGHTER

Queen Victoria's Favourite Granddaughter: Princess Victoria of Hesse and by Rhine, The Most Consequential Royal You Never Knew

by
Ilana D. Miller

QUEEN VICTORIA'S FAVOURITE GRANDDAUGHTER

PRINCESS VICTORIA OF HESSE AND BY RHINE, THE MOST CONSEQUENTIAL ROYAL YOU NEVER KNEW

ILANA D MILLER

PEN & SWORD HISTORY

AN IMPRINT OF PEN & SWORD BOOKS LTD.
YORKSHIRE - PHILADELPHIA

First published in Great Britain in 2024 by
PEN AND SWORD HISTORY
An imprint of
Pen & Sword Books Ltd
Yorkshire – Philadelphia

Copyright © Ilana D Miller, 2024

ISBN 978 1 39906 626 6

Typeset in Times New Roman 10/12 by
SJmagic DESIGN SERVICES, India.
Printed and bound in the UK by CPI Group (UK) Ltd.

Pen & Sword Books Limited incorporates the imprints of Atlas, Archaeology,
Aviation, Discovery, Family History, Fiction, History, Maritime, Military,
Military Classics, Politics, Select, Transport, True Crime, Air World, Frontline
Publishing, Leo Cooper, Remember When, Seaforth Publishing, The Praetorian
Press, Wharncliffe Local History, Wharncliffe Transport, Wharncliffe True Crime
and White Owl.

For a complete list of Pen & Sword titles please contact
PEN & SWORD BOOKS LIMITED
George House, Units 12 & 13, Beevor Street, Off Pontefract Road,
Barnsley, South Yorkshire, S71 1HN, England
E-mail: enquiries@pen-and-sword.co.uk
Website: www.pen-and-sword.co.uk

or

PEN AND SWORD BOOKS
1950 Lawrence Rd, Havertown, PA 19083, USA
E-mail: uspen-and-sword@casematepublishers.com
Website: www.penandswordbooks.com

Contents

Acknowledgements

I would like to express my gratitude to:

The late HRH Queen Elizabeth II for her gracious permission to print quotes from the Royal Archives and specifically from the digitised Queen Victoria's Journals. For cheerfully checking citations, I would like to thank, Julie Crocker, the Senior Archivist at the Royal Archives.

The late HRH The Duke of Edinburgh for graciously taking the time to answer questions about his grandmother, Princess Victoria.

The Hartley Library Archive & Special Collection, University of Southampton for allowing to me to quote the Broadlands and Mountbatten archives.

The Hessisches Staatsarchiv for permission to use letters.

The Hemmelmark Archives, Alexander von Solodkoff as well as Duchess Donata and Duchess Edwina of Mecklenburg for permission to use letters from Princess Irène.

The Hoover Institute for their entire file about Princess Victoria's arrangements for Grand Duchess Elisabeth's burial in Jerusalem.

Professor Will Lee and David Chavchavadze, for providing unpublished materials from the Grand Duke Dmitri Archive.

Coryne Hall for using portions of the Grand Duchess Xenia archive.

Arturo Beèche for his help and giving permission to use the beautiful photographs, all from the Eurohistory Archive. For graciously reading the text and making crucial suggestions and additions. And, for always encouraging me to expand my royal history horizons. David Higdon-Beèche for reading parts of the text and making suggestions.

Charlotte Zeepvat for making the beautiful family trees.

Katrina Warne, John Van der Kiste, Greg King and the late Christopher Warwick for their generous and constant help and advice.

Acknowledgements

Sarah-Beth Watkins, Laura Hirst, and Karyn Burnham, for their help shepherding this work to completion and all their helpful comments and answers to questions.

Gentle readers: Mike Michelson and Tom Heller.

I also appreciate the kindness and companionship of my dear friends, Lisa Davidson, Liz Freedman, Jeri Gaile, Georgia Taylor Michelson, Tom Miller, Lisa Rosenstein Miller, Judy O'Brien, Charles Stewart, Lynn Superstein-Raber, Jane Tippett, and, never least, Stephen Fisch.

I remember with great love Soozi Parker Levin, always supportive and encouraging – will miss you always.

I also remember with great fondness the wonderful and always delightful Patricia Mountbatten.

Next, to my wonderful family Scott, Lisa, Spencer, Erika, Sydney, Zac, Becca, Aaron, Ana, Gabby, Jonah, Benjamin, Adam, Corey, Melissa, Charlotte, Augusta, Madeline, my very dear parents, Sherman and Gloria Miller,

… and, lastly, Tom.

List of Personages and their Relationship

TO **Princess Victoria of Hesse and by Rhine** *later* **Princess Louis Battenberg** *later* **the Marchioness of Milford Haven** *and lastly* **The Dowager Marchioness of Milford Haven (VMH)**

Albert, Prince of Saxe-Coburg & Gotha, Prince Consort. Married to Queen Victoria. VMH's maternal grandfather.

Albert Victor, Prince of Great Britain and Ireland, Duke of Clarence and Avondale (Eddy). Eldest son of Bertie and Alexandra, brother of George, Maud, Victoria, and Louise. VMH's first cousins.

Alexander III, Tsar of Russia. VMH's first cousin by marriage.

Alexander, Prince of Battenberg (Sandro). Prince of Bulgaria, Count Hartenau, Prince Louis of Battenberg's brother, and Moretta's erstwhile suitor. VMH's cousin and brother-in-law.

Alexander, Prince of Hesse and by Rhine, Prince Louis' father. VMH's father-in-law.

Alexandra (née Denmark), Queen of Great Britain and Ireland, Empress of India. Married to Bertie. VMH's aunt by marriage.

Alexandra Feodorovna, Tsarina of Russia (Alix). VMH's youngest sister.

Alfred, Prince of Great Britain and Ireland (Affie). Duke of Edinburgh, Duke of Saxe-Coburg & Gotha. Queen Victoria's second son, married to Marie Alexandrovna. VMH's maternal uncle.

Alice, Princess of Battenberg, Princess Andrew of Greece. VMH's daughter and mother of Prince Philip, the Duke of Edinburgh.

Alice, Princess of Great Britain and Ireland, Grand Duchess of Hesse and by Rhine. Queen Victoria's second daughter. VMH's mother.

Alice, Princess of Albany, Countess of Athlone. Leopold's daughter, Queen Victoria's granddaughter. VMH's first cousin.

Arthur, Duke of Connaught. Queen Victoria's third son, married to Louise of Prussia. VMH's maternal uncle.

Augusta Viktoria, Princess of Schleswig-Holstein-Sonderburg-Augustenburg (Dona) German Empress, Queen of Prussia. Wife of Kaiser Wilhelm II (Willy) German Emperor, King of Prussia. VMH's cousin by marriage.

Beatrice, Princess of Great Britain and Ireland, Princess Battenberg. Queen Victoria's youngest daughter. Married to Prince Henry (Liko) of Battenberg. VMH's maternal aunt and sister-in-law

Edward VII, King of Great Britain and Ireland, Emperor of India. (Bertie). Queen Victoria's eldest son. VMH's maternal uncle.

Elisabeth, Princess of Hesse and by Rhine (Ella). Married to Grand Duke Serge of Russia. VMH's younger sister.

Elisabeth (née Prussia), Princess of Hesse and by Rhine. VMH's paternal grandmother.

Ernst Ludwig, Grand Duke of Hesse and by Rhine (Ernie). Firstly married to Princess Victoria Melita of Edinburgh (Ducky), secondly to Eleonore of Solms-Hohensolms-Lich. VMH's brother.

George, Prince of Battenberg, 2nd Marquess of Milford Haven (Georgie). VMH's son.

George V, King of Great Britain and Ireland, Emperor of India. Married to Princess Victoria Mary of Teck (May). VMH's first cousin.

Heinrich, Prince of Prussia (Henry *or* Harry). Second son of Vicky, brother of Willy. VMH's brother-in-law.

Helena, Princess of England (Lenchen). Married to Prince Christian of Schleswig-Holstein-Sonderburg-Augustenburg, mother of Helena Victoria and Marie Louise. Queen Victoria's third daughter. VMH's maternal aunt.

Henry, Prince of Battenberg (Liko). Brother of Louis, married to Beatrice, Queen Victoria's son-in-law. VMH's cousin and brother-in-law.

Irène, Princess of Hesse and by Rhine. Married to Prince Heinrich of Prussia. VMH's younger sister.

Julie, Princess of Battenberg. Married to Prince Alexander of Hesse and by Rhine. VMH's mother-in-law.

Karl, Prince of Hesse and by Rhine. VMH's paternal grandfather.

Leopold, Prince of Great Britain and Ireland, Duke of Albany. Queen Victoria's fourth son, husband of Helena of Waldeck and Pyrmont. VMH's maternal uncle.

Louis, Prince of Battenberg, 1st Marquess of Milford Haven. Brother of Marie, Sandro, Liko, Franzjos. VMH's husband.

Louis, Prince of Battenberg, Lord Louis Mountbatten, and The Earl Mountbatten of Burma (Dickie). VMH's son.

Louise, Princess of Battenberg, later Lady Louise Mountbatten, later Queen of Sweden. Married to Gustav VI Adolf, King of Sweden. VMH's daughter.

Louise, Princess of Great Britain and Ireland, Marchioness of Lorne, Duchess of Argyll. Queen Victoria's fourth daughter. Married to the Marquess of Lorne, later the Duke of Argyll. VMH's maternal aunt.

Ludwig III, Grand Duke of Hesse and by Rhine. VMH's paternal great-uncle.

Ludwig IV, Grand Duke of Hesse and by Rhine. VMH's father.

Marie, Princess of Battenberg, Princess of Erbach-Schönberg. VMH's sister-in-law

Marie Alexandrovna, Grand Duchess of Russia, Duchess of Edinburgh, Duchess of Saxe-Coburg & Gotha. Married to Affie. VMH's aunt by marriage.

Marie, Queen of Romania (Missy). Daughter of Affie and Marie of Edinburgh. VMH's first cousin.

Nicholas II, Tsar of Russia (Nicky). Married to Alix of Hesse. VMH's brother-in-law.

Sergei Alexandrovich, Grand Duke of Russia (Serge). Husband of Ella of Hesse. VMH's brother-in-law.

Victoria, Princess Royal of Great Britain and Ireland, German Empress, Queen of Prussia (Vicky). Queen Victoria's eldest daughter. VMH's maternal aunt.

Victoria, Princess of Prussia (Moretta). Vicky's second daughter, engaged to Sandro, ultimately married Prince Adolph of Schaumberg-Lippe.

Victoria Melita, Princess of Great Britain and Ireland (Ducky), daughter of Affie and Marie. Married firstly to Ernie, secondly to Grand Duke Kyril of Russia. VMH's first cousin.

Wilhelm II, German Emperor, King of Prussia (Willy). Son of Vicky. VMH's first cousin.

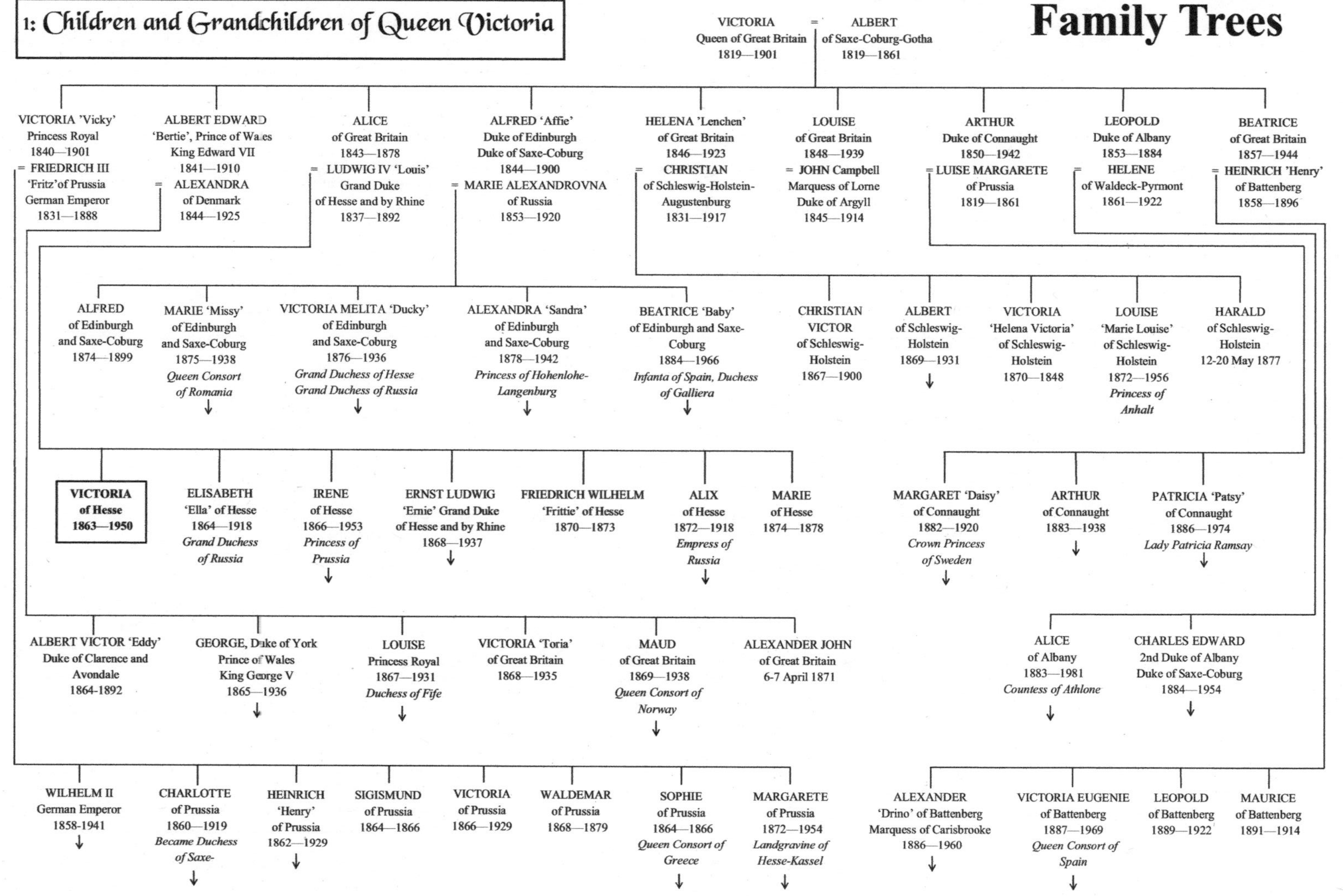

1: Children and Grandchildren of Queen Victoria

Family Trees

VICTORIA
Queen of Great Britain
1819—1901
=
ALBERT
of Saxe-Coburg-Gotha
1819—1861

VICTORIA 'Vicky'
Princess Royal
1840—1901
= FRIEDRICH III
'Fritz' of Prussia
German Emperor
1831—1888

ALBERT EDWARD
'Bertie', Prince of Wales
King Edward VII
1841—1910
= ALEXANDRA
of Denmark
1844—1925

ALICE
of Great Britain
1843—1878
= LUDWIG IV 'Louis'
Grand Duke
of Hesse and by Rhine
1837—1892

ALFRED 'Affie'
Duke of Edinburgh
Duke of Saxe-Coburg
1844—1900
= MARIE ALEXANDROVNA
of Russia
1853—1920

HELENA 'Lenchen'
of Great Britain
1846—1923
= CHRISTIAN
of Schleswig-Holstein-
Augustenburg
1831—1917

LOUISE
of Great Britain
1848—1939
= JOHN Campbell
Marquess of Lorne
Duke of Argyll
1845—1914

ARTHUR
Duke of Connaught
1850—1942
= LUISE MARGARETE
of Prussia
1819—1861

LEOPOLD
Duke of Albany
1853—1884
= HELENE
of Waldeck-Pyrmont
1861—1922

BEATRICE
of Great Britain
1857—1944
= HEINRICH 'Henry'
of Battenberg
1858—1896

ALFRED
of Edinburgh
and Saxe-Coburg
1874—1899

MARIE 'Missy'
of Edinburgh
and Saxe-Coburg
1875—1938
Queen Consort
of Romania

VICTORIA MELITA 'Ducky'
of Edinburgh
and Saxe-Coburg
1876—1936
Grand Duchess of Hesse
Grand Duchess of Russia

ALEXANDRA 'Sandra'
of Edinburgh
and Saxe-Coburg
1878—1942
Princess of Hohenlohe-
Langenburg

BEATRICE 'Baby'
of Edinburgh and Saxe-
Coburg
1884—1966
Infanta of Spain, Duchess
of Galliera

CHRISTIAN
VICTOR
of Schleswig-
Holstein
1867—1900

ALBERT
of Schleswig-
Holstein
1869—1931

VICTORIA
'Helena Victoria'
of Schleswig-
Holstein
1870—1848

LOUISE
'Marie Louise'
of Schleswig-
Holstein
1872—1956
Princess of
Anhalt

HARALD
of Schleswig-
Holstein
12-20 May 1877

VICTORIA
of Hesse
1863—1950

ELISABETH
'Ella' of Hesse
1864—1918
Grand Duchess
of Russia

IRENE
of Hesse
1866—1953
Princess of
Prussia

ERNST LUDWIG
'Ernie' Grand Duke
of Hesse and by Rhine
1868—1937

FRIEDRICH WILHELM
'Frittie' of Hesse
1870—1873

ALIX
of Hesse
1872—1918
Empress of
Russia

MARIE
of Hesse
1874—1878

MARGARET 'Daisy'
of Connaught
1882—1920
Crown Princess
of Sweden

ARTHUR
of Connaught
1883—1938

PATRICIA 'Patsy'
of Connaught
1886—1974
Lady Patricia Ramsay

ALBERT VICTOR 'Eddy'
Duke of Clarence and
Avondale
1864-1892

GEORGE, Duke of York
Prince of Wales
King George V
1865—1936

LOUISE
Princess Royal
1867—1931
Duchess of Fife

VICTORIA 'Toria'
of Great Britain
1868—1935

MAUD
of Great Britain
1869—1938
Queen Consort of
Norway

ALEXANDER JOHN
of Great Britain
6-7 April 1871

ALICE
of Albany
1883—1981
Countess of Athlone

CHARLES EDWARD
2nd Duke of Albany
Duke of Saxe-Coburg
1884—1954

WILHELM II
German Emperor
1858-1941

CHARLOTTE
of Prussia
1860—1919
Became Duchess
of Saxe-

HEINRICH
'Henry'
of Prussia
1862—1929

SIGISMUND
of Prussia
1864—1866

VICTORIA
of Prussia
1866—1929

WALDEMAR
of Prussia
1868—1879

SOPHIE
of Prussia
1864—1866
Queen Consort of
Greece

MARGARETE
of Prussia
1872—1954
Landgravine of
Hesse-Kassel

ALEXANDER
'Drino' of Battenberg
Marquess of Carisbrooke
1886—1960

VICTORIA EUGENIE
of Battenberg
1887—1969
Queen Consort of
Spain

LEOPOLD
of Battenberg
1889—1922

MAURICE
of Battenberg
1891—1914

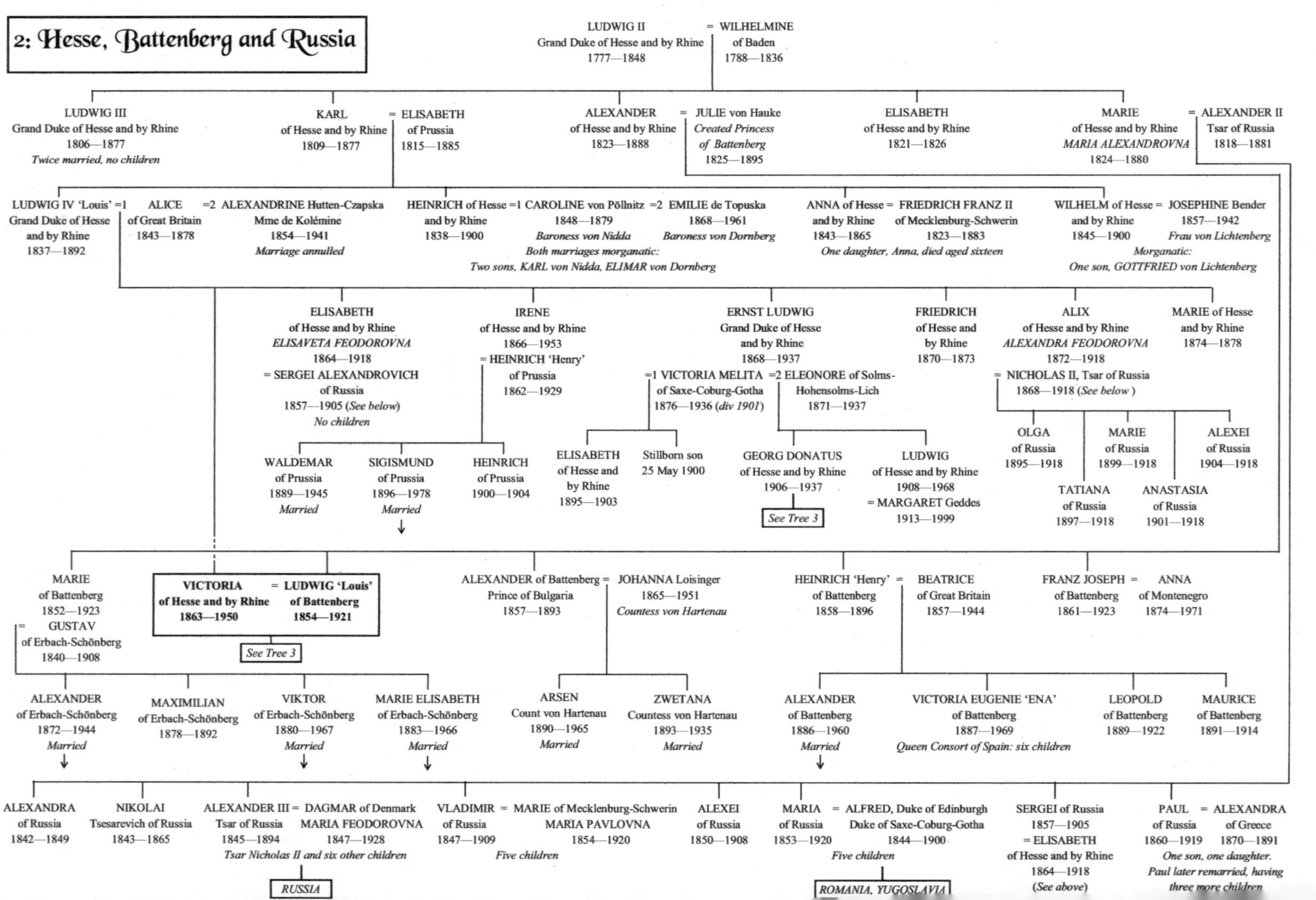

2: Hesse, Battenberg and Russia

LUDWIG II
Grand Duke of Hesse and by Rhine
1777—1848
= WILHELMINE
of Baden
1788—1836

LUDWIG III
Grand Duke of Hesse and by Rhine
1806—1877
Twice married, no children

KARL
of Hesse and by Rhine
1809—1877
= ELISABETH
of Prussia
1815—1885

ALEXANDER
of Hesse and by Rhine
1823—1888
= JULIE von Hauke
Created Princess
of Battenberg
1825—1895

ELISABETH
of Hesse and by Rhine
1821—1826

MARIE
of Hesse and by Rhine
MARIA ALEXANDROVNA
1824—1880
= ALEXANDER II
Tsar of Russia
1818—1881

LUDWIG IV 'Louis' =1
Grand Duke of Hesse
and by Rhine
1837—1892
ALICE
of Great Britain
1843—1878
=2 ALEXANDRINE Hutten-Czapska
Mme de Kolémine
1854—1941
Marriage annulled

HEINRICH of Hesse =1 CAROLINE von Pöllnitz =2 EMILIE de Topuska
and by Rhine
1838—1900
1848—1879
Baroness von Nidda
1868—1961
Baroness von Dornberg
Both marriages morganatic:
Two sons, KARL von Nidda, ELIMAR von Dornberg

ANNA of Hesse = FRIEDRICH FRANZ II
and by Rhine
1843—1865
of Mecklenburg-Schwerin
1823—1883
One daughter, Anna, died aged sixteen

WILHELM of Hesse = JOSEPHINE Bender
and by Rhine
1845—1900
1857—1942
Frau von Lichtenberg
Morganatic:
One son, GOTTFRIED von Lichtenberg

ELISABETH
of Hesse and by Rhine
ELISAVETA FEODOROVNA
1864—1918
= SERGEI ALEXANDROVICH
of Russia
1857—1905 (See below)
No children

IRENE
of Hesse and by Rhine
1866—1953
= HEINRICH 'Henry'
of Prussia
1862—1929

ERNST LUDWIG
Grand Duke of Hesse
and by Rhine
1868—1937
=1 VICTORIA MELITA
of Saxe-Coburg-Gotha
1876—1936 (div 1901)
=2 ELEONORE of Solms-
Hohensolms-Lich
1871—1937

FRIEDRICH
of Hesse and
by Rhine
1870—1873

ALIX
of Hesse and by Rhine
ALEXANDRA FEODOROVNA
1872—1918
= NICHOLAS II, Tsar of Russia
1868—1918 (See below)

MARIE of Hesse
and by Rhine
1874—1878

WALDEMAR
of Prussia
1889—1945
Married

SIGISMUND
of Prussia
1896—1978
Married

HEINRICH
of Prussia
1900—1904

ELISABETH
of Hesse and
by Rhine
1895—1903

Stillborn son
25 May 1900

GEORG DONATUS
of Hesse and by Rhine
1906—1937
See Tree 3

LUDWIG
of Hesse and by Rhine
1908—1968
= MARGARET Geddes
1913—1999

OLGA
of Russia
1895—1918

MARIE
of Russia
1899—1918

ALEXEI
of Russia
1904—1918

TATIANA
of Russia
1897—1918

ANASTASIA
of Russia
1901—1918

MARIE
of Battenberg
1852—1923
=
GUSTAV
of Erbach-Schönberg
1840—1908

VICTORIA
of Hesse and by Rhine
1863—1950
= LUDWIG 'Louis'
of Battenberg
1854—1921
See Tree 3

ALEXANDER of Battenberg =
Prince of Bulgaria
1857—1893
JOHANNA Loisinger
1865—1951
Countess von Hartenau

HEINRICH 'Henry' =
of Battenberg
1858—1896
BEATRICE
of Great Britain
1857—1944

FRANZ JOSEPH =
of Battenberg
1861—1923
ANNA
of Montenegro
1874—1971

ALEXANDER
of Erbach-Schönberg
1872—1944
Married

MAXIMILIAN
of Erbach-Schönberg
1878—1892

VIKTOR
of Erbach-Schönberg
1880—1967
Married

MARIE ELISABETH
of Erbach-Schönberg
1883—1966
Married

ARSEN
Count von Hartenau
1890—1965
Married

ZWETANA
Countess von Hartenau
1893—1935
Married

ALEXANDER
of Battenberg
1886—1960
Married

VICTORIA EUGENIE 'ENA'
of Battenberg
1887—1969
Queen Consort of Spain: six children

LEOPOLD
of Battenberg
1889—1922

MAURICE
of Battenberg
1891—1914

ALEXANDRA
of Russia
1842—1849

NIKOLAI
Tsesarevich of Russia
1843—1865

ALEXANDER III = DAGMAR of Denmark
Tsar of Russia
1845—1894
MARIA FEODOROVNA
1847—1928
Tsar Nicholas II and six other children
RUSSIA

VLADIMIR = MARIE of Mecklenburg-Schwerin
of Russia
1847—1909
MARIA PAVLOVNA
1854—1920
Five children

ALEXEI
of Russia
1850—1908

MARIA = ALFRED, Duke of Edinburgh
of Russia
1853—1920
Duke of Saxe-Coburg-Gotha
1844—1900
Five children
ROMANIA, YUGOSLAVIA

SERGEI of Russia
1857—1905
= ELISABETH
of Hesse and by Rhine
1864—1918
(See above)

PAUL = ALEXANDRA
of Russia
1860—1919
of Greece
1870—1891
One son, one daughter.
Paul later remarried, having
three more children

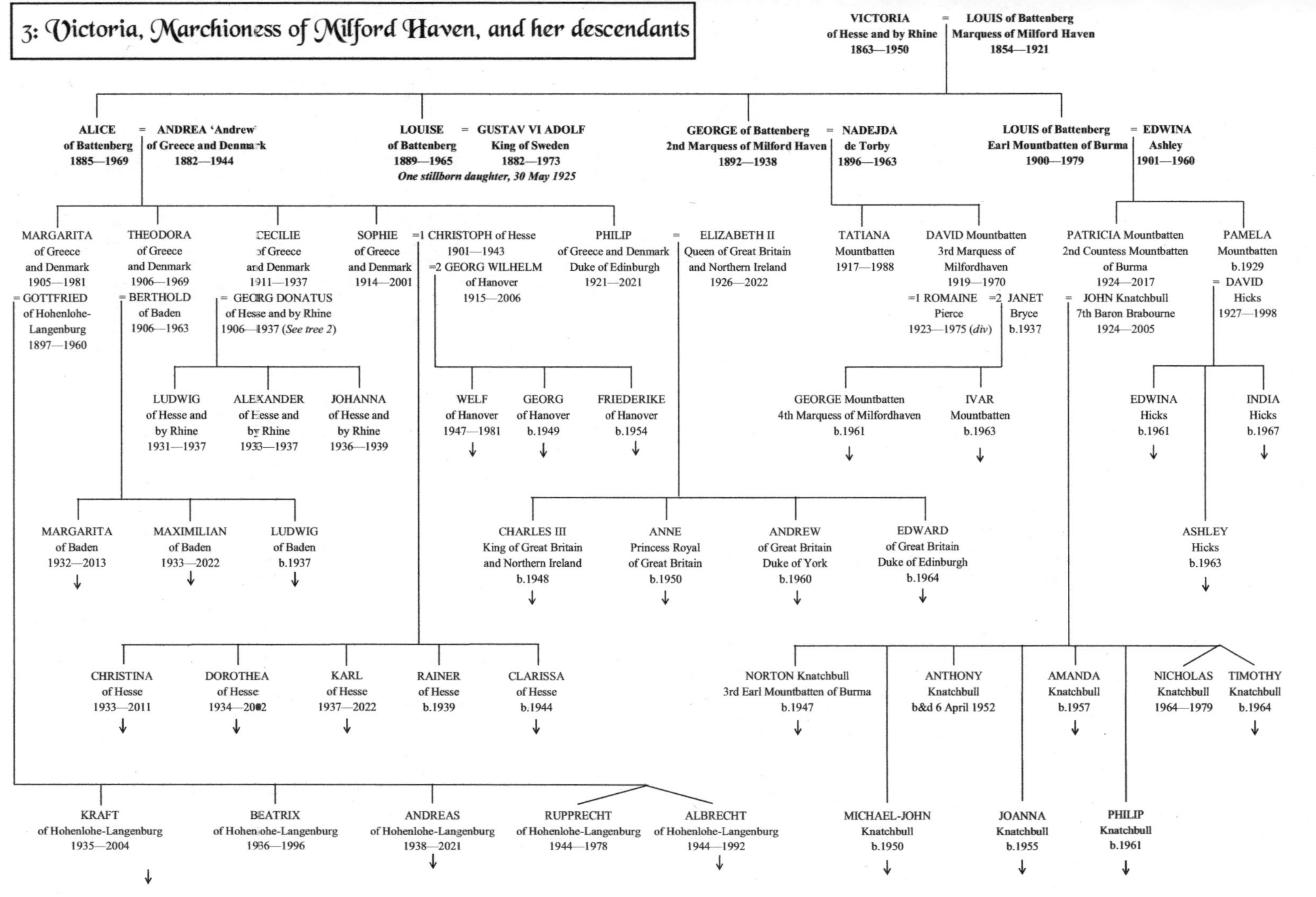

3: Victoria, Marchioness of Milford Haven, and her descendants

VICTORIA of Hesse and by Rhine 1863—1950 = LOUIS of Battenberg Marquess of Milford Haven 1854—1921

ALICE of Battenberg 1885—1969 = ANDREA 'Andrew' of Greece and Denmark 1882—1944

LOUISE of Battenberg 1889—1965 = GUSTAV VI ADOLF King of Sweden 1882—1973
One stillborn daughter, 30 May 1925

GEORGE of Battenberg 2nd Marquess of Milford Haven 1892—1938 = NADEJDA de Torby 1896—1963

LOUIS of Battenberg Earl Mountbatten of Burma 1900—1979 = EDWINA Ashley 1901—1960

MARGARITA of Greece and Denmark 1905—1981 = GOTTFRIED of Hohenlohe-Langenburg 1897—1960

THEODORA of Greece and Denmark 1906—1969 = BERTHOLD of Baden 1906—1963

CECILIE of Greece and Denmark 1911—1937 = GEORG DONATUS of Hesse and by Rhine 1906—1937 (See tree 2)

SOPHIE of Greece and Denmark 1914—2001 =1 CHRISTOPH of Hesse 1901—1943 =2 GEORG WILHELM of Hanover 1915—2006

PHILIP of Greece and Denmark Duke of Edinburgh 1921—2021 = ELIZABETH II Queen of Great Britain and Northern Ireland 1926—2022

TATIANA Mountbatten 1917—1988

DAVID Mountbatten 3rd Marquess of Milfordhaven 1919—1970 =1 ROMAINE Pierce 1923—1975 (div) =2 JANET Bryce b.1937

PATRICIA Mountbatten 2nd Countess Mountbatten of Burma 1924—2017 = JOHN Knatchbull 7th Baron Brabourne 1924—2005

PAMELA Mountbatten b.1929 = DAVID Hicks 1927—1998

LUDWIG of Hesse and by Rhine 1931—1937

ALEXANDER of Hesse and by Rhine 1933—1937

JOHANNA of Hesse and by Rhine 1936—1939

WELF of Hanover 1947—1981

GEORG of Hanover b.1949

FRIEDERIKE of Hanover b.1954

GEORGE Mountbatten 4th Marquess of Milfordhaven b.1961

IVAR Mountbatten b.1963

EDWINA Hicks b.1961

INDIA Hicks b.1967

MARGARITA of Baden 1932—2013

MAXIMILIAN of Baden 1933—2022

LUDWIG of Baden b.1937

CHARLES III King of Great Britain and Northern Ireland b.1948

ANNE Princess Royal of Great Britain b.1950

ANDREW of Great Britain Duke of York b.1960

EDWARD of Great Britain Duke of Edinburgh b.1964

ASHLEY Hicks b.1963

CHRISTINA of Hesse 1933—2011

DOROTHEA of Hesse 1934—2002

KARL of Hesse 1937—2022

RAINER of Hesse b.1939

CLARISSA of Hesse b.1944

NORTON Knatchbull 3rd Earl Mountbatten of Burma b.1947

ANTHONY Knatchbull b&d 6 April 1952

AMANDA Knatchbull b.1957

NICHOLAS Knatchbull 1964—1979

TIMOTHY Knatchbull b.1964

KRAFT of Hohenlohe-Langenburg 1935—2004

BEATRIX of Hohenlohe-Langenburg 1936—1996

ANDREAS of Hohenlohe-Langenburg 1938—2021

RUPPRECHT of Hohenlohe-Langenburg 1944—1978

ALBRECHT of Hohenlohe-Langenburg 1944—1992

MICHAEL-JOHN Knatchbull b.1950

JOANNA Knatchbull b.1955

PHILIP Knatchbull b.1961

Prologue

I discovered Princess Victoria quite by accident.

I was wandering around a used bookstore in Santa Monica and as usual I meandered into the British History Section. At that point, my interests were Queen Victoria and her large family, having been introduced to them by Elizabeth Longford's benchmark biography of the queen, *Born to Succeed*. As a graduate student I was given free rein to choose my books and I delved into the queen, her children, their spouses and ultimately her grandchildren.

In a dusty corner of this bookstore, I found a thin volume entitled *Advice to My Granddaughter*. This little book contained a selection of letters from Queen Victoria to her granddaughter and namesake, Princess Victoria of Hesse and by Rhine. On its cover was a smiling queen and her young granddaughter in her wedding finery. Intrigued, I opened to the photographs.

What fell open in the section was a photograph of an unusually attractive young couple, an older man, and a baby. The date was 1885 and the background was Osborne House on the Isle of Wight. The handsome young gentleman, like the older man, had the beard and moustaches that were so fashionable at the time. The young woman was sitting and looking at the camera as though she were about to speak or in the middle of a sentence. The young man is her husband, Prince Louis of Battenberg, and they are sitting with Victoria's father, the Grand Duke Ludwig IV of Hesse and by Rhine. The baby they are holding is the couple's first child, Princess Alice, the future mother of Prince Philip, the Duke of Edinburgh.

When I began to read the book, I learned that young Victoria was the eldest daughter of Queen Victoria's second daughter, Alice. I knew that Alice was the first of the queen's children to die. Her death occurred during an outbreak of diphtheria at her residence. She was in her mid-thirties at the time and left five young children, the eldest being Victoria, 15, and the youngest, Alix, 6. It was also here that I read that Alice's mother, the queen, took over the raising of the five grand ducal children with copious letters of advice and visits telling the Hessian children 'Think of me as your mama.'

Through years of research, I have gotten to know Princess Victoria and have come to admire and cherish a woman about whom I have only read. At a particularly young age, Princess Victoria carried the responsibilities of caring for her bereft family. It is through her intelligence, compassion, pragmatism, and tenacity that she brought her family through the tragedy of losing their mother. In the lament that many strong women of the time may have voiced, she was heard to remark that she should have been born a man.

It was Princess Victoria who would later hold her own husband and children together through the disasters that befell the Hesse family, the Romanovs, the Battenbergs and later the Mountbattens. Ultimately, it was she who had a major influence in shaping *her* son, Earl Mountbatten of Burma and her grandson, Prince Philip, the consort of Queen Elizabeth II.

The sense of duty and public service that infused the life of Queen Elizabeth II may have been inherited at least partly from many different sources. Its basis may not only come from her indomitable parents, George VI and his wife, Queen Elizabeth, but also from her grandmother, Queen Mary. It is my opinion that it may also have come from Queen Mary's dear friend, Elizabeth's first cousin twice removed. A cousin whom the queen respectfully called 'Aunt Victoria'. Certainly, that sense of duty was impressed firmly upon Prince Philip.

I have written extensively about Princess Victoria, in articles and books as well as spoken to several conferences about her. My book *The Four Graces: Queen Victoria's Hessian Granddaughters* had initially been conceived as a biography of Victoria but evolved into a biography of the four Hessian sisters: Alix (who became Empress Alexandra Feodorovna of Russia), Ella (who became Grand Duchess Serge of Russia), and Irène (who married Kaiser Wilhelm's brother, Prince Henry of Prussia).

But Victoria – what of her?

She married her first cousin once removed Prince Louis of Battenberg, a morganatic, or unequal, branch of the Hessian family, and lived, on first inspection, a private life. There were no grand marriages, no traumatic assassinations, no constant court life or even scandals. Instead, she was in many ways a simple naval wife. Prince Louis, who had been born in Graz, Austria became a naturalised British citizen at 13, and rose through the ranks of the Royal Navy. He became First Sea Lord in 1912 and to the undiscerning eye, it seemed that Princess Victoria was content to be a traditional helpmeet to her husband.

Closer examination, however, proves that Victoria was more than the sum of her parts. From a very early age she had been instructed by her mother to do public service, and she likewise imbued that quality in her own children and grandchildren. Hence, doing her duty to herself, her family and her country was something very strongly engrained in her character.

Though she did lead a private life, it was nevertheless a significant one. A life that I think should be illuminated as we begin to shed more light on the roles played by women of the past. Her life began as one of Queen Victoria's first lot of grandchildren in the 1860s and concluded just after the birth of Princess Anne, the current Princess Royal.

She witnessed first-hand the zenith and then the fall of many of the great dynasties of Europe. In between, her life sparkled with christenings, weddings, coronations and jubilees. In addition, she was one of the very close confidants of her grandmother, Queen Victoria – closer to her than many of the others in the queen's large and fascinating family.

The way that Victoria came to terms with what would be a tumultuous time in history both for herself and her family is a valuable as well as absorbing story. It is the way that one woman coped with grand tragedy on both a personal and a global scale. These large historical events shaped the woman. Her own development, helped by her mother, Alice, and her grandmother Queen Victoria, moulded her into a strong and steadfast character that was the bedrock of her family.

Her story draws to a close with:

The Lord Chamberlain is commanded by
Their Majesties
to invite The Dowager Marchioness of Milford Haven
to the Ceremony of the Marriage of
Her Royal Highness The Princess Elizabeth,
with
Lieutenant Philip Mountbatten, Royal Navy
. in Westminster Abbey,
on Thursday, 20th November, 1947, at 11.30 o'clock, a.m.[1]

But it begins in a small bedroom in Windsor Castle with a window that overlooks the beautiful Long Walk.

Chapter 1

The Useful Daughter

Queen Victoria didn't trust German doctors.

Look at what they had done to her first grandchild, Prince Wilhelm of Prussia (later Kaiser Wilhelm II). Because of an extremely complicated breech birth, Willy – as he was called in the family – would be forced to endure a withered left arm for his lifetime. It was perpetually shorter than his right arm and would be one of the sources of anger and resentment he harboured toward his mother, Princess Victoria Adelaide Mary Louisa of Great Britain (Vicky), later the German Empress, and *her* mother, Queen Victoria.

Indeed, if the queen had had her way, her two daughters, both married to German princes, would have come home to have their babies. Though that idea never sat well with either Vicky or the queen's second daughter Princess Alice, their mother got her wish on one occasion. Alice, at that time, Princess Ludwig of Hesse and by Rhine, was heavily pregnant with her first child. She and her husband, Prince Ludwig, were attending the wedding of her brother, Albert Edward, to Princess Alexandra of Denmark in March 1863. The queen saw with satisfaction that she could urge her daughter to stay in England for her confinement.

Princess Alice Maud Mary, Queen Victoria's third child and second daughter, was born 25 April 1843, at Buckingham Palace. As a child, she was considered extremely intelligent, and would later become an extremely spiritual, artistic, and liberal person. She had a great curiosity and a noteworthy sense of social justice – most unusual for royalty at that time. Had her older sister Vicky not been considered brilliant and highly talented, there is little doubt that Alice would have been the shining light of her family. However, instead, she grew up in the shadow of her elder sister. Eventually, she would have four sisters and four brothers.

Their education, contrary to the usual roles of the day, would be the province of their father, Prince Albert. It was he who would develop the curricula that their governesses and tutors would follow. As Alice matured, it was obvious she was more like her father in temperament – strong, gentle, yet soulful and introspective to the point of melancholy. However, she had a strong social conscience and wanted to be useful in her life, not just decorative. Having said that, she grew into an exceptionally attractive young woman.

As Alice's seventeenth birthday approached, the queen began to invite suitors to the palace. Among several others who were vetted, in the summer of 1860 Victoria invited princes Ludwig and Henry – the two sons of Prince Karl, the brother of the childless Grand Duke Ludwig III of Hesse and by Rhine – to Ascot. About six months later in late November, Ludwig was invited to Balmoral. The couple were conspicuously left alone on several occasions so they could have the required conversation and Ludwig could make the proposal that all expected.

Alice accepted him, on the condition that her parents approved. She whispered to her mother that Ludwig had made his proposal, and would it be all right with her parents? The queen said, 'Certainly', and that she would summon Ludwig in later. Afterward, Victoria repaired to her room to crochet in order to calm her nerves.

Though Alice's parents gave their consent to the match, the couple had to wait a year until Alice was 18. Queen Victoria liked her future son-in-law; he was, she thought, friendly, unassuming, 'honest, modest, warm-hearted, [and] high-principled....'[1] The queen believed her daughters should always be of use to her and had misgivings about any of them getting married. In this case, however, it was the wish of Prince Albert, and those wishes were sacred.

With Alice and Ludwig, the queen envisioned the young couple visiting England frequently during their marriage to be at her beck and call. They would have no significant duties in Darmstadt, the capital of Hesse and by Rhine, until Ludwig became the Grand Duke. That eventuality seemed far in the future with at least one heir in front of him. Victoria happily contemplated that her second daughter would have all her babies in her mother's house. Certainly, all the children would have British nurses and nannies.

Meanwhile, the year 1861 was a difficult one for the royal family. Queen Victoria's mother had died in March of that year and, consequently, she was in a state of emotional and mental paralysis. Some months before her mother's death, she had embraced mourning following the death of her brother-in-law Fürst Ernst of Hohenlohe-Langenburg. For the queen, death and loss were insurmountable. In her sorrow she took no account of the grief of those around her. Prince Albert took on more and more of the queen's responsibilities while Alice tried to care for her mother and bring her back to some form of normality.

Thereafter, Alice was a witness to her father working himself to death while her mother was busy seeing to the nation and meeting with prime ministers. As the year drew to a close, Prince Albert fell gravely ill. He was worn out with work, depression and in a weakened state of health. His despair in no small measure was affected by the news from Lisbon of the tragic deaths of several Coburg cousins, among them King Pedro V. It fell to Alice to nurse her father during this last illness and at that time she served as his confidante. Prince Albert died 14 December 1861 possibly of typhoid, or more modern theories speculate it might have been stomach cancer or even Crohn's Disease. The queen was led out of the room in hysterics.

Again it fell to Alice to be 'in charge' of the queen, and according to her sister, Helena, 'the gay, bright girl seemed all at once to have changed into the thoughtful woman'.[2] Alice moved into the bedroom next to the queen and for some time afterward took her mother's orders, 'carried messages between her and her ministers and altogether acted with great presence of mind, zeal and intelligence where all was consternation and confusion'.[3]

For a young woman of 18, Alice acted in a commendable manner, doing her best to lift the queen out of her grief, though she too was grieving. Eventually, Victoria began to recover and took charge of her household once again – but never as before.

First and foremost, Albert's wishes were paramount and one of the things he had most desired was for Alice's marriage. The queen felt that weddings were solemn occasions, and so had no problem with the wedding taking place during her mourning period. That didn't mean that the occasion should be joyous, with champagne corks popping, but it should take place nonetheless.

The wedding, which was private, was celebrated at Osborne on the Isle of Wight on 1 July 1862, with a relatively small group of guests in attendance. Unfortunately for the bride, the atmosphere couldn't have been more funereal. Alice's brothers, especially Alfred (known as Affie), and sisters were weeping – not for joy, but because their dear papa was not there. 'Her sorrowing mother'[4] the queen was sitting to one side, claiming to remain calm, while others saw her weeping copiously. She wrote:

> It was a terrible moment for me … The service then commenced, … Alice answered so distinctly and was fully of dignity and self-possession. L[udwig] also answered very distinctly. I restrained my tears, and had a great struggle all through.[5]

Alice, however, *was* calm and poised. Ludwig's Hessian family was present as well as the late Prince Albert's brother, Ernst II, Duke of Saxe-Coburg & Gotha, who gave the bride away, and Queen Victoria's elder half-sister, Fürstin Feodora of Hohenlohe-Langenburg. The couple spent their honeymoon in St Clare, Springvale near Ryde, on the Isle of Wight.

A day later, her mother praised her in a letter to Vicky, who was unable to attend: 'What I shall not forget is Alice herself, and her wonderful bearing – such calmness, self-possession and dignity, and how really beautiful she looked, so tall, and graceful, and her voice so sweet.'[6]

Alice, however, was cleverly able to obviate her mother's feelings that she was joyful. The young woman was acutely aware of her mother's sadness. Alice, while happy at least at the onset of her marriage, was careful not to let the queen see that she was 'too happy'.[7] Instead, she concealed much from Victoria throughout the ordeal of her father's death and the continuous mourning. This would be a source of contention for the two women; however, it was the best way for them to conduct a modestly cordial relationship.

The happy couple left for their home in Hesse on 9 July 1862.

The Grand Duchy of Hesse and by Rhine was in western Germany. A sizeable German state, Hesse is nestled snuggly in the Rhine River valley, dotted with charming and picturesque hamlets, villages and towns, as well as castles and palaces.[8] It was considered the oldest ruling Protestant Dynasty in the world and boasted Charlemagne as one of its ancestors. It was then tied to the Holy Roman Empire until the empire was broken up.

Hesse and by Rhine was one of several branches of the House of Hesse that were divided under Philip the Magnanimous about 1565. He had four sons and divided their legacy in four sections: Hesse-Rheinfels, Hesse-Marburg, Hesse-Cassel and Hesse-Darmstadt. Much later, having thrown their lot in with Napoleon in 1806, Hesse-Darmstadt became a Grand Duchy, and Landgraf Ludwig X became Grand Duke Ludwig I of Hesse and by Rhine. By 1870, Hesse and by Rhine would be absorbed into what would become the Second German Reich.

While this may not immediately seem germane to the tale, another bit of Hessian history must now be added.

Ludwig II, son of Grand Duke Ludwig I, married Princess Wilhelmine of Baden in 1804. The couple were not particularly happy, but nevertheless, Wilhelmine did her duty and produced 'an heir and a spare' for Ludwig and then the two mutually agreed to live in separate establishments.

Grand Duchess Wilhelmine had two surviving children while living separately from her husband. She had her own establishment, and figuring prominently at this small court was the young and attractive Swiss Baron, August Senarclens de Grancy, who had initially entered the service of Ludwig II. His official position was equerry to the Grand Duchess, and they lived together in a charming house, Heiligenberg, near Darmstadt and above a little village called Jugenheim.

The results of their 'companionship' were Prince Alexander and Princess Marie. The Hereditary Prince Ludwig, however, 'did not raise a whisper in protest and recognised them all as his own'.[9] Clearly, they were not. As Prince Alexander's daughter-in-law, Princess Victoria would write later about his murky parentage, 'honi soit qui mal y pense!'[10]

Later, when the Tsarevich Alexander of Russia was looking for a bride, he looked no further than Hesse – and Marie, the ostensive daughter of Wilhelmine and Ludwig II. The couple were married in 1841 and would later become Tsar Alexander II of Russia and Tsarina Maria Feodorovna. The question of the bride's parentage raised no rumours in the Russian court, because the Romanovs had their own skeletons.

When his sister married, Marie's brother Alexander – who had to make his way in the world – thought that it would be an excellent opportunity for him too. The handsome young man became quite a favourite in the Russian court. While there, Alexander searched for a bride, and proposed to several aristocratic ladies, including the daughter of Tsar Nicholas I. Though unsucessful there, he next set his sights on the Russian aristocrat, Countess Sophie Shuvaloff. She toyed with him, and they passed letters back and forth with the help of Sophie's confidant, Countess Julie von Hauke. Sophie's parents, however, quickly put a stop to it.

Alexander then fell in love with the go-between, Countess Julie. Throughout the time that she was sending messages back and forth between Alexander and Sophie, she had been 'filled with a consuming passion for him[,]' and made herself available.[11] This was not considered a good match for the brother of the Tsarina. Falling in love, however, had very little to do with future pedigree or solvency, and the ensuing pregnancy settled the matter – the couple eloped. They eventually settled in Hesse and their home, Heiligenberg, where Alexander's mother had lived for so many years.

Julie, who made it her business to be understated and likeable, was granted the title of Countess of Battenberg, and later Princess of Battenberg, by Alexander's eldest brother, the now Ludwig III of Hesse and by Rhine. Their children were Marie, Louis, Alexander, Henry and Francis Joseph. This family soon became a great favourite of Queen Victoria who especially liked Princess Julie because of her self-effacement and unobtrusiveness. Less well known, however, was that Julie was fiercely protective of her brood and had an iron will.

Meanwhile, Ludwig II was succeeded in 1848 by his genial and odd son, Ludwig III. Ludwig III had married Princess Mathilde of Bavaria but their union was childless, and Mathilde died in 1862. It was clear that Ludwig III's brother Karl, and thereafter Karl's son – also Ludwig – would be the heirs.

Prince Karl and his wife Princess Elisabeth of Prussia were a most devoted couple. Karl was timid and had a delicate constitution, suffering often from bronchitis and migraines. His wife was nervous that the children's uproarious behaviour would be too much for him. Nonetheless, they would play a significant role in the lives of Ludwig and Alice. Elisabeth, too, was shy, and deeply religious. However, she was also extremely broadminded and very tolerant of new ideas. Her granddaughter Victoria wrote that 'I can remember her listening with an amused smile at my lecture on Home Rule of Ireland and the advantages of socialism when I was about 16.'[12]

Young Ludwig and Alice would make their home in Darmstadt, which served as the capital of Hesse and by Rhine. The town was lovely; lying on flatlands, it had narrow cobbled streets and squares, as well as Rococo buildings and fountains. It had always been a culture-loving place and most of the Grand Dukes encouraged endeavours in art and music. It had an impressive opera house and most of the foremost opera singers of the day performed there, including the incomparable Jenny Lind. The Grand Dukes also befriended and encouraged great German intellectuals including Schiller, Goethe and the Brothers Grimm. This was a tradition that Alice was happy to maintain.[13]

Alice was sincerely welcomed to Darmstadt. The town, with its population of about 30,000, was gaily decorated with bunting and flags. The young girls who lined the streets, were dressed in white and wore flowers, while the bells all over the town rang. Welcoming speeches were made, and Alice was overwhelmed with the joy and loyalty of her new subjects.

Alice delighted in the beauty of the town and surrounding countryside. A young Englishwoman and memoirist, Meriel Buchanan, described it this way: 'Darmstadt was a pretty little town where nearly every house had its own garden, and all the broad white streets were shaded by chestnut trees, lime trees and acacias.'[14] It sounds like an idyllic place to live and to raise children. But, like any marriage and new living situation, there were challenges.

When Alice arrived in Darmstadt, young Princess Marie of Battenberg, the daughter of Julie, observed:

> I often felt sorry for her, she was so kind and so congenial to us, more so than our Hesse relations, and in a different way … It interested me also to hear people speaking of the complete absence of Court usages in her house, and of her intercourse with people of the middle classes, who were 'not eligible' for presentation.[15]

But even in the initial joy of her marriage, her empathetic heart continued to ache for her mother, whose grief seemed incalculable to the entire family. Alice constantly wrote to Victoria asking if any of her grief had lifted. In the depths of her mourning, the queen was insensitive to the bereavement of her own children. She almost seemed to guard her loss jealously and shared her grief with her family only with great reluctance. The queen wanted 'no implied strictures from [Alice] and made it clear that what she did want was unadulterated sympathy, or better still her company'.[16]

The Hesse and by Rhine family had a variety of homes in the region. There was the Old Palace in town, the Pavilion at Prinz Emil Garten and Wolfsgarten, a lovely simple residence outside of Darmstadt. As well, there was a castle in Friedberg and hunting lodges at Kranichstein, Seeheim and Auerbach, as well as a very old Castle at Romrod. However, initially, there was no appropriate residence for Alice and Ludwig in Darmstadt proper. As a result, they would spend the first years of their married life in a house in the Upper Wilhelminenstrasse then a part of the Village of Bessungen which would later become part of Darmstadt. It was a relatively simple gentleman's residence with a large garden in front reaching down to the Heidelberger Strasse.

Alice, who was in no way a snob, didn't care for the society of the 'upper classes' of Darmstadt; she may have considered the life they led pointless as well as tedious. Indeed, while the town itself was elated to have the second daughter of Queen Victoria as their future Grand Duchess, the 'upper classes' of the town were less than impressed. Alice was more comfortable spending time with the British ex-patriots, the artists and musicians who either lived there or frequently visited. Alice fully embraced the cultural life of Darmstadt and many of her interests lay in theatre, opera and many other artistic pursuits.

She listened to music and played the piano well. Indeed, she could hold her own when playing duets with the great Romantic composer, Johannes Brahms, whom her daughter Victoria thought of as a shy and uncouth man.[17] Alice was a voracious reader, a trait she passed on to her eldest daughter, and preferred an intellectual life to a social one. This endeared her to many, but as might be expected, did not make her popular with the old guard of the Grand Duchy.

Alice also had a spiritual side and questioned so much that was seen and unseen. She conferred with the philosopher and theologian, David Strauss, who lived in Darmstadt during the early years of her marriage. It was he who pioneered the idea of an historical Jesus as opposed to a divine one. Alice enjoyed his company and went through a period of questioning her faith.

Queen Victoria was distressed by these ideas and later cautioned her granddaughter, Victoria 'I would <u>earnestly</u> warn you against trying to <u>find</u> out the <u>reason</u> for & explanation of <u>everything</u>. ... [I]n the end [it will make you] miserable.'[18] There is little doubt that the queen would have warned Alice about this as well. Though in Alice's case, the constant questioning contributed to her tendency toward melancholy. She looked for answers in science and philosophy but always came back to faith.

During these early years, Alice's ideas for the Grand Duchy coalesced. She believed that people could be helped by charity and welfare without a loss to their dignity. She was very much a progressive reformer, although her daughter Victoria would later deny that Alice was either a liberal or a socialist. Nevertheless, she inculcated her daughters and son with these ideas and as adults, they would pursue such philosophies in myriad ways.

Alice embarked on plans to improve the lives of the people, and especially the women, of the Grand Duchy. To that end, she founded the Alice Hospital and the Darmstadt Red Cross. She consulted with Florence Nightingale about the training of nurses, and the first matron of the hospital trained under Miss Nightingale. Alice herself, would later be called the 'Florence Nightingale of Darmstadt'. She promoted modern ideas of nursing, helped the poor, orphans, unwed mothers, and interested herself in education for girls, training them as clerks and in handicrafts.

She was a fervent supporter of women's rights, and many of her societies – under the umbrella of the women's union called the *Alice Fraüenverein* (Alice Women's Association) – were for the betterment of women. Eventually, there were many associations under that umbrella, such as an orphans' home and the Alice Bazaar – where poor ladies could create little works of arts and crafts, which they sold. She was, without question, a true First Lady of Hesse, or as they called her a *Landsmütter* (Mother of Her Country).

Soon after settling in Darmstadt, the newlywed couple drove out into the country to visit Prince Alexander and Princess Julie. Alice enjoyed the company of her husband's uncle, and his charming wife, consequently, Ludwig and Alice would spend much time at Heiligenberg.

However, Alice became bored by the German tradition of eating dinners earlier than was the custom in England. Grand Duke Ludwig held on to this custom and gave family dinners every Sunday at 4.30 pm. For Alice, they spoiled the entire Sunday – a day when all the family were at home. She had been used to eating luncheon at 2.00 pm in England, and so before long she eschewed these dinners entirely and dined at home, which annoyed the Grand Duke.[19] For Alice, it was just another way of asserting her independence.

As time went on, it became obvious that although she had married a man for whom she had a great affection, he was in no way her intellectual equal. Their marriage was not a meeting of minds and spirits and may have only temporarily been one of hearts. Ludwig did not share her great curiosity, nor was he a deep or critical thinker. In addition, when it came to emotions, he was very shy in expressing them.[20] This was something he would pass on to his first daughter, Victoria, who would have difficulty articulating her deepest feelings.

In November 1862, Alice and Ludwig returned to England to visit Queen Victoria. The visit was not without friction, because the queen was still annoyed that Alice was not constantly on hand. At this point, Alice was in the middle of her first pregnancy and the couple planned to stay for eight months so, to her mother's satisfaction, it seemed likely that the baby would be born in England.

The purpose of the visit was to attend the wedding of Alice's oldest brother, Bertie. He had chosen a Danish princess to be his bride, Princess Alexandra the daughter of King Christian IX and his wife Queen Louise. Like Alice's wedding, this was certainly not meant to be a festive occasion and the queen watched mournfully from the sidelines. Queen Victoria's journal is again full of the misery she felt at most of her children's marriages. As always, she thought of her own needs first.

On the evening of the wedding, she wrote in her journal: 'I quite overlooked Alice coming in, looking extremely well in a violet dress, covered with her wedding lace, and a violet velvet train, … [with] L[udwig] in the Garter robes leading her.'[21]

Just a little under a month later, at 4.45 am on 5 April 1863, Alice gave birth to her first child, a girl. According to Queen Victoria's wishes, not only was the child born in England, but she was born at Windsor Castle in the Lancaster Tower, alongside the Tapestry Room. The room looked straight on to the Long Walk.

The new-born daughter would be one of seven children born to Alice and Ludwig, five of whom would survive to adulthood. The queen wrote to her eldest daughter, Vicky with a small gibe:

> Alice's Child is to be called Victoria Alberta Elisabeth, Matilde Marie & will be called Victoria, – the 1st of our gd. children that will be called after either of us. This I know was not your fault – but it grieved me.[22]

The queen continued:

> I shall take great interest in our dear little grand-daughter, born … in
> the very bed in which you were all born, … She is very like Alice,
> has a long nose and beautiful, long fingers ….[23]

The queen couldn't resist remarking that though the baby had a resemblance to
her lovely daughter, she still found babies frog-like and unattractive. She was
also appalled that Alice intended to breastfeed her children. She considered it
animalistic and repulsive.

Vicky's answer was more cheerful, if a little wistful: 'The dear little girl – what
a little darling it must be … It will become the favourite of all your Grandchildren
now – I do not doubt as you were present when it came into the world.'[24]

Letters of congratulations were sent to the queen on the auspicious occasion of
the first birth of a grandchild in England. Queen Victoria's uncle, King Leopold
I of the Belgians remarked upon the happiness of a safe birth and that Alice came
through the ordeal strong and healthy. Certainly, as in all families at that time,
childbirth was a risky business, and it was always a blessing when mother and baby
came through unscathed.

The baby was christened at Windsor on 27 April. Vicky would be one of
her godmothers as well as Queen Victoria's half-sister, Feodora of Hohenlohe-
Langenburg. The queen detailed the event in her journal:

> At 1, Alice, L[udwig], & the dear Baby came to my rooms, the former
> looking so pretty in a grey dress … P[rin]ce Alexander [of Hesse and by
> Rhine] & the other sponsors stood next to me, Alice & Louise opposite.
> … The following are the names she received: Victoria, Alberta, Elisabeth,
> Matilda [after the Grand Duchess of Hesse], Marie [after Queen Marie
> Amelie, widow of Louis Philippe] … The sponsors were myself, Mary
> [Adelaide of Cambridge), P[rin]ce Alexander (representing the Gd
> Duke of Hesse) Bertie, & L[udwig's] brother Henry. … The baby was
> brought in to be looked at and much admired.[25]

Alice recovered at Osborne, but by the next month the little family was back in
Darmstadt in their house in Bessungen.

Queen Victoria would be frustrated in her efforts to have all of Alice's children
born in England; the rest were born in Darmstadt. After Victoria came Elisabeth,
who was born at their first home in Bessungen. When their residence, the New
Palace, was built, Irène was born there, as were the rest, Ernst Ludwig, Friedrich,
Alix and lastly Marie.

The queen thought of Alice as undutiful and disloyal, and for a time, it appeared
that mother and daughter would continue to be at odds. What the queen failed to
understand was that travelling with such a large retinue (equerries, nurses, nannies,
etc.) was expensive, and until Alice and Ludwig became the Grand Ducal couple,
they were relatively strapped for cash.

The queen often wrote to her elder daughter, Vicky, complaining about Alice; how too much was made of her when she went to Berlin; how she had the audacity to ask her, the queen, for pearls for each of her daughters. Did she understand how much pearls cost? Alice, she believed was bossy, tactless, and never fell in with her mother's plans.

Vicky had the unenviable task of being in the middle since she was close both to her mother and her sister. She constantly wrote letters to the queen praising Alice and saying positive things about her. Far from annoying the queen, as time went on, the feelings of anger and resentment faded out and Alice and her mother would retrace some of their old and close relationship. It would, however, be a more adult relationship. Because Alice lived in a different country, she individuated from her mother. In this, she set a powerful example for her daughters.

Despite their disharmony during the first years of her marriage, Alice wrote constant letters to her mother reporting on baby Victoria's progress and how much she was admired. She told her mother the baby was healthy and that by June, she was sitting up, looking around and laughing in the most alert way. She also mentioned that she could hear the baby shrieking; she wasn't much of a crier, but passionate nonetheless.

Victoria's first summer was spent at the hunting lodge of Kranichstein. It was one of the oldest buildings in the Darmstadt area dating back to 1329. The property had a vineyard and made its own wine. It was described as an 'old, grey palace, whose walls were mirrored in the still waters of the pond, like the palace of the Sleeping Beauty, dreaming in the silence of the autumn woods.'[26] The queen visited this lodge often and scratched her name on a windowpane during one of her stays. The dining hall was the biggest room of the house, with Queen Victoria paying for a remodelling job that made the ceilings higher. Much later, it would be turned into a museum.

It was also that first summer that Alice, Ludwig and Victoria stayed at Heiligenberg with Uncle Alexander and Aunt Julie. There was a large pack of children: the five Battenbergs, the youngest of Tsarina Marie's children, Grand Dukes Sergei and Paul, as well as Grand Duchess Marie and little Victoria playing around the palace. Life there was carefree, especially for the Tsarina. Here in the hills, she could shed the fears of assassination and the tight security under which she had to live in Russia. Here, there were no anarchists trying to destroy her or her family. Here, she could rest as the illness of consumption slowly and inexorably continued to weaken her, while her unfaithful husband, Tsar Alexander II dallied and eventually began a second family.

Among the things that irritated the queen most about the summers spent with the Battenbergs and the Romanovs was that Alice got along so well with the Russian Imperial family. Queen Victoria thought Russian society villainous and atrocious, probably an old prejudice from the Crimean War. Individual family members might be nice, but overall she had no use for the country or the people. She was convinced it had a bad climate, an autocratic government and was completely insecure. She did not believe any of her family members should go there, never mind marry there. Certainly, in that last, she was correct.

Nevertheless, as the families grew their children spent a great deal of time together in the beautiful verdant hills. Located on the road through Seeheim, it too was a vineyard region. The area was hilly, full of trees and fields, and the roads, lined with green ivy-wrapped trees were narrow, steep, and winding. Just below the property there was a leafy path leading to the mock ruins of a medieval abbey. It was constructed in the nineteenth century and used for play or contemplation.

Heiligenberg had two towers, one with a clock, and a very large courtyard. A ballroom would be added in 1873, along with more gardens, playhouses, and bathhouses. From the house there is a panoramic view of the Rhine Valley and Jugenheim. Past the mock ruins, there is a mausoleum containing memorial plaques of various members of the Battenberg family and Prince Alexander and Princess Julie are buried there.

The eldest boy in the Battenberg household was Louis. He was born 24 May 1854 in Graz, Austria-Hungary. He was an especially good-looking little prince and at the age of 8, attended Alice's marriage to Ludwig. He was also very talented in art and language and at that tender age could speak Italian and Russian as well as his native German.

As a young boy, he was extremely impressed with the uniform of the British Royal Navy. Prince Alfred (Affie), the second son of Queen Victoria, told him bold and exciting stories of what was the largest and most powerful navy in the world. Affie was equally impressed by the lad's keen interest and 'encouraged him in his ambition to join the service'.[27] Though his parents were sceptical of Louis' joining a foreign navy, the boy was also encouraged by Alice to do so. Young Louis became a naturalised British citizen, with Alice as his sponsor, at the age of 13 and was accepted as a cadet at 14.

Chapter 2

'The child born under
your roof....'

Meanwhile, baby Victoria was considered quite advanced for her age. She had started talking by the age of 9 months, and her relations would say that from then onward, she never stopped. She spoke German before English, but soon became fluent and was writing in both by the time she was 7 years old.

The family continued their treks back and forth to see grandmama in England and in the following year, 1864, there came another addition to the Hesse family. Elisabeth Alexandra Louise Alice was born at Bessungen on 1 November 1864. Ella, as she was called, was described as an exceptionally beautiful child. She and Victoria were raised as a very close twosome, Alice writing to her mother that 'this little pair of sisters is so nice, and they can be such friends to each other'.[1]

They shared intimacies and bedrooms like so many sisters close in age. They were also a study in contrasts, while Victoria was intellectual, garrulous, endlessly curious, and heedless of her clothes and hair, Ella was more spiritual, though at the same time fashion conscious. While Victoria was a wild child, full of mischief, romping around and climbing trees, Ella loved to play with her dolls and was always neat, clean and sedate. The princesses took dance classes, which Victoria despised, thinking them very feeble and affected, while Ella was plainly more feminine in her likes and dislikes. Despite, or because of their differences, these two sisters would be close and devoted their entire lives.

Victoria wrote: 'I was definitely a tomboy up to the age of 14 … I ruled all the younger with a rod of iron, though my sister Ella being nearest my age, would rebel sometimes against too much ruling.'[2]

Alice came to Darmstadt with a substantial dowry of £30,000 and with it, the family was able to build their own residence near the centre of town. The New Palace was completed in 1866. It was built in the Renaissance style in a botanical park and was surrounded by lawns and flower gardens. People considered the house very English, 'more a Victorian Piccadilly mansion'[3] and quite unsuited to its surroundings. Others thought it bourgeois with its furniture from Maples of London. The fabrics for the upholstery and draperies were chintz and the rooms were filled with portraits of Queen Victoria and Prince Albert, as well as photographs of the children and the rest of the family. The children's nurseries were at the top of the house over their parents' rooms and looking into the gardens.

For Alice, the house was reminiscent of Osborne, a scene of many happy memories. While the house had its detractors, others thought it lovely. Alice's admirer Princess Marie Battenberg wrote: 'I liked, too, the way in which her rooms were arranged, and the real luxury which she developed in the "New Palace".'[4]

❋ ❋ ❋

War came on 27 June 1866. The Austro-Prussian war was fought on the pretext of a complicated question involving the administration of the Schleswig-Holstein duchies which Austria and Prussia held jointly. In reality, Prussia was flexing its militaristic muscles and the Prussian Chancellor Otto von Bismarck wanted to unite all the Germanic peoples under the same *Reich*. Alice, who was again pregnant, sent Victoria and Ella to their grandmother at Windsor for safety.

Hesse had joined the seven-week war on the Austrian side, which was the losing side. Dynastic alliances tested family bonds as Alice and Vicky were placed on opposing sides of the conflict. Alice visited hospitals and the wounded doing what she could to ease the sufferings of the town. And, like her father, she tended to tire herself out with overwork. Her mother and sisters, aware of this tendency, were extremely troubled that she was going about these activities so late in her pregnancy.

It was miraculous that in the middle of a heatwave, she was safely able to give birth on 11 July 1866; Irène Louise Maria Anna was born at the New Palace. Ludwig was away, fighting at the head of the Hessian Regiments at the front, so Alice was without husband or family at the birth. Alice called the infant, Irène, which is the Greek word for peace, although she decided to put off announcing the name until a peace, or at least an armistice, came. Alice's health during this time was not good. As well as being in a weakened state after giving birth and with extreme fatigue, she suffered from neuralgia and rheumatism.

As August came, Hessians were starving, and Alice and her new-born had little food. The Prussian troops occupied, looted and brutalised the Hessians. Communication was forbidden with any Hessian soldiers in the field, so Alice could not communicate her plight to Ludwig. In August, the Treaty of Prague formally ended the war and by the end of the month, the two little princesses were safely returned to their mother. Queen Victoria said goodbye to them, writing in her journal on 23 August 1866:

> [I took my] leave with much regret of darling little Victoria & Ella, who are such little loves. They have been quite like my <u>own</u>, during these last two months & are really 2 as handsome, clever & engaging Children as it is possible to see.[5]

The charm of the two Hessian princesses had overcome Victoria's usual dislike of babies. Of course, this may have strongly had to do with the fact that she knew they would eventually go home.

By September, the peace was concluded. The Hessians were assessed an indemnity of 3 million florins (approx. £41 million in today's currency). It was a crippling sum for the financially strapped Grand Duchy to pay, and it took them years to do so. Fortunately, the occupation lasted only six weeks and the plundering and terrorising was stopped.

Life slowly returned to normal, and Alice began to teach the 3-year-old Victoria to read with flash cards. The following year, an important member was added to the household. Mrs Mary Anne Orchard (Orchie) arrived to take charge of the nurseries and the three little girls who occupied them. Working with a German and English maid under her, she organised a strict routine that they and the new babies that would soon arrive, would follow throughout their childhood. These routines were typical of Victorian upper-class children.

Orchie woke and dressed the children at six o'clock, gave them bible lessons in the morning. They breakfasted at seven o'clock and were outside at least twice a day, riding, exercising and being trundled about on some excursion or other. They were encouraged in any physical activities and took long walks no matter the weather. They had their lunch at around eleven, and then lessons until two. They ate typical English nursery foods and had their mealtimes following the same English routine by which their mother had been raised.

At about the age of 4, Victoria was made to write a 'thank you' note to her grandmother for a birthday present. It was handwritten in pencil. By then, Alice had engaged a teacher, Mr Geyer, who was excellent with small children. Lessons were to be every other day and Alice called them 'little lessons'. He and later governesses would urge Victoria to write these 'bread-and-butter' notes for the various little gifts which the queen sent. This would begin a consequential correspondence that would last until the queen's death in 1901.[6]

The two would exchange news, opinions, discuss family members and political issues. The queen would instruct and advise, which Victoria dutifully accepted, and there was a feeling in all the correspondence that Victoria wanted her grandmother to love, approve and be proud of her. However, Victoria would never have lectured Queen Victoria about utopian socialism or how royalty was an anachronism the way she would later do with her paternal grandmother. As Victoria wrote, her other grandmother, Princess Elisabeth, was far more tolerant.

Unlike most royal mothers, Alice took an active role in the raising of her children. It was more common for the small children of upper-class families to be bathed, spruced up and set before their parents for an hour or so in the late afternoons. Alice had breast-fed her children, and later spent time supervising their lessons and involved in all their scholastic progress.

As mentioned, when the Hessian brood were children, their favourite place during the summer was Kranichstein. There were horses, dogs, endless rowing at the lake, and for her father and the other gentlemen, hunting. Victoria wrote about learning to ride there on a pony her Aunt Beatrice had given her. Victoria called the pony 'Dread' after a character in *Uncle Tom's Cabin* and the pony is buried at Heiligenberg.

The three young girls' behaviour was wilder than their contemporaries, as Alice believed they should develop their own personalities. Because of that, Victoria scorned what she called the 'sedately brought up Darmstadt girls....'[7] She disdained their tendency to cry when they got hurt for which she 'cordially despised them'.[8] The 'Darmstadt girls' families began to eschew the dubious honour of playing with the Hessian children. However, the Hesses were not much bothered as they had always enjoyed their own company best anyway.

In the summer of 1868, Alice was pregnant again and the Hessian family spent the months of June and July with Queen Victoria. Mother and daughter's relationship remained cool. The thorn in the queen's side was not that the family did not come to visit often enough, or that Alice continued to breastfeed (which irked the queen no end), it was another family matter completely.

At the end of 1865, Queen Victoria's third daughter, Helena (Lenchen), became engaged to Prince Christian of Schleswig-Holstein-Sonderburg-Augustenburg. Beside the political difficulties of the match, Alice had vocally made her objections that the prince, who was fifteen years older than Lenchen, was too old. Alice felt that her mother was marrying this daughter off to an impecunious prince who would raise no objections to living with or at least close to his mother-in-law. Lenchen, Alice thought, was sacrificed for the queen's needs.

The queen was furious with Alice and called her sly and abominable.[9] That, along with the queen's other complaints, made the estrangement complete, and their relationship was frosty for several years. Vicky, however, worked hard in her role of peacemaker telling her mother in April of that year: '[Y]ou need not dread her visit. She is so gentle and amiable and so delighted at the thought of going to England as she looks forward to meeting you so much.'[10]

Eventually, the queen was convinced. That June she wrote: 'Alice is not strong — but most kind, amiable, gentle and sensible ...! .... And all is most comfortable between her and Lenchen.'[11] It was questionable whether the friction was between Alice and Lenchen, but nonetheless all told, their visit was a success. Much of the tension of the first years of marriage ceased between Alice and her mother.

On 25 November 1868, Alice gave birth to the long-awaited male heir. He was named Ernst Ludwig. Victoria wrote later that his double name was borne by a Hessian Landgrave in the seventeenth century, a combination of Saxon Ernst and Hessian Ludwig. However, everyone in the family called the baby Ernie. Victoria was disappointed that it was a boy as she would have much preferred another sister.

Ernie was christened in December of that year and Princess Marie Battenberg noted that he 'sneezed, quite unembarrassed'.[12] Two-year-old Irène, the perennial middle child, only worried that someone had done something to the baby.

Meanwhile, Victoria continued to be a rapid learner, and Alice was delighted by her progress. She told Queen Victoria that her 'facility in learning is wonderful, and her lessons are a delight'.[13] Not only was she highly intelligent according to her mother, but she was a lovely and stout child. Queen Victoria shared this opinion, writing to Vicky that the two eldest, Victoria and Ella were attractive and 'Victoria most engaging. [But] Irène is very plain.'[14] The queen frequently commented on the looks of her children and grandchildren and had no qualms about being completely candid. However, it was known and acknowledged by Alice that Victoria was a favourite of the queen's. She wrote: 'The child born under your roof and your care is of course your particular one, and later, if you wish to keep her at any time when we have been paying you a visit, we shall gladly leave her.'[15]

The family did a great deal of travelling, Alice enjoyed visiting her beloved sister Vicky in Berlin, and of course travelling to England to see grandmama. They visited Potsdam in 1869, where a compound of royal palaces lay outside of Berlin. There the four Hessian children played with their Prussian cousins, Wilhelm, Charlotte and Henry. According to Vicky, the cousins got along well together and didn't argue. They attended military parades and a special state ballet in honour of the Khedive of Egypt. Victoria and Charlotte sat with his young son who looked bored and uncomfortable. The two girls decided to take turns kissing him to make him feel more welcome.[16]

For summer vacations they went to the Belgian seaside resort of Blankenberge. It was not as expensive as some of the more luxurious beach hotels and Ludwig could only afford to take his family there every other year. The children recalled playing croquet, making sandcastles and taking donkey excursions. Victoria also wrote about the bathing machines in vogue at the time. These were horse-drawn carriages with dressing rooms that were drawn into the sea. The bathers could emerge without being seen by the other beachgoers in order to protect their modesty.

Summers were also a time for visits from Alice's English family. Victoria's cousin Marie Louise, the younger daughter of Lenchen and Prince Christian, particularly remembered spending many of her summers in Darmstadt with her Hessian cousins. They stayed at Wolfsgarten for much of the time, which was about an hour outside of Darmstadt, but Marie Louise remembered going to her first opera and to the theatre in town. Many of the celebrities of the day came to Darmstadt. Victoria wrote about having seen the great actress Eleonore Duse, as well as seeing Jenny Lind sing. And although Miss Lind was a very old lady by then, Victoria was struck by her clear and beautiful voice.

Another very welcome visitor from England was Alice's younger brother Leopold, who suffered from haemophilia and was mostly kept under the queen's stifling wing. As he grew older, Leopold sought an independent life away from his mother. In Darmstadt, he could feel independent with his sister and family who treated him like the adult he was. He quickly became a favourite with his nieces and nephew. More important, he became an intimate confidant of their father, and they became as close as brothers.[17]

In the beginning of 1870, Victoria, Ernie and their father came down with scarlet fever. Once again, Alice assumed responsibility for the nursing – steering all three clear of an often-fatal disease. But that was not the worst of the trials of that year. On 19 July 1870 war was once again declared, this time between what was now a coalition of German states and France. The Franco-Prussian War was the conflict Otto von Bismarck needed to rally all Germans behind the Prussian flag.

At least this time, Alice and Vicky were on the same side and could commiserate with one another as they both nursed with a fanatical zeal. While Ludwig commanded a division on the battlefield, Alice organised the nurses. She filled her days visiting four hospitals in addition to the newer ones that she had set up for this emergency. In her compassion, she nursed the French and German wounded just the same.

During this time, she brought her little daughters Victoria and Ella with her. The two visited soup kitchens and helped their mother carry bowls of hot soup to those in need. The family housed two wounded officers in the New Palace and Victoria recalled: 'One was very ill with typhoid and the younger had a shattered leg and liked to show us bits of bone he kept in a pill box.'[18]

A preliminary peace was concluded in February 1871 after a crippling siege of Paris. The Treaty of Frankfurt was signed, and the war concluded in May 1871, though most of the decisive victories, including a Prussian victory at the Battle of Sedan, were achieved in 1870. The result was a humiliating defeat for France and the solidification of the Second German *Reich* – the German Empire; Vicky was now poised to become an Empress when her husband inherited the crown. As for France, this defeat not only brought about a republic, but also planted the revanchist seeds that in due course would bring war to the Continent.

Alice, who had been pregnant since the start of the Franco-Prussian war, gave birth to another boy on 7 October 1870. This little one was called Friedrich ('Frittie') Wilhelm. Victoria described him as a pretty and winsome child. Soon after his birth, he showed signs of bruising and was diagnosed with the family curse: haemophilia.

The winter of 1870 was an especially cold one. Victoria remembered the acute pain and suffering of having her first case of chilblains and bad circulation. Chilblains is an inflammation of the hands and feet due to exposure to extreme cold. She would suffer from this for the rest of her life. Her handwriting in her later letters in the 1930s and 40s was particularly shaky and she attributed this to chilblains.

Despite being on the winning side with Prussia in the war, the Hessians were still paying back the indemnity that had been levied upon them earlier. Alice and Ludwig were relatively poor and had to continue to make economies. Despite these distractions, Victoria maintained her correspondence, writing little letters to her grandmother. One thanked her for the pearls, which the queen sent at birthdays and Christmases despite her complaints, and the news that she had a new governess, Fräulein Kilz. In another letter she told the queen how Frittie was such a pretty little boy and Ernie made him laugh so loud that it astonished the family. Victoria also lamented in the same letter that papa was away. During her childhood and teens, papa was frequently absent. Whether it was the army, or later just out shooting, papa was never around when needed.[19]

In September 1871, the entire Hesse family went to visit the queen at Balmoral in Scotland and moved with her thereafter to Sandringham. Victoria's Uncle Bertie, Alice's eldest brother, the Prince of Wales, contracted typhoid fever and the family stayed so that Alice could be one of his nurses, along with his wife, Princess Alexandra, and his other sister, Lenchen. Concurrently, all the Hessian and Wales children got whooping cough and needed to be moved away to Buckingham Palace, where the queen looked after them.

It was November by this time, and they quickly recovered from the disease, but were not permitted to be reunited with their mother. Instead, they moved to Windsor with the other children, the Waleses – Albert Victor, George, Louise, Victoria and Maud, as well as their Aunt Beatrice, Queen Victoria's youngest child, who was only six years older than Victoria – all watched over by Queen Victoria. All the children had memories of playing hide and go seek in the Windsor Grand Corridor, and behind pieces of furniture. They played with their aunts' and uncles' toys in the old nurseries and read their books and were able to draw their Aunt Beatrice into their games. The queen didn't mind having a slew of grandchildren under foot, but the Hessian children, true to form, were quite noisy – she had often to send pages to tell them to keep it down.

Victoria remembered being combed, cleaned and dressed up in beautiful dresses of white lawn with coloured satin-sashes and being brought with her brothers and sisters to see the queen. They were shushed and admonished and brought to the Queen's Tower. The children would quietly enter and be given tea. On their very best behaviour, their governess Fräulein Kilz was questioned by the queen about the children's deportment and any transgressions that had been committed. She looked terribly sad about those, Victoria reported, but also remembered seeing a twinkle in her eye, and soon would smile the sweet little smile that her family knew was rare.

Bertie was finally out of the woods by about January 1872, and the Hessian family went home after four months in England. By then, Alice was once again pregnant, and gave birth on 6 June 1872 to Victoria Alix Helena, who the family called Alix. They might have named her Alice, but Alice hated how the Germans consistently 'murdered' her name and so came up with this compromise.[20] Alix was blue-eyed with golden hair and had a sunny disposition as a child. Alix adored her eldest sister and clearly looked up to her. Throughout her life, Alix thought Victoria was extremely clever with a clear and active mind.[21]

Victoria and Ella spent the time of their mother's confinement at Heiligenberg with Uncle Alexander and Aunt Julie. Alice was slow to recover and struggled to regain her former strength. They played with Henry and Franz Joseph who were more their age. Franzjos, as he was known in the family, was bookish and later became an academic. He evidently found his young cousins too boisterous to be around for long. He would send them off on errands in order to read in peace.

Alice continued ailing. She seemed spent from childbearing and overwork. Nevertheless, she continued working no matter the danger to her wellbeing. Victoria, at 9 years old, saw this tendency in her mother and worried about it. She wrote to her grandmother from the family home at Kranichstein describing the symptoms. 'Mama returned from Baden yesterday, and is laid up with a feverish attack and rheumatism so that she can not write.'[22] And again, some months later, that mama was not feeling well, with what appears to be migraines. It was a constant refrain.

In April 1873, Victoria reached her tenth birthday. Despite still being a child, her commanding character was already formed. She was intelligent, talkative, bossy, but always empathetic to the suffering of those around her. She was also a strong and confident girl who began to take charge of her mother, much as her mother had taken charge of Queen Victoria after the death of Prince Albert. Somehow, Victoria sensed she was the stronger and her mother needed her protection. In her letters to the queen, she continued to discuss the litany of Alice's physical complaints, and the hope that her beloved mother would soon be better.

Like her mother, Victoria was an insatiable reader and rarely without a book in her hand. Her tastes were varied, and her interests spanned from philosophy, geology and archaeology, to later, *Gone with the Wind* or an Agatha Christie mystery. She simply had an unquenchable thirst for knowledge and the experiences that books could provide. Her brother wrote, 'Few women have read as widely as she has. What is more, she almost never forgets what she has read.'[23]

She even managed to turn a photography session into an opportunity to read. In her memoirs she described the long and boring photography sessions she and her siblings had as children. They were quite popular in the Grand Duchy and postcards and photographs of them were always wanted. Since photography was a tedious process in those days, Victoria always had a book to hand. Sometimes, in desperation, she would grab any book that might be on the photographer's table. She kept track of all the books she read in little notebooks that she kept up to date from a small girl to old age. She would often critique the books and was known in the family for always being able to recommend something good to read.

This idyllic childhood was interrupted on 29 May 1873 when tragedy struck her 3-year-old brother Frittie. Alice was practicing the piano, and Frittie and Ernie were playing in adjacent rooms and leaning out the window shouting at each other. Frittie climbed on a chair and accidently fell out. Though he appeared to have escaped serious injury, later that evening he suffered a haemorrhage and died.

The entire family was in shock, and it affected the children deeply. It gave Victoria a fear of the disease which lasted her entire life. Ernie was deeply disturbed by this and all deaths and abandonments. He said, according to his mother, 'When I die, you must die too, and all the others; why can't we all die together? I don't like to die alone like Frittie.'[24] As a consequence, his older sisters tended to coddle him and encourage his sensitive side.

Alice didn't fully recover from the death of Frittie and was never the same. Victoria continued to worry about her mother and wrote often to her grandmother about her fears. Even more, Victoria fretted about her health saying '[Mama]has had a bad sore throat for the last day or two and Sunny [Alix] had one too,' and in the same letter, 'I hope I may be able to become what you wish for I should very much like to be a comfort to Mama.'[25] Nevertheless, only several months after the death of Frittie, Alice was again pregnant. Marie Victoria Leopoldine, or 'May', was born in 1874.

As would happen after family tragedies, there was a sense that things must go on, and the strong members of the family must be the ones to show the way. This was something imbued in Victoria at a young age with the death of her little brother. The characteristic of resilience would never leave her.

❀ ❀ ❀

As Victoria and her sisters grew, their mother and grandmother began mapping out their futures. The queen thought that Alice's growing girls were quite superb. She wrote:

> The children really are (I am speaking quite impartially) perfect dears, some of them strikingly handsome, and so lovable and well brought-up. The two eldest, Victoria and Ella, a wonderfully pretty girl, are with us here and bring life into the house.[26]

The queen, no doubt, had more confidence in her impartiality than she should; but perusing her letters, it is clear that she may have held back a compliment, but never a criticism. She was not alone in her admiration of Ella, however. She was considered by many one of the most beautiful princesses in Europe, even as a young child.

Despite her daughters' pulchritude, Alice wanted her daughters to have a say in their own destinies, be they marital or otherwise. She wrote to her mother:

> You say rightly, what a fault it is of parents to bring up their daughters with the main object of marrying them … I want to strive to bring up the girls without seeking this as the sole object for the future … A marriage for the sake of marriage is surely the greatest mistake a woman can make.[27]

❀ ❀ ❀

In 1875, Victoria wrote to her grandmother that her great-uncle, Grand Duke Ludwig III, did not look well. The time was drawing near that Victoria's grandfather would become the Grand Duke.

Meanwhile, Victoria was becoming a young lady. She, like her sisters after her, would be tall, slender and graceful. Her brother wrote in his memoirs that she had 'very aristocratic features and resemble[d] mother more closely than any of the rest of us'.[28] Her hair was red gold and she had blue-grey eyes. She loved her studies and, like her mother, wanted to know the 'whys and wherefores' of everything. She was excellent in arithmetic, though she couldn't comprehend geometry, but also excelled in science and history, as well as loving – like every good citizen of Darmstadt – music, theatre, opera and dance.

She continued to be extremely voluble (her grandmother Victoria called her a 'gasbag') and loved the clash and controversy of heated debate. As a result, she was stubborn and often argumentative. She tried to emulate her mother by embracing causes and considered herself a strong progressive. She proclaimed against the concept of monarchy, though as she grew older, she was more content with her position in life and moderated her positions. She continued to, as her brother Ernie put it, 'rule the roost'. He went on to say, 'Apart from being the most intelligent, she was also, as the eldest, the most forceful and we always did what she said.'[29] She felt that as her mother seemed more absorbed in her work, and had less strength, that it was up to her to help with the younger children.

She was wrong though. Alice noticed a great deal about her children, and particularly her eldest and wrote to the queen:

> Victoria is immensely grown, and her figure is forming. She is changing so much — beginning to leave the child and grow into the girl. I hear she has been good and desirous of doing what is right; and she has more to contend with than Ella, therefore double merit in any little thing she overcomes, and any self-sacrifice she makes.[30]

Being 'good' was evidently harder for Victoria than it was for Ella or her other sisters.

Soon Alice decided that Victoria was prepared to take the Oxford Examinations for Young Girls. These were a difficult set of examinations that would test her abilities in reading, writing, mathematics and science. Victoria had a distinct advantage as a constant reader, and had much practice in composition since she wrote so many letters. She commented how her ideas and thoughts would flow into her letters, while her younger sisters sat, biting their pens.[31]

On 20 March 1877, Ludwig's father – Prince Karl – died, thereby making Ludwig the heir to the Grand Duchy. Karl's health had been compromised by chronic bronchitis, and a delicate constitution in general. Victoria described her grandfather as a kind man whom the children adored. Several months later, the Grand Duke, who Victoria had noticed was unwell, died. By summer 1877, Victoria's father was Grand Duke Ludwig IV of Hesse.

The family's financial circumstances changed for the better as there was no longer a need to scrimp and save as they had done in the past. Nevertheless, Alice worked as hard as ever, and Victoria continued to write about how tired and white she looked and how overwhelmed she now was with the official functions of the Grand Duchy.

Another important member of the household was added during this time. It was the children's beloved governess Margaret Hardcastle Jackson, whom the children called 'Madgie'. She, like Mrs Orchard, stayed until all the girls grew up and eventually ended her days in a grace and favour house given for her use by Queen Victoria. Madgie had what were considered to be very modern ideas, meaning she was tolerant and broad-minded. She had a deep sense of probity and hated gossip, malicious or otherwise, which she passed on to her charges. She also emphasised Alice's view of social justice and taught the children that their position 'is nothing save what their personal worth can make it',[32] and that they should always be modest and unselfish.

In the summer of 1878, the family took a trip to England, staying with the queen. Victoria and Ella fondly remembered sightseeing in London and playing with the Wales children. The two young princesses were invited to a large garden party at Marlborough House, the home of their Uncle Bertie and Aunt Alexandra. Victoria particularly remembered leaving the party and that she and Ella had been rowed around a lake at Buckingham Palace by their very handsome cousin, Prince Louis Battenberg, who at that point was a sub-Lieutenant in the Royal Navy. He was staying at Marlborough House and was a great favourite of Uncle Bertie. The young prince had always been a glamorous figure to Victoria, and so smart-looking in his Royal Navy uniform. She also never forgot what she considered his great kindness to two schoolgirls by their 'English Cousin'.

During that idyllic summer, the family stayed for some time at Eastbourne in East Sussex. The sojourn was undertaken at the queen's expense since Alice continued to be ill and drawn. Nevertheless, though it was supposed to be a rest, Alice could not resist visiting hospitals and opening charity bazaars when called upon. She went as far as becoming a patroness of the Albion home in Brighton, which was a home for rehabilitation of prostitutes.[33] This was Alice's last visit to England.

❋ ❋ ❋

In winter 1878 Victoria, who had been reading *Alice's Adventures in Wonderland* to her brother and sisters, complained of a sore throat. She was quickly put to bed with hot milk and a hot water bottle. A physician was sent for and she was diagnosed with diphtheria. Quickly, the entire family, excepting Alice and Ella, came down with the dreaded disease. The queen, desperate to do something, sent her personal physician, Sir William Jenner to help the beleaguered family. The queen, who received daily and sometimes hourly reports, wrote: 'I am miserable … Poor dear Alice, and she so delicate herself.'[34]

Alice threw herself into nursing her four sick daughters and remaining son, while Ella was sent to her grandmother Elisabeth. Alice moved from sick room to sick room while the family physicians tried to match her twelve-hour nursing schedules. Soon Ludwig, too, came down with the disease. Tragically, little May died on 16 November, aged 4. Alice held back telling the other children about the death of their sister, but eventually told her remaining son, Ernie, who was slowly convalescing from the illness. To comfort him, she gave him a kiss and with that, Alice also contracted the disease.

The illness and exhaustion took their toll on Alice, and with the dreaded anniversary of her father's death on 14 December imminent, there was no improvement. The queen continued to receive nearly hourly reports on the health of her daughter. The evening before, 13 December, Alice had been conscious, and had visits from her family as well as Sir William. She died in her sleep, early the next morning. Physicians concluded that since only members of the family were infected by the disease that it must have been contracted through kisses. Though it was unclear how Victoria got the disease, there was some discussion about the sanitary conditions of the drainage in the New Palace.[35]

Although Queen Victoria's relationship with Alice had always been a little bumpy, she was much beloved in Britain. She was well remembered for her sacrifice and love while caring for her father, the prince consort, and the support she was to her mother thereafter. This child, who was so much like Albert, had also had an iron will when it came to her own children and husband. She was first lady of Darmstadt for most of her time there and felt it her first duty and obligation to be present in the Grand Duchy. Like Albert, she did something the queen could not understand; she worked herself to death.

The queen was immediately informed:

> This terrible day come round again! … I met Brown coming in with 2 bad telegrams; I looked first at one from L[udwig], which I did not at first take in, saying: 'Poor Mama, poor me, my happiness gone, dear, dear Alice. God's will be done.' (I can hardly write it!)
>
> That this dear, talented, distinguished, tender hearted, noble minded, sweet child, who behaved so admirably, during her dear Father's illness, & afterwards, in supporting me … should be called back to her Father, on this very anniversary, seems almost incredible, & most mysterious![36]

Chapter 3

Not marrying for marrying sake….

Queen Victoria wrote to her beloved granddaughter: 'Think of me as your mama.'[1]

She articulated the devastating loss to the family in terms that only emphasised their grief. The queen wrote to Victoria:

> [she] gave her precious life for you all! – You must treasure her in your hearts as a <u>Saint</u> — one who is rare in this world! It is a great <u>privilege</u> to be her Child — but it is <u>also</u> a great responsibility to become <u>really worthy</u> of her — to walk in her footsteps — to be unselfish, truthful, humble-minded, <u>simple</u> — & to try & do <u>all</u> you can for <u>others</u> as <u>she</u> did! —[2]

She encouraged Victoria to wallow in the deep mourning into which she herself had descended. However, Victoria, like her mother Alice, saw no purpose in this. Even as a teenager, she was pragmatic and independent. Victoria managed her position well and refused to be mired in gloom. Underneath her sensible exterior, however, was a sensitive and vulnerable interior.

Victoria, who was now fully recovered from her illness, was 15 years old, and she took over the family with the help of her sister Ella and various family members. It seemed the weight of the responsibility fell to her, and because of her maturity and strength of character, she could shoulder it. She wrote: 'My childhood ended with her death for I became the eldest and most responsible of her orphaned children.'[3]

Victoria was fortunate to have an outlet such as her grandmother and she poured her heart out to her saying,

> It is too dreadful, that after we all had recovered our own darling Mama should fall sick too, & that her illness should take such an end…. [I]t is very hard for us, & without her … it does not seem like home anymore.[4]

During this time, Victoria was the rock and strength of the family. Her weekly letters from Queen Victoria, while often doleful, were also supportive and full of advice, but they were just letters. She told her grandmother that her 'father was somewhat lost as the head of the household of growing children … all these cares were borne by my mother',[5] so Victoria stepped in. Ludwig IV reacted to the death of his wife by being away most afternoons shooting, or later spending it with his mistress. He seemed to be just as much of an orphan as his children.

As soon as all the children had recovered, they went to Osborne. Always empathetic like her mother, Victoria wrote to the queen: 'I know how sad it will be for you to see us arrive! But please take comfort that it is just what dear Mama would like best – to know we are with You.'[6] Uncle Leopold, a family favourite, was there to amuse them and then would accompany them on their sad pilgrimage to their home. Victoria wrote to her grandmother that it was sad going through it again.[7]

Thereafter, Leopold would visit Darmstadt every year until he was married, though he was often laid up for weeks on end with episodes of haemophilia. He was 'a delightful uncle to us all, only ten years older than myself', Victoria wrote.[8] Leopold was the most cultivated of the queen's sons and influenced Victoria's growing taste in art and literature. Moreover, when he was there, there was someone for Ludwig and the children to go to when there was free time. Someone 'who went out with us like Mama did so that we did not notice how different everything was....'[9]

Victoria's letters to her grandmother often expressed her father's loneliness. She wrote about their daily routine after Mama was gone:

> We breakfast & lunch with Papa in the visitors room just over the entry to the house ... In the evening we stay with Papa generally, as we used to do, untill [sic] it is time to go to bed. — The worst time is coming down to breakfast, & passing Mama's room, where we used to go in often & say good morning, it is all so quiet & empty now.[10]

There is a desolation in such letters. Certainly, she and Ella were despondent, but the three younger children, Irène, Ernie and Alix were visibly more so. Irène, who felt outshone by her elder sisters was lost without her mother's support and encouragement. Alix, who had been called 'Sunny' as a child, was very much less so now. She seemed to wallow in dolefulness, which her cousin Marie Louise commented on in her memoirs. She mentioned that, being the same age, she and Alix were very close but observed (something which now seems greatly ironic) that there was, 'a curious atmosphere of fatality about her. I once said ... "Alix, you always play at being sorrowful: one day the Almighty will send you some real crushing sorrows and then what are you going to do?"'[11]

Ernie, who suffered so when his little brother died, again proclaimed how he wished that they could all join hands and die together. He was terrified of dying alone and would have abandonment issues his entire life. His remaining sisters would continue cosseting him and doing their best to protect him from life's tragedies.

Ella returned home several days after Alice's death and remarked how dreadful Ernie looked, and so terribly sad. Mostly, the family could not realise the reality of the loss. 'It seems like a horrible dream.'[12] After Alice's death, the hunting lodge at Kranichstein was closed. The residence of choice was now Wolfsgarten, where Alice had never lived. The charming house located between Frankfurt and Darmstadt would become their new summer home. It sat in a deeply wooded area, with a garden full of pergolas, ivy and roses. A visitor described the compound:

> Opposite the big red palace, where the Grand Duke and any Royal guests stayed, were the stables with their clock tower and green painted doors, and on either side of the courtyard were small, low-built, one-storied houses occupied by the suite and any other visitors who might be staying. People had breakfast in their own little houses, but for lunch and dinner everybody went across to the big palace, and on rainy days wooden planks were laid down from house to house to enable people to go to and fro without getting their feet wet.[13]

The house itself was in the art nouveau style, decorated in deep colours such as blue and green, with red furniture.

After the Hessian family returned from the long and therapeutic visit to Osborne, Queen Victoria sent several family members to stay in Darmstadt, including Uncle Leopold and Uncle Bertie as well as Aunts Vicky, Helena, Louise and Beatrice. Victoria, always observant, wrote that in movement and manner, Aunt Louise reminded Victoria most of her mother, while Aunt Vicky sounded so much like Alice, that when they were both alive, the children could never be sure who was calling them.[14]

※ ※ ※

The three eldest sisters were called 'the Three Graces' for their beauty and style. As they grew, they came to rely on the queen's advice on a myriad of topics including marriage, but while they always listened, they did not always obey. Ella, for example, was infatuated with her Russian cousin Serge Alexandrovich, the son of Alexander II and Marie Feodorovna. While Queen Victoria had nothing personal against the young man, she deplored any of her granddaughters marrying in Russia. She constantly proclaimed her dislike of Russia and strongly urged Victoria to convince her sister not to go to that 'awful place'.

However, Ella did have another admirer – that was Aunt Vicky's son, Willy, the future Kaiser Wilhelm II. He was attending the university in Bonn and frequently visited his Hessian cousins. Even at that young age, Willy was pompous and bossy. He would take Victoria and Ella on rides or walks around the country, and would insist that they sit while he read passages from the bible. He wanted to marry Ella and proposed to her in 1878 when she was just 14; she gently turned him down. She had already made up her mind to marry Grand Duke Serge Alexandrovich, spurning all other suitors. It was said that he never spoke to her again. According to Ernie neither 'his mother [Aunt Vicky] nor mine wanted anything of it because of their close relationship'. Thereafter, Willy hated Serge, going 'after him in every possible way'.[15]

Willy introduced Victoria, at 16, to what was probably her worst habit – a lifelong addiction to tobacco: 'I remember secretly smoking up chimneys and out of the windows at the hotels. Though my father did not object to my smoking, Miss Jackson [their governess] did, authorised thereto by Grandmama.'[16]

Victoria kept abreast of current events from newspapers and those of her father's papers she was permitted to see. Her letters to her grandmother were peppered with her political observations and opinions. For example, in September 1879 the personnel at the British Embassy were slaughtered by a mob of Afghani soldiers and townspeople. She told her grandmother: 'We were so shocked to hear of the treacherous way in which your embassy was massacred. Papa has been away shooting & I therefore opened the tellegram [sic].'[17]

As Victoria advanced into her mid-teens, her confidence about her self-expression temporarily diminished. Maybe the absence of her mother accounted for this as well as the fact that she constantly observed to both of her grandmothers that papa was extremely lonely and always seemed to be away. Perhaps Queen Victoria sensed this, and she wrote: 'You must *try & write* what you feel & think too as you get older.'[18]

Victoria strove to be candid with her grandmother, reporting as accurately as she could the progress, or lack thereof, of her siblings. She was especially anxious about Ernie, who was recalcitrant and lazy. The queen wrote back that Victoria should make sure that the others were 'very punctual ab[ou]t their lessons'.[19] Though it was unfair to put the burden of her four siblings on her and not her father, Victoria was easily able to handle it. She noted that Grandmother Elisabeth spent a great deal of time with them, hearing their lessons, taking them to lunch and of course, listening to Victoria's arguments about numerous subjects.

The family continued to enjoy visits to Jugenheim – often to see the Battenberg family, but also when the Russian Empress and cousins came to stay. Queen Victoria worried about the girls going 'all Russian', and Victoria tried to counter that charge:

> Every body has always been very kind, but I do not believe if they were a hundred times more kind they would make us a bit Russian, they have such odd manners & say such odd things to each other & even once about the English that it made one quite angry … The cousins are very tall & lazy & never seem to know how to amuse themselves, they talk very little & don't seem to know what to say, so that after we have talked about the weather & the roads, they generally are silent or talk among themselves.[20]

The queen had to be satisfied with Victoria's observations, but it was never Victoria about whom she was anxious. It was Ella, and later, sweet, simple Alix. Victoria had no such inclinations.

The dreaded first anniversary of Alice's death was coming around and the shock and numbness was beginning to abate. As Victoria sorted out her feelings, she realised that much of those feelings were a struggle to maintain some kind of normality. A year having gone by, sometimes if felt natural for her mama to be gone, and sometimes it didn't. Having encouraged the 16-year-old to express herself, Victoria was doing so as thoughtfully and as accurately as she could. The queen was pleased with her development telling her that so much depended on her 'as the eldest'.[21]

In March 1880, Victoria and Ella were confirmed together. Though it was unusual for the queen to travel for family events, she felt the obligation, as a surrogate mother, to attend. The queen described the event in her journal, saying that Victoria and Ella, dressed in white, looked extremely nervous. However, both young girls acquitted themselves admirably, repeating the Catechism and answering all the questions so well. Though this ceremony was a coming of age, the two didn't come out socially until Victoria was 18 and Ella 17.

During those months after the confirmation, the girls constantly asked for, and were given, advice from their grandmother. About Victoria's deportment, the queen warned 'You must learn to be *posée* [level-headed], not talk too much or too loud – but take your place as your beloved Father's eldest daughter ...!'[22] She deplored Victoria's endless talking, her constant reading, and disliked the fact that she was learning to ride fast horses and shoot. She told her granddaughter, 'it is not lady like to kill animals & go out shooting – & I hope that you will never do that. It might do you g[rea]t harm if that was known as only fast ladies do such things.'[23]

Victoria and Ella were constantly anxious about how they appeared to Darmstadt society. The girls realised that they had to participate in these social occasions but needed more guidance than their father could provide, or any of the ladies-in-waiting. The queen tried her best to fill the void and wrote long letters about how the two should conduct themselves.

Her granddaughter wrote:

> Papa is going to be inviting a few people to dinner now & then as he must see them sometimes & it is quite nice for us. I have begged him not to have any real parties yet — & I am sure will not wish it as Ella is only 16 & I not so very much older. I know too that dear Mama was never very anxious about our knowing & seeing all the people here....

And...

> [a]s we are so many, we never feel the want of acquaintances as single girls would & these here generally behave as if we were a sort of demi-god, or are rather vulgar ... Papa has much to do ... & leaves it to us so I thought it would be right to ask you.[24]

Indeed, the queen felt exactly the same way, not just about deportment and table issues, but also about marriage. In this way, she was very forward-thinking. She wrote:

> You are right to be civil & friendly to the young girls you may occasionally meet … — but *never* make *friendships*; girls friendships & intimacies are very bad & often lead to great mischief — … dear Mama was quite of the same opinion. … And at the dinners remember *not* to talk too much & especially *not* too loud & not *across the table….*
>
> There is another *most important* thing wh[ich] you are *quite old* enough for me to speak or write to you about. Dear Papa will, I know, be teazed & pressed to make you marry, & I have told him you were far too young to think of it, & that your 1st duty was to stay with *him*, & to be as it were the Mistress of the House … I know full well that *you* … don't wish *to be married* for *marrying's sake* & to have a *position*.[25]

Victoria wrote back most appreciative of her counsel and promised to never be like so many German princesses – only looking for a good match.

For the next few years, the family struggled with the loss of Alice. Ludwig sought to introduce Victoria and Ella into society, but without an older woman around, it was more difficult for the girls to present themselves, they both felt insecure about the social scene. Their father treated them both as adults and Victoria commented to her grandmother that all the men did was to pay her compliments and she 'hated such stuff'.[26] Later she described a ball that she attended and how she danced with her uncle and some other gentlemen but felt that she wasn't a great success. She was far more engrossed in helping her siblings in their lessons and social interactions.

Her young brother Ernie continued to be of particular concern, and Victoria wrote endless letters to her grandmother about his lack of discipline and concentration. Moreover, he was far more respectful of their Uncle Leopold than he was of his own father. Victoria was contrite in her dealings with Ernie and regretted her scolding and dictating to him. She thought he seemed to have a lack of pride and wasn't ashamed that he was backsliding.

Victoria was more interested in talking about political subjects with her grandmother. She wrote lengthy letters to the queen about the assassination of Tsar Alexander II on 13 March 1881. The queen's son, Alfred, was married to the late Tsar's only daughter, Marie and Victoria empathised with her aunt by marriage about this tragic loss saying, 'It must have been horrible for poor Aunt Marie who was his favourite child.'[27] Only a month later, she commiserated with her grandmother on the death of her favourite prime minister, Benjamin Disraeli, Lord Beaconsfield, saying 'He was such a great statesman that he will be a great loss to the country as well as yourself.'[28]

There was, however, good news that spring. Uncle Leopold, whom his mother thought would never marry, found himself a bride – Princess Helene of Waldeck & Pyrmont. The Hessian family was particularly pleased since they knew how much he yearned for a family, independence and normality – and the fact that the couple met in Darmstadt. The queen, who hoped he would spend his life being her unpaid secretary, was quite shocked about it. Nevertheless, she consoled herself by telling her daughter Vicky that Victoria and Ella liked the young lady.

Their marriage, in April 1882, would be a happy, though short one. The couple had two children: Charles Edward, who later became the Duke of Saxe-Coburg & Gotha; and Alice, who in 1981 was the last of the queen's grandchildren to die.

Meanwhile, despite what the queen might have thought, Victoria and Ella were looking around at the men of their acquaintance. Victoria commented in a wistful and thoughtful mood:

> Time seems to me to go very fast. It sometimes seems as if it were only yesterday that we were all romping about with May in Mama's room after tea – & now we are big girls & even Alix is serious & sensible & the house is often very quiet.[29]

Victoria did not possess the beauty of her sisters Ella and Alix, but in photographs she is tall with a sweet, open and engaging look, with her hair arranged in a haphazard fashion with the fashionable fringe and knotted in the back. She was never interested in fashion or clothes and was carelessly untidy about her appearance. In later years, one of her cousins described her as looking like a 'ragbag'. Her brother wrote of her that she, 'would have been a suitable woman for a great prince because she had the right temperament for it. Clever men coming into contact with her have often said to me "A woman like that is absolutely unique."'[30] Though this sounds patronising, it was meant as a great compliment to Victoria.

During this time, Victoria and the queen were well-aware of where Ella's affections lay – Serge Alexandrovich. Because of this, Queen Victoria presented alternatives to Ella, and discussed the various matches endlessly with Victoria. One such young man was Hereditary Grand Duke Friedrich of Baden, the eldest son of the Friedrich I, Grand Duke of Baden. Queen Victoria wheedled young Victoria into trying to find out if Ella would be open to such a match. Victoria was quick to say that she and Ella never talked about these things, though that hardly seems likely.

The truth was that Ella told Victoria that she found Fritz, as he was known in the family, very solemn and much too good a person for her taste. And, besides that, '[Papa] would [never] oblige any of us to marry against our inclination'.[31] The queen was extremely disappointed about Ella's refusal. She would have been furious if she had known that Victoria agreed with Ella, that Serge was a far more appealing suitor than either Fritz or Willy. The queen reiterated her wishes that Ella not think of marriage for a year or two. But Ella was not the only one thinking of marriage.

Prince Louis Battenberg, the eldest son of Prince Alexander of Hesse and by Rhine and Princess Julie Battenberg, now about 27 years old, was considered quite the 'man about town'. He had been a great favourite of his cousin, the Prince of Wales, and was often invited to Marlborough House, the Waleses' home in London. Louis had accompanied the prince to India in 1875-76 and was part of the North Atlantic Squadron. He was also an extremely cultured and intelligent person. He played the piano and drew. In fact, some of his drawings of the India journey made it into *The Illustrated London News*, when the official illustrator of the tour fell ill.

With his good looks, charm and tall figure, he got the reputation as something of a Lothario, so it was unsurprising that when Louis met the prince's former mistress, Lillie Langtry, the two embarked on a short affair and Lillie gave birth to an illegitimate child in 1881, who she would raise as her niece. Though the baby was most likely not his, Louis nevertheless made a financial settlement on the child.

This was several years before he came home to Hesse on a long leave during the winter of 1882–3. He had just come off a posting on the HMS *Inconstant* after being decorated for bravery during the Anglo-Egyptian War. Some wags noted the name *Inconstant,* implying that when Mrs Langtry became pregnant, Louis left her. However, Louis was relatively impecunious, and lived only on his navy pay. Certainly, as Jane Austen wrote, young men needed something to live on as well as young women. He was convinced by his parents to continue his naval career and did so.

During that winter, he and Victoria spent a great deal of time together going for long drives around the area in a pony cart or taking long walks in the forests. Victoria, always eager for knowledge no doubt wanted to hear all about his adventures in the navy. She commiserated with him about the anti-intellectual and anti-foreign sentiment expressed by some of his fellow officers. Louis was a prince and there was a great deal of jealousy over what was considered the preferential treatment granted him. These issues would hound Louis until he felt the need to resign in 1914.

However, that was a long way in the future as Louis and Victoria spent time together that spring of 1883. She and Ella had been invited to visit the queen at Balmoral, but Victoria wrote that she was not keen to go. It was obvious to anyone looking that her hesitation was her enjoyment of Prince Louis' company. Her sister Ella told their father: 'If Victoria does not go with me to Scotland she will become engaged to Louis Battenberg.'[32]

So, Victoria stayed behind, and the inevitable happened. In June 1883, Louis proposed, and Victoria accepted. Louis wrote to his cousin, George of Wales (the son of Uncle Bertie):, 'I have a great piece of news to tell you. Our mutual Cousin Victoria has promised to be my wife! – I can't tell you how happy I am. She is such a lovely darling girl, as you know.'[33]

Victoria, too, was elated. Not only was Louis handsome, intelligent and kind, but she revelled in the fact that he was 'lower' than she on the social scale since it gratified her liberal leanings. Those leanings didn't necessarily gratify her grandmother since they were anti-royalist, and the queen initially wasn't pleased about Victoria's engagement. She felt that Victoria should stay home and care for her siblings, but she very soon came around. Not only were the Hessian children excited about acquiring a brother-in-law, but the queen, who notoriously loved a handsome face, succumbed very quickly to Louis' charms.

Reaction from the British family was mostly positive if a little guarded. Queen Victoria's son Arthur wrote that he was quite surprised to hear of Victoria's engagement to Louis Battenberg, and he hoped his mother was pleased. 'I have always liked him very much & I think he will make her a good husband, I only wish his rank were a little higher & that they had little more money between them.'[34] That, of course, was the rub. Victoria's family had not been overly endowed with the world's goods until her father became the Grand Duke, and in the Battenberg family it was always known that each of the sons would have to make their own way.

Sir Henry Ponsonby, the queen's private secretary, put it another way when he described Victoria as:

> bright, lively but full of strange ideas … Some say that she has shown her condemnation of princely titles by insisting on marrying a semi-Prince, going as low as she could in the scale of Princes without hurting susceptibilities. They will have no money from Hessian Parliament as she's not marrying a real Prince.[35]

Reaction from family members from the Continent wasn't so affirming. The Prussians, namely Victoria's first cousin Willy, were quite contemptuous of the engagement. His own sister, another Victoria or 'Moretta', had a secret *tendresse* for Louis' brother, Alexander – or 'Sandro', as he was known in the family.

Alexander had been named Prince of Bulgaria in 1879 under the auspices of his uncle, Tsar Alexander II, and the German Chancellor Otto von Bismarck. After Alexander II's death, his son became Tsar Alexander III. He disliked Sandro; moreover, Sandro was proving not to be a biddable Russian puppet. Moretta, a highly romantic and impressionable teenager fell instantly in love with Sandro the handsome Battenberg prince. They came to an understanding, but Willy and his grandfather, Kaiser Wilhelm I, were against the marriage, as was Alexander III, or 'Sasha'.

Naturally, the Prussians and Sasha were averse to any marriages with Battenbergs. Not only because of politics, but also because, as the Prussians said, the family were not of *geblüt* [stock], or quite 'of the blood'. They voiced their objections which made Queen Victoria furious. She said quite decidedly that she disliked the Prussian prejudices against the Battenbergs. The queen despised such snobbery. She wrote to the Empress Augusta, the wife of Kaiser Wilhelm I,

> With regard to Victoria's engagement, it is precisely because she is
> so talented that she should not have made a conventional marriage
> with some prince who would have called *a good match*, but would
> otherwise have offered no advantages. The English element in Louis
> Battenberg attracted her very much, since she is herself so very
> English.[36]

There is an element of a jibe there since the Prussians had never quite got used to
Vicky's Englishness. Nevertheless, the Prussians were powerless to prevent the
engagement of Victoria and Louis.

That summer, Victoria was invited to spend time alone with her grandmother at
Osborne. The queen liked to do this with her daughters and granddaughters, while,
as she put it, they were just themselves. Afterward, one supposes that husbands and
children would have made the queen secondary, however, that was hardly the case
with her own daughters at least. She was more than irritated when Louis showed up
at Osborne while Victoria was spending her last maiden days.

> Louis Battenberg is coming here tomorrow & I shall be very pleased
> to see him. But I much regret that what I *told* Papa nearly a *month
> ago* has *not been listened to* & that he is coming to be at Cowes with
> Uncle Bertie, for I wished to have you to *myself*, & as you *are*, for
> the *last* time – [37]

Afterward, Victoria very timidly hoped that her grandmother, who notoriously
hated engaged couples because of possible public demonstrations of affection, did
not mind Louis' visits too much and that she was not vexed.

She was.

The queen was also displeased with Louis' friendship with the Prince of Wales.
She warned her granddaughter against the temptations of Marlborough House –
meaning the dinners and soirees that were given there, of which the queen strongly
disapproved. She was sure that Victoria would be a good and steady wife and that
she would find her happiness as a homemaker. Victoria listened and learned. She
was never what might be called a party girl, she was more interested in cerebral
pursuits. What made her match with Louis so appropriate was that he, too, was
ultimately more interested in those kinds of pleasures.

The queen did, however, tell Victoria that she would attend her wedding in
Darmstadt – something she had not done before. Victoria was thrilled that her
grandmother would do her such an honour, but of course, that would mean far
more work for her since she would be the one to organise the wedding, set for mid-
April 1884.

In the same letter in September 1883, the queen lamented Ella giving up a good
match with dull Fritz of Baden, and sticking to her preference for Serge. She told
Victoria that she was sure the Russians were moving heaven and earth to get her.[38]

However, by October, the match was a *fait accompli*. Ella, who had refused
him just three weeks before, was now engaged to Serge and it would be announced

in February 1884. Again, the queen stated that she had nothing against Serge personally, but that Russia was the real enemy. Finally, she knew when to back down and accepted the couple.

In her letters to Victoria in November, she proceeded to give both girls marital advice:

> So many girls think to marry is *merely* to be independent & amuse oneself – whereas it is the very *reverse* of independence – 2 wills have to be *made* to act together & it is *only* by *mutual* agreement & *mutual yielding* to one another that a happy marriage can be arrived at.[39]

Excellent advice, though, the queen herself often did not follow it during her own marriage.

Back in Darmstadt, Victoria became introspective:

> This old year is now at an end, & the new one, which is to bring such a change in my life is close but I feel that I know what I am about to do & that you will be kind & good to me as you have always been & therefor, I can look forward with pleasure.[40]

Serge visited Darmstadt in the new year, and his engagement to Ella was officially announced. He was an enigmatic man who commanded love and respect from his family, but later, when he was made Governor of Moscow, he was almost universally loathed. He was described as an Anglophobe, cold reserved, with grey-green eyes, unpopular even at home. 'Ella,' wrote Sir Henry Ponsonby, 'has got her fine bold Russian. He isn't handsome, but she likes him and prefers him to the gentle but rather dull Baden prince who was told off for her.'[41]

Ella was eager for the queen to like him and for him to make a good impression. She was able to get her siblings in on the act to persuade her grandmother. Ella wrote, 'Serge remains still a week I think, he was very much pleased by your kind message & with the others thank you many <u>times</u> for having thought of them all.'[42] Then Irène told her grandmother 'I assure you the more one sees of him the nicer one thinks of him.'[43]

These comments may be a matter of protesting too much. Serge was known to have a cruel and coercive nature. To Ella he was a pedantic martinet who scolded her like a schoolmaster when she did, or wore, something of which he disapproved. He was, however, a deeply religious man who was loved by his relatives and had 'the loftiest principles coupled with a character of the rarest nobility.'[44]

The queen later pronounced that Serge was 'nice'.

Those first months of 1884 were filled with preparations for Victoria and Louis' wedding. Queen Victoria's attendance made it an international event and the arrangements even more complex. Since the queen was coming, other royal houses also wanted to attend. Not only the Prussians would be there, but also members of the Romanov, Habsburg and Scandinavian royal families, as well as German nobility, and a large contingent of British aunts and uncles, including the Prince and Princess of Wales. With no mother to assist her, Victoria organised the wedding with lots of admonitions from her grandmother about the way she wanted things prepared. Ella helped, but at that point she was busy arranging her own wedding, which would take place in St Petersburg.

The queen's instructions included which rooms she would occupy in the New Palace, where the other royalty would be housed, and when they would be allowed to come. She was quite adamant that she wanted her daughter Vicky to come only a day before the rest of the relations. Vicky, she thought, was altogether too high and mighty and unpleasant when in Germany.[45]

In attendance would be young Sandro, who hoped to see more of Moretta. Too many Battenbergs would irritate the Prussians, but one imagines the queen and Victoria thought the more Battenbergs, the better. So, there were many balls in the air for young Victoria to juggle. It was difficult, but she was able to handle much of what was to come with assurance.

Just as things were coming to fruition, the family experienced a great tragedy. Prince Leopold, the Duke of Albany, and Victoria's favourite uncle, died in Cannes at the end of March 1884, after a fall. It was sudden and Victoria wrote to her grandmother that she felt stunned. 'Dear Uncle was so kind & loving to us all, such a friend to Papa that this sorrow now is very hard to bear.'[46] The wedding was postponed, but only until the end of April, since the queen thought that May weddings were bad luck and she still planned to attend.

The sequence of events that unfolded before the wedding were worthy of a drawing-room farce.

Grand Duke Ludwig had not remarried after the death of Alice, but that didn't mean he lacked for female company. At around the time that Victoria's wedding arrangements were being made, the grand duke was conducting an affair with Alexandrine de Kolemine. Originally a Polish countess, Alexandrine had lived in Darmstadt for some years and was divorced from Alexander de Kolemine, the Russian *chargé d'affaires* in Darmstadt. Far from being upset by their father's affair, Victoria and her sisters liked her and were glad their father had found happiness. The family was no stranger to morganatic marriages since both Ludwig IV's brothers had married unequally.

Around five days before what was being called 'the wedding of the decade', Ludwig told his daughter that he wanted to marry Alexandrine. Moreover, he wanted Victoria to tell her grandmother and see what she thought about the match. Victoria was horrified to have to be the messenger of such news, and felt it was unreasonable that she would have to be the one to inform the queen. In addition, she was tired, depressed over her uncle, and felt that the timing couldn't have been worse. However, she dutifully told her grandmother of her father's plan to marry.

The queen was quite clear on the subject. Though she understood that Ludwig wanted female companionship, the lady in question was a divorcee and of another religion. Since there were unmarried daughters at home this was an untenable situation. If her father insisted on marrying the countess, then she, Queen Victoria, could not have him as close as before. She was so decided about this that she put it in writing in a letter to Victoria closing with, 'For all our sakes I entreat him to delay *at any* rate so serious & I must fear, fatal a step.'[47]

Victoria reported her grandmother's feelings to the grand duke who became angry at Victoria. He was baffled as to why the queen would be against such a union. Victoria, who was becoming more and more wearied could hardly worry about her father's romantic problems.

The queen arrived with her retinue a few days before the big event. Accompanying her was her youngest daughter, Beatrice. This would prove to be another headache for Victoria. Queen Victoria imagined that her 'Benjamina', as she called Beatrice, would be with her as unpaid companion, secretary and general dogsbody always. She was determined that Beatrice would never marry, and so not only did she not meet any eligible young men, but they were actively kept from her. No one was supposed to mention marriage or romance in her presence. Prince Louis related an incident where he went to a family dinner and sat between the queen and Beatrice, who didn't say a word. Later, he was told that the queen had 'sent word to the First Lord of the Admiralty that she wished me to be employed exclusively on foreign stations. She was afraid I might want to marry Aunt Beatrice!'[48]

Beatrice was thus successfully kept away from Louis, but while in Darmstadt for the wedding she met Louis' brother, Henry, known in the family as 'Liko'. A romance ensued and Beatrice was completely bowled over by Liko, who was something of a dandy. He looked extremely attractive in his white uniform, tight britches, and highly polished boots. The sight of him was nearly too much for the matronly princess. Undoubtedly Victoria, always very observant, saw what was going on, but already had more than enough on her plate.

When the big day arrived, Victoria was ill from having eaten too much lobster the previous night, as well as hobbling around on an ankle that she injured while attempting to leap over a coal scuttle! She was 21 and as irrepressible as ever. The queen reported in her journal: 'Poor Victoria was not feeling well, so she could not come to breakfast … Poor Victoria continued to feel very unwell … She could not come to luncheon.'[49] The queen sent her personal physician, Sir James Reid, to tend to the young bride and determined that Victoria had been so anxious and so involved with wedding preparations that she forgot to eat. When she did, the lobster was too rich for her digestion.

She did pick up later in the afternoon and dressed in white satin with her mother's wedding lace festooned with roses, orange blossoms and myrtle. She wore a Honiton point lace veil which did not cover her face, a diadem of sapphires and diamonds given to her by Louis' parents and a wreath of orange flowers and myrtle on her head.

The streets were filled with cheering crowds as Victoria, Grand Duke Ludwig, and the queen rode together to the old Grand Ducal palace, former residence of the counts of old Hesse-Darmstadt. They were excited to see the eldest child of their Grand Duke marry, even if the marriage itself was not considered spectacular. More likely, it was the enthusiasm of seeing so many other royals who had flocked to the event, as well as the doyenne of monarchs – the Queen-Empress Victoria.

Louis and Victoria had a short civil ceremony performed by the prime minister and thence on to the chapel in the old palace to have the religious ceremony. Victoria entered the chapel, limping slightly, with her father and new father-in-law, Prince Alexander. Louis, looking splendid in full British naval dress with the Grand Cross of the Order of Bath and the Star of the Hessian Order of Louis and Chain around his neck, entered between Princess Elisabeth of Hesse and Princess Julie Battenberg. The queen was impressed and said that they were a handsome couple. She advanced with 'evident emotion'[50] and kissed her granddaughter while her new grandson-in-law kissed her hand at the conclusion of the ceremony.

The wedding breakfast was held at the New Palace, and according to Princess Marie of Erbach-Schönberg, they were very happy.[51] When all the toasting was done, Louis and Victoria drove off to Heiligenberg for the honeymoon. The queen, who had not attended the banquet, saw the couple off and 'followed them to the door … We saw them get into the carriage amidst a shower of rice & slippers.'[52]

The following morning Louis wrote a letter to his parents. For those who wonder about the devotion of royal married couples, this was a confirmation of a very strong commitment between the young pair:

> My dearest parents,
> I want to take this opportunity on the first morning of my married life to say to you what my heart was too full to express yesterday. I thank you with all my heart and soul for the great and endless kindness and love you have shown me all my life. You have given me the opportunity to bring home my beloved Victoria as my wife, and few men can have found such an angel as she is. To my life's end I shall owe you my thanks for that. My happiness is so overwhelming that I cannot yet take it all in, and my heart is full of thankfulness to everyone who has helped me to find it. I can look into the future with confidence, because I am sure that our married happiness will resemble yours – I cannot wish and hope for more, for such perfect domestic happiness as yours must be the rarest that two people on this earth have ever enjoyed.
> God bless you and reward you for all you have done for me.
> Ever your grateful and loving son,
> Louis[53]

Chapter 4

'…first great grandchild born in England!'

While Louis and Victoria were enjoying their honeymoon at Heiligenberg, surprising events were unfolding back in Darmstadt.

On the night of the wedding, Victoria's father secretly married his mistress, Madame de Kolemine. Victoria, who was usually deputised to break bad news to the queen, was unavailable. Eventually, Queen Victoria's lady-in-waiting, Lady Ely, was forced to tell her the unabridged story, and the entire affair sat poorly with Grand Duke Ludwig IV's former mother-in-law. She was extremely displeased and dispatched the matter swiftly.

The Grand Duke must annul the marriage at once, since the reputation of the lady was such that his younger unmarried daughters could not be put in her care. The Prince of Wales, Uncle Bertie, was dispatched to inform him of the queen's wishes. He acquiesced meekly; Madame de Kolemine was bought off, dismissed from Darmstadt and retreated to Moscow with love letters and blackmail threats. She remarried and outlived the grand duke.

It was but a ripple in the family, and the grand duke was consoled by continuing in the queen's good graces and by a long visit to Balmoral. It was certainly a puzzle why he would do such a thing while the entire house was filled 'to the rafters with the very people most likely to object[.]'[1] Perhaps he was pressured into it, perhaps he was carried away by love, it would be difficult to say. Nevertheless, Victoria wrote: 'The episode was a nine days scandal in the whole of Europe, and a painful one for my father, alas.'[2] Naturally the snobbish Prussians were not to be polluted with such behaviour and were ordered by Chancellor von Bismarck to leave at once.

Meanwhile, Louis and Victoria happily contemplated their future together. While at the Battenberg family home, they were visited by the queen, Beatrice and young Alix. The queen thought Heiligenberg lovely somewhat in the Italian style and surrounded by terraces and trees. She described their arrival, 'L[ouis] & Victoria received us at the door of the very large sort of hall … They showed us over the house, which is very pretty … The young Couple's rooms are upstairs, & very nice & cheerful, quite English looking.'[3]

After luncheon, Louis 'remained for some time alone' with Queen Victoria.[4] One cannot help but wonder what they discussed. Was it Louis' brother's troubles in Bulgaria? Or perhaps it was what the queen had observed between Henry and Beatrice during the wedding festivities?

The newlyweds left Heiligenberg on 10 May and arrived at London the following day. Throughout Louis' professional life, the couple would move around a great deal and usually live in rented houses. Heiligenberg, however, was the place that they would always consider home, and where they would spend as much time as possible.

Their first rented home was Sennicotts in Chichester in Sussex, chosen because Louis was now a Commander in the Navy and needed to be in easy reach of Portsmouth. It was there that he would take command of the Royal yacht, an appointment he was less than thrilled with, as it smacked of nepotism.

Victoria penned an account of their first weeks together in a letter to Ernie. She described rambles and excursions all around the neighbourhood. She enjoyed being a navy wife and loved the time that she and Louis spent together taking rides in their pony cart. It was the perfect rural setting with good roads and tidy little villages.[5]

Victoria felt it her duty to continue to advise her siblings during the first years of her marriage. Ernie would come into a substantial amount of chiding to do better. She sweetened the pill with amusing descriptions of her new married life. The remaining children in Darmstadt, Irène and Alix, also came under her motherly wing since Ella was to be married in June.

Victoria and Louis were in their home barely a month before they were off to Darmstadt at the end of May. Along with the entire family, they travelled on to St Petersburg. It took three days by train to get from Darmstadt to their destination. The wedding was a magnificent affair, with the entire family in attendance excepting the queen, whose views on Russia were well-known, and Willy, who had vowed never to see Ella again. The queen made sure to tell Victoria to admonish Ella never to write anything confidential through regular mails – a caveat prompted by the fact that the secret police were so pervasive. She also expressed her fervent desire that such magnificence and riches would not spoil Ella.

The Hessian party were met at the station by Grand Duke Serge, his Preobrajensky Guard, having joined the train at the border, and his elder brother Alexander III (Sasha); they were cheered by the crowd as they were driven in gilded coaches. Victoria was impressed with the richness and utter grandeur of the scenery. She would soon discover that everything in Russia was on a majestic scale. She was also aware of the massive amount of security necessary to protect the Romanovs from assassination attempts, and was surprised at the cheering reception with which the Hesses were greeted. She knew well that the Imperial family were mostly feared, not loved. They later learned that these demonstrations had been staged.

They went first to Peterhof on the Gulf of Finland. Grand Duke Ludwig and his unmarried children, Irène, Ernie and Alix, stayed in the Grand Palace, while Louis and Victoria stayed next door in the Benois wing. They had arrived a week before the wedding and had time to explore the gorgeous complex of palaces, parks, waterfalls, gardens and fountains. The beauty and sumptuousness of her surroundings surely impressed Victoria, but not enough to ever want to succumb to its attraction as it would two of her sisters. Perhaps, it was her egalitarian nature or her revulsion at the unimaginable luxury juxtaposed against the inconceivable poverty, but she never felt the same yearning her sisters felt.

Alix, who was just 12 at the time, adored everything about Russia. She was among the few family members who truly loved the enigmatic Serge. He teased her, saying that as a little girl he had seen her in the bath. It was at this time that her real and growing attachment to her older cousin, Nicholas, the tsarevich, began.

On the morning of 15 June 1884, Victoria, Irène and Alix as well as Sasha's wife, the Empress Marie Feodorovna, helped Ella dress. Her wedding finery was extremely elaborate, her dress was of very heavy white and cloth of silver, as well as both a crown and a diamond tiara on her head. Her earrings were so heavy they had to be supported by wires that dug into her head. The crowns and earrings had belonged to Catherine the Great. In her right shoe she had a 10-ruble piece for good luck – which of course squashed her toes.[6] There were ceremonies in both the Russian Orthodox and Protestant faiths and the wedding breakfast was long and formal.

Victoria sympathised with her sister for having to endure such a long day in such uncomfortable attire, but was more concerned that Sasha had snubbed her husband. Louis came into the banquet room with his family after the wedding and was astonished when he was seated with officers of the *Osborne*. It was preposterous since Louis and Sasha were first cousins. Victoria was very upset that stiff Russian protocol placed Louis 'below the salt', thus befitting his morganatic status. Though he was offended, the other celebrants thought he preferred sitting with his navy fellows. Louis later said he was glad he lived in England where such pettiness did not exist.[7] Victoria, untypically, said nothing about the matter, not wanting to spoil her sister's celebrations. The grand duke, Victoria's father, later said something to Sasha, and Sasha shrugged his shoulders and remarked that the Prussians had wanted it that way. It is difficult to believe that if the tsar had wanted Louis to sit with his family, he wouldn't have been asked to do so.

There is much speculation on why this was so. Did he subscribe to the Prussian snobbery? Or perhaps it was jealousy because all the brothers were tall, slender and handsome, while Sasha was tall, but built like an overfed bear and not particularly attractive. The truth was that Sasha hated the Battenbergs.

Ella and Serge would make their home at the Sergueivjia Palace in St Petersburg and Illinskoje by the left bank of the Moskva River, sixty kilometres outside of Moscow. Illinskoje was much more of a family home and a place to relax. It was a wooded country estate with cottages and a working farm. The drive to the main house, which was a large oak structure, was bordered by lime trees and it was furnished in the British way with chintzes and imported pieces. The back of the house faced the river with a broad terrace where they could breakfast and sit, while the front had a pillared portico.

Victoria quickly observed that the relationship between Ella and Serge was more master and pupil than husband and wife. He was quick to reprimand Ella if she made any sort of mistake no matter where or in front of whom. She would meekly reply in the French that many in the Imperial family spoke, 'Mais, Serge....'. '[T]he expression of her face was like that of a schoolgirl detected in some fault.'[8] These were the observations of Princess Marie of Edinburgh, Ella's first cousin and daughter of Queen Victoria's second son, Alfred. Marie worshipped beauty and therefore adored Ella, who she thought was one of the most beautiful women she had ever seen; she also adored Serge.

Queen Victoria had thoughtfully sent the royal yacht *Osborne* to pick up English and Danish royalty after the festivities. The yacht was an elegant paddle-steamer and the cruise back to their various destinations was wonderful. One imagines them talking about the wedding and the festivities before and after this majestic event. Little Alix was no doubt pondering her infatuation with the older Nicholas, while Victoria was smarting over the insult to her husband.

With the summer before them, Louis and Victoria settled back in Sennicotts. Victoria spent a great deal of time walking and driving around the countryside, visiting the little town of Romsey, which would play an important role in her family in the years ahead. Their marriage fell into the patterns that could be expected from two strong and intelligent characters. They were competitive and on occasion there were quarrels. Victoria was careless and sometimes even slovenly in her appearance, which grated on Louis. However, Louis admired Victoria's analytical and questioning mind, and, overall, they seemed entirely devoted.

Louis settled in his husbandly role and wrote to a friend:

> Now that I am married, I positively hate going to a ball, as I could not dance with the only woman I could care to ... She is really more English than German, and we invariably speak English together, which may seem strange at first sight. She is a regular sailor's wife, and takes an immense interest in all naval matters ... [S]he is ready to go anywhere with me.[9]

It was during that first summer together that Victoria learned she was expecting a child. Naturally, the queen was very interested in this piece of news and continuously inquired about her health. 'I hope you walk regularly every day? It is the one thing to be attended to.'[10]

While she was preparing to be a mother, she also continued her role as surrogate mother to her siblings. Ernie, who was 12 at this time, seemed to thrive more on praise than criticism. Victoria now wisely cheered him instead of berating him: 'I hope I shall hear only praise from Herr Müther & that you have been working hard & getting on nicely like a great big fellow of your age should, if he ever wishes to become a real man & a sensible prince.'[11]

She encouraged him to take charge and comfort his family when they felt sorrowful. It was especially important as the unhappy month of December came around. She told him '[y]ou must brighten Papa & girls up, if they feel sad and be a help and comfort to Papa like a loving thoughtful boy, as dear Mama would have wished'.[12]

It was also during this summer and autumn that the drama between Queen Victoria and Beatrice played out. Beatrice took a stand with her mother and told her she wanted to marry Liko, Louis' brother. Indeed, the young man stayed with Louis and Victoria at Sennicotts while he was courting Beatrice. The queen, however, refused to discuss it and so the two did not speak for nearly six months. Instead, they passed notes to one another at the breakfast table. It was an intolerable situation but for perhaps the first and only time in her life, Beatrice went against her mother.

Beatrice remained steadfast; by November, with a little encouragement from her now beloved Louis, it appeared that Queen Victoria was getting used to the idea. By December, after Henry got up the nerve to ask the queen for Beatrice's hand, she allowed the couple to become secretly engaged. In March 1885, the queen permitted a public announcement to be made.

The drama of their courtship caused a furore in Berlin. Because Liko came from morganatic stock, the Prussian royal family looked down on him as they had on his brother. It turned out that the queen was angrier about this than losing a daughter. She quoted Lord Grenville who said: 'If a Queen of England thinks a person good enough for her daughter what have other people got to say?'[13] Uncle Bertie of Wales was also happy about his sister's proposed marriage – he said that she had found her Lohengrin (a legendary knight of the Holy Grail). Victoria told Ernie, '[A]s long as he shows tact and discretion in political, social and family matters, everything should go smoothly.'[14]

The queen's conversion to the idea of her daughter marrying was not as difficult as she might have thought. She wrote to her daughter Vicky in Berlin:

> I am surprised at myself – considering the horror and dislike of the most violent kind I had for the idea of my precious Baby's marrying at all (never personally against dear Liko) how I should have been so much reconciled to it now that it is settled. But it is really Liko himself who has so completely won my heart.[15]

The queen disliked the idea of having a beloved and useful daughter and companion being taken from her. However, she quickly settled the problem by making a condition of her consent that the couple live with her always. This circumstance may have been difficult for Liko, but there was the compensation of having a much better position than he had had as a younger son, as well as being the son-in-law of Queen Victoria. If he had anything to complain about, he did it to himself – at least for the time being.

Now there was the excitement of a wedding to plan. Victoria looked forward to the strong Hessian and Battenberg presence that would attend. She apprised her young brother about the situation saying:

> Liko has just left us for Darmstadt. I am sure you were surprised & pleased at his engagement to Aunty. Grandmama is full of plans for

> the wedding already. She wants it to take place here at Whippingham
> in July & you are all to come. Aunty wants to have eight of her nieces
> as bridesmaids.[16]

She also schooled him in how to address his letters to her: 'Princess Louis Battenberg', as he had obviously addressed them incorrectly. Then she discussed the arrangements she had made for when the family arrived at Osborne, where the wedding would take place. Far from resenting Victoria's organising, arranging and orders, they loved her for it and seemed lost without her. Therefore, she spent a good deal of time giving directions on where to stay, what to wear and, more importantly, where they should buy their clothes: England.

But, at least for a short period, Victoria was more absorbed in the coming birth of her first child.

Her grandmother insisted on being present at the birth and of course, since Victoria lived in England, the child would be born there. Louis and Victoria had been in Osborne at the beginning of 1885, but in February they travelled to Windsor where Victoria awaited the birth. They stayed in the Tapestry rooms where Victoria had been born and enjoyed being in such a 'grand' place on their own.

Arriving some days after the couple, the queen was told on 24 February that Victoria had gone into labour and Louis had sent for a doctor. Though the queen hated such things as confinements, in the absence of Victoria's mother, her grandmother stayed by her side, stroking her arms, wiping her forehead, and giving comfort when she could. Victoria laboured through the night with the queen and Louis at her side.

The following day late in the afternoon a baby girl was born. The queen noted: 'The relief was great, for poor Victoria had had such a long hard time, which always makes one anxious. How strange & indeed affecting, it was, to see her lying in the same room, & in the same bed, in which she herself was born.'[17]

Both Louis and Victoria were thrilled at their new addition as was the entire family. They were not only happy but also relieved that Victoria had come through the labour safely. Sister Irène wrote to the queen that '[w]e were so pleased to hear of the Birth of Victoria's little girl. Your first great grandchild born in England!'[18]

The baby was called Victoria Alice Elisabeth Julie Marie, after her grandmothers and great-grandmothers. She would be known in the family as Alice. Alice was christened in the spring in Darmstadt, and it was an occasion with the entire family present.

While recovering from the childbirth, Victoria found time to write to Ernie and tell him about the baby:

> I hope you will think her pretty when you see her. She has nice big
> dark grey eyes, which everybody says will turn brown soon & a pair
> of capital eyebrows, such as I never possessed, so I should say she

will be more like L[ouis] than me – but at present she has got a true baby's face, with a nice little nose & a mouth, which she opens like a fish.[19]

Victoria often said that the baby looked like the Battenbergs. Indeed, Alice was lovely and would go on to be called one of the most beautiful princesses in Europe.

Alice was a sweet but mischievous child and the stories of her making her great-grandmother laugh are legion. There is a photo of Queen Victoria with Alice on her knee surrounded by her mother and her Aunt Beatrice. The queen's eyes are shut and there is a smile on her face as though she couldn't stop giggling. Unquestionably, Alice had done something outrageous to make her laugh. Once, when Alice was about 4 or 5 and had been bathed and dressed to appear before her great-grandmother, she had been instructed to kiss the queen's hand, but when the moment arrived, she refused to do so. Queen Victoria scolded her saying 'Naughty Alice', whereupon the child replied, 'Naughty grandmama!'. At which point, she was quickly taken out of the room.

Alice would go on to be Princess Andrew of Greece, and her youngest child, born in 1921, was Prince Philip later the Duke of Edinburgh and the husband of Queen Elizabeth.

Victoria and her little family were slated to go back to Darmstadt for the christening which would take place, along with Ernie's confirmation, in April 1885. Victoria's other grandmother, Princess Elisabeth, who had so been looking forward to seeing her first great-grandchild, died that March at the age of 69. Louis and Liko rushed ahead to attend her funeral.

Victoria returned in the beginning of April and Queen Victoria once again went to Darmstadt for the occasion. Before she arrived in Darmstadt the queen took the opportunity to write to Victoria some of her thoughts about Louis. Though she was always susceptible to a handsome face, she did not suffer fools lightly. If Louis had not measured up, the queen would have said so quite decidedly. Instead, she had come to love Louis like a son and would later have him as one of the executors of her will: 'Let me just add … how I have learnt to esteem your dear Louis – what a motherly feeling I have for him & what an exceptionally tender kind & excellent Husband you have in him! – You can never show him too much devotion & affection.'[20]

Victoria had a difficult time sharing her feelings openly and the queen often scolded her for not showing enough warmth for her husband. That is interesting coming from the woman who disliked public displays of affection. For Victoria, the things that were deepest in her heart were the things that she had the most difficulty in expressing outwardly.

She responded that she would not,

> forget what you say about my duty to Louis, & indeed it will be easy to fulfil it, for I love him with all my heart & if I have seemed to

> think of Papa more than him, it is only because I am so afraid of my
> happy married life making me neglect poor Papa, who has always
> been the kindest of fathers to me.[21]

From Darmstadt Louis went back to sea, and this would form the pattern of their lives. Louis would often be absent, but because Victoria was an independent woman of great inner resources, she travelled, visited extended family members in Russia and Germany, pursued her own interests, and raised her children. In fact, for someone who had been the mother and father of her siblings through most of her teen years, this was an ideal arrangement for her. She would never dwell on the loneliness of being, for all intents and purposes, a single mother, but would make the best of the situation.

While Louis was away in those first years, Victoria spent a great deal of her time in Darmstadt. Later, when Louis came home from his voyages, they spent more time at Heiligenberg. However, as long as her grandmother was alive, she would spend time with her.

※ ※ ※

Just before Beatrice's wedding, which would take place in July 1885, the Sandro/Moretta drama continued to absorb the family. In fact, the Prussians would not attend Beatrice's wedding because of what they considered a very unsuitable entanglement.

Victoria had been following the couple's predicament, as well as the politics in Bulgaria, for a long period. She had compassion for her lonely brother-in-law and knew how urgently he wanted a wife. However, she also felt that his wavering, and eventually giving up the throne of Bulgaria, was the sign of a weak spirit. As time went on, she was less critical of Sandro.

※ ※ ※

Beatrice and Liko were married at St Mildred's, Whippingham, on the Isle of Wight. Naturally there was a great presence of family and friends. The Russians and Scandinavians and many of the German families attended, but the Prussians, as noted, were conspicuous by their absence. In any case, they were not invited since the queen wished to avoid all controversies and problems.

Although Beatrice had a natural tendency to plumpness, by her wedding day she had lost weight as a result of the Prussian's loud disapproval and the ridicule in the continental newspapers; nevertheless, she looked lovely. Liko, of course, looked extremely handsome in his uniform with his tight breeches and his shiny boots.

Victoria and baby Alice stayed at Kent House, which belonged to her aunt, Princess Louise, the queens' daughter. She was occupied with seeing to her family and their arrangements. They were to come over on HMY *Victoria and Albert*, and she arranged the cabins so that everyone was comfortable. The entire party would arrive 20 July, three days before the wedding, which was set for the 23rd.

Ironically, Victoria's mother-in-law, Princess Julie Battenberg, was a bad sailor and was uneasy about the crossing from Flushing to the Isle of Wight. It was an arduous journey and took sixteen hours over rough seas. Louis' sister Marie also talked about the terrible seasickness that many in the party suffered. 'My maid,' she said, 'was literally howling with the misery.'[22]

When they reached the Isle of Wight, the Archbishop of Canterbury, who was to perform the ceremony, was white with the remnants of seasickness and fatigue. After the service, the roads were lined with cheering crowds and holiday makers. The wedding breakfast was served in tents with guests paying tribute to both Queen Victoria and the bridal couple. The company was serenaded with ten pipers in Highland dress.

In the evening, there was a state dinner, where no doubt the queen and Grand Duke Ludwig commiserated with one another about their various losses. In all events, Queen Victoria came to love Liko. He was not overly intelligent, and because of this, his mother wondered what Beatrice saw in him. Nevertheless, he had a great deal of charm, curiosity and was interested in everything. Princess Marie observed that they were very happy together.

Victoria was happy that year because Louis was promoted to commander. He went on half-pay and stayed with her and Alice through the winter. They printed and assembled a pamphlet detailing his sister Marie's visit to Sandro in Bulgaria. She wrote a fascinating account describing the food, the sights and sounds in and around Varna and Sofia. Louis had learned how to print when he was a boy, 'when it was still the fashion for young Princes to learn some handicraft'.[23]

During these years, the crisis in Bulgaria came to a boiling point. There were not only elements from Russia who wanted Sandro gone, but several camps in the Bulgarian army who supported the tsar and plotted to seize control of the government and force him to leave. They carried out a plan to kidnap Sandro at gunpoint, along with his youngest brother Franzjos, and put them on a steamer out of the country. Louis was able to intercept his brothers at Breslau, east of Berlin, which at the time was part of Germany.

The Bulgarians were outraged by the kidnapping and demanded the return of their prince. Sandro returned to Sofia in August 1886 and was received with great enthusiasm. At the beginning of September, Sandro sent a coded telegram to Alexander III saying that as the tsar had given him the crown, Sandro would return the crown back to him if he desired. The telegram was made public and Sandro was seen as capitulating. Given such an obvious choice, the tsar told Sandro to go.

Both Louis and Victoria felt his biggest mistake was that he had too high of an opinion of his cousin, who made no secret of his dislike. Another German, Prince Ferdinand of Saxe-Coburg & Gotha, was invited to rule in his place. He would be far more amenable to the Russians' wishes and Bismarck's machinations.

Prince Louis had harsh words for his duplicitous cousin. In a letter to Queen Victoria, he was blunt:

> I would point out that ... [no one] has the slightest influence on the
> Emperor Alexander ... He is stupid & dull, consequently suspicious.
> This hatred for Sandro has increased with every abortive measure
> undertaking against the object of his hatred ... It has long ago ceased
> to be a political question with him – he hates Sandro & will hate him
> to his dying day ... happily [he] can no longer harm [him].[24]

A year later, Sandro officially gave up Moretta and wrote a letter to her breaking the engagement. Obviously, the whole situation had gone on for much too long, and Sandro had been lonely in Sofia for all those years. In 1889 he married a beautiful opera singer, Johanna Loisinger, and took on the title of Count Hartenau. He did so to prevent embarrassment to the family. The marriage was seen by many observers as a statement that he would never again seek the Bulgarian crown. Victoria was philosophical about the marriage that some might have called a misalliance. She wrote to her father that: 'the poor man has had to go through so much in the past few years, has lost so much and led such a lonely miserable life, this marriage will perhaps make him happier than anything else could. I believe Frl. Loisinger has an unblemished reputation.'[25]

But further, 'this marriage is a grief to us, as he could have done so much better for himself & such marriages are always risky.'[26]

The couple had two children, Svetlana and Assen. Tragically, Sandro died of appendicitis in 1893 at the age of 35. The Bulgarian people had loved their handsome prince, who had so desperately tried to free them from Russian influence and had clamoured for him to be returned after his death. He was buried in Bulgaria.

Victoria had a final word to say about him: 'Sandro had none of the born politician's subtlety and his talents were decidedly military ones.'[27] His obituary in *The Times* of London was sympathetic and remarked that 'his name will always occupy an honoured place in the early history of the Bulgarian Principality'.[28]

Chapter 5

'…my advice [is] never listened to….'

During those years, Victoria spent a lot of time with family members and travelled a great deal with Alice. When Louis went to sea, she would most likely be with her father and siblings who were still at home in Darmstadt.

Though Victoria was a grown woman, the queen continued to give her advice about every aspect of her life. Victoria remained an avid reader and continued to keep her lists of books. She was interested in everything and willing to give any book a try. In a letter from 1885, the queen admonished Victoria to read only good and improving books, not 'materialistic & controversial ones for they are bad for everyone'.[1] There is little doubt that Victoria listened carefully to her grandmother, but didn't always do as she advised.

Alice and Victoria spent Christmas 1886 in Darmstadt and were joined by Louis, who now commanded the HMS *Cambridge*. The celebrations were delightful and Irène wrote to her grandmother that, Alice, 'the dear Baby is delightfully fat & pretty with such a merry laugh'.[2]

Ernie spent a few years at the University of Leipzig and passed his military exams becoming a member of the First Guard Regiment in Potsdam. In 1886, Victoria wrote him a letter of congratulations on his eighteenth birthday. It was important to her for the young man to understand that he had grown up just as his mother would have wished. Victoria knew that she had been hard on him after their mother died and wanted him to know:

> Now that you too are no more a child; & ask you to believe that
> I really love you very much, though we don't speak about it & that
> whatever the future may bring you may be sure this won't chang…
> [K]now that I will always do my very best to help you, for dear
> Mama's sake & for your own.[3]

The sentiments she expressed in this letter would never change. Victoria could be bossy and preachy to her brother, but she was also capable of praising him when it was due, and was always scrupulously fair. Though it has been written that Ella was more of a mother to Ernie after the death of Alice, Victoria would always be the bedrock of Ernie's life. In the future when they were on opposite sides in the Great War, their relationship would be soonest mended afterward.

Irène, the perennial middle child, now comes to the forefront of the family. It was a little drama, and it only took a small amount of time to resolve, but it was probably the first and only time that she was the central character in the family.

Irène was nearing 20 at this point and of marriageable age. In 1886, Irène and her father went to St Petersburg and Queen Victoria became wildly suspicious. She was worried about some atrocious Russian getting their claws into her tender granddaughter and wrote to Victoria:

> I must tell you how annoyed & grieved I am at dear Papa & Irène's going to Petersburg – now – after the monstrous way in wh[ich] dear Sandro has been treated ... I think it most unfortunate. And then for poor Irène, it is most awkward for no end of reports have been spread ... I shall never forgive it, if she also is to go to that horrid, corrupt Country – & I sh[ou]ld break with Papa if he did it![4]

The queen could have hardly been clearer than that. Victoria quickly reassured her that there was no such idea in the wind. Her father and Irène had promised a visit to Ella for a while and there would have been great disappointment had they not gone. She went on to say that Irène had absolutely no predispositions in that direction.

Irène's actual predispositions, however, would not please her grandmother much more. She had known her Prussian cousin, Prince Henry, the second son of her Aunt Vicky and Uncle Fritz, her entire life and they had fallen in love. In the beginning of 1887, Irène announced that she and Henry were engaged. Though it was certainly not as distasteful as a Russian engagement, her grandmother was not happy because she disliked Henry. She considered him heedless and non-intellectual. And worse, he was unkind about Liko marrying Beatrice.

There were also questions and concerns about first cousins marrying. However, Aunt Vicky was especially happy about Irène, whom she loved like a daughter. The deepest cut of all for the queen was that she only found out about the engagement in the newspapers. Irène had not had the courage to break it to her.

An angry letter went to Victoria filled with the queen's shock and dismay about the situation. Irène, she wrote had 'deeply hurt' her. She had assured the queen over and over that she would never make such an engagement and then did so. 'How can I trust her again after such conduct?'[5] Her anger was quickly spent and the queen, ever the pragmatist, reconciled herself to the matter, but felt that her granddaughter would be treated badly in the Prussian court.

Ultimately the Hessians embraced Henry as they had Louis and Serge and absorbed him into their family group. Ernie, who was sensitive to all of his sisters' feelings, told Victoria that Irène was extremely content and a 'more dear boy one really could never have seen'.[6] Victoria wrote to her grandmother that she found Henry to be a 'very nice fellow – frank good natured & full of high spirits',[7] and that he had acted in a very conciliatory way around Sandro.

Though it cost her, Irène was firm in her desire to marry Henry and attempted to convince her grandmother that she was wrong about him; 'Harry [as he was called in the family] is really the good angel here ... that I scarcely deserve him.'[8] In the end, a more inoffensive couple could not be found. They were perfectly happy together and were called 'the Very Amiables' by their family. The Grand Duke was fond of his new son-in-law and Irène envisioned the coming years in which her father would visit Berlin often. Queen Victoria invited Henry to the forthcoming Golden Jubilee. The queen had other concerns: the marriage of her last Hessian granddaughter, Alix. In comparison, a Prussian marriage was to be embraced.

The queen wasn't about to let Alix slip out of her fingers and go to repugnant Russia. She had new candidates for Alix: one of Bertie's sons, either Albert Victor or George. While she asked Victoria to intercede with her father to make sure that some Russian didn't 'snap her up',[9] she was also frustrated and wrote to Victoria: 'I feel very deeply that my opinion and my advice are never listened to and that it is almost useless to give any.'[10]

Of necessity, Queen Victoria's attention went from marital machinations to the preparations for her Golden Jubilee. Around 20 May of that year, however, Victoria contracted typhoid and was laid up for an entire month. She was extremely ill and had a dangerously high fever. Louis nursed her through her illness and she was given anti-febrin, which had only recently been shown to reduce fever. The queen was kept abreast of developments by Irène who wrote that '[d]ear L[ouis] is so touchingly devoted to her & she feels quite unhappy when he is away from her'.[11] The queen took this opportunity to remind Victoria, as if she didn't know, how lucky she was to have such a devoted husband, she wrote: 'You have been most tenderly loving nursed by one of the kindest & best of Husbands whose love & unbounded devotion you can never sufficiently repay.'[12]

Other family members were also concerned about Victoria. Uncle Affie wrote to his mother that he had just heard of her illness and its seriousness and expressed the wish that 'she will be strong enough by then [the jubilee] to come to England with the other guests'.[13] Thankfully, she was soon on the mend and would be able to attend the jubilee the following month, although she would be severely limited as to the festivities and ceremonies that she would be able to attend.

Victoria would have been heart-broken to miss the celebration and the chance to be with her entire family. Not only that, but during the time of her illness she was unable to see little Alice, who was just starting to talk. Her babble was unintelligible as was often the case, but Victoria hated missing any part of her little daughter's development.

Victoria and her family travelled to England around 15 June, they accompanied the queen from Windsor to Buckingham Palace on the 20th and stayed with her there. Victoria, sensibly, refrained from attending the dinner parties or other evening festivities.

The jubilee was considered to be the zenith of Queen Victoria's reign and the celebrations were attended not just by her family, but also by most of the top dignitaries of the known world at that time. The following day there was a service of Thanksgiving at Westminster Abbey. The queen's sons, sons-in-law, and grandsons rode in the procession, as well as Victoria's Louis. Aunt Vicky's husband, Uncle Fritz, got the loudest cheers as he rode by looking strikingly handsome in his uniform and his dignified bearing; what the crowds didn't know was that Fritz was mortally ill with throat cancer. He had had several throat operations before the festivities and was in quite a bit of pain. During the service, Queen Victoria embraced Vicky the longest when the princesses lined up to kiss her hand. The *Te Deum,* an organ composition by Prince Albert, was played, and then 3,000 schoolboys joined to sing *God Save the Queen.*

On the 22 June, the queen and most of her family members returned to Windsor where Victoria continued her convalescence. By July, she was well enough to travel back to Darmstadt with her family.

In the same month, Louis was appointed second in command to the HMS *Dreadnought.* Once again, for many this smacked of favouritism and there were murmurs because Louis had not quite lost his German accent nor his Germanic phrasing. His way of coping was not to pay attention but just get on with his duties.[14]

Louis had his defenders. There was a letter written to *The Times* of London by a certain A. Cooper Key, dated 4 August 1887. The writer expressed his astonishment at the criticisms that were levelled at Louis. He knew the prince and said, 'without hesitation that his abilities and his professional knowledge – both practical and theoretical – fully qualify him[.]' The writer further expressed his disbelief that Louis had not been promoted sooner.

That October, Victoria and Alice set out for Malta. They were joining Louis at his new post at the strategic cross-roads of the Mediterranean and Southern Italy – Britain's stepping-stone to the Middle East, Africa, and India. They joined Uncle Affie, who was the Commander-in-Chief of the Mediterranean Fleet, and his wife Grand Duchess Marie Alexandrovna. The Battenbergs arrived in Valetta, the capital city, and initially stayed with the Edinburghs in San Antonio.

The exoticism of the island fascinated Victoria. It was the home of many wayfaring and battling cultures. She explored the ruins of the Phoenicians, Carthaginians, Romans, Arabs and Normans. The Knights of St John or Hospitaller originated from Malta and only added to the mystery and fascination of the island. They had defended the area from Muslim invasions and were a stop for the crusaders on their way to the Holy Land. Being a bastion of Southern Europe, it was chock-full of defensive forts and battlements. Its language, Maltese, which is a mixture of Arabic, Italian, Sicilian and Spanish, is the only Semitic language written in Latin letters.

San Antonio was a lovely little town with an opera house, shuttered windows, colonnaded porches, and gardens with Mediterranean flowers. The people were smiling, relaxed and extremely hospitable. Victoria enjoyed her stay and commented that there were more goats than people. She especially appreciated the temperate climate. As someone who suffered from poor circulation and chilblains her entire life, she loved the warm summers and the cool, mild winters.

She adored exploring the unusual landscape of the island where she cultivated her interests in botany, cartography and archaeology. It was a period where she became better acquainted with Uncle Affie, Aunt Marie (Sasha of Russia's only sister) and their lovely daughters. The Edinburghs' eldest child was their only son, Alfred Jr., then came Marie, called Missy in the family, who became the colourful and flamboyant Queen Marie of Romania. The next was Victoria Melita, called 'Ducky', who had a sadder destiny much closer to the Hessian family – more on that later. The third sister was Alexandra, called Sandra, and the youngest, Beatrice or Baby Bee, would later marry an Infante of Spain. Bee was a playmate for her cousin Alice.

Victoria, though over ten years older than Missy, enjoyed wild gallops with her young cousins and was often scolded by their mother for riding around like hooligans. These gallops would end at various parts of the island where al fresco picnics and teas would be set up.

Victoria described her relaxed activities to her family:

> Here we are leading a quiet pleasant life, making driving expeditions of an afternoon or taking long rides of which the 3 girls are passionately fond. They all ride very nicely & don't know what it is to be nervous. Alice & Baby Bee romp & play together & I am sorry to say quarrel besides – they are both rather spoiled so their games often end in pitched battle, in which poor Baby Bee generally comes off worse, as Alice slaps & even bites her, before she has time to realize what is happening.[15]

By the following month, Louis was back from the sea, and they were able to move into their own house at Number 1, Molino Avento. It was a tiny corner house with no nursery, so the flat next door was also rented. Their dining room was comparatively small and could only seat six, but they were constantly entertained by Uncle Affie either in large parties or *en famille*. The social life was brisk for the naval officers and Victoria and Louis went out frequently.

Victoria did not neglect her grandmother and wrote copious letters describing her sojourn on the island. The queen was delighted with these letters and told her: 'Your descriptions of … your life at Malta are very vivid & enable me to follow all in thought.'[16] Nor did she forget Ernie lecturing him about bad spelling saying that George [Prince George of Wales, later George V]

> is nearly as bad on this point, but in French chiefly & like a sensible fellow does dictations in that language with cousins under Aunt Marie, who is very strict & also makes him read French aloud. He is much at San Antonio & also comes here sometimes & all are fond of him.[17]

George, at this moment in time, was very fond of his first cousin Missy, and wanted to marry her, but Aunt Marie was determined that none of her daughters should marry Englishmen. She disliked England – the climate, the food, and had clashed with her mother-in-law over precedence. Here in Malta, however, she was the first lady, even if it was a small island. George would go on to marry Princess Victoria Mary of Teck.

It was as the year was closing that there were several family issues on Victoria's mind. She wrote to the queen that Alix would be confirmed in the late spring and that Miss Jackson, who had been with them since the summer before their mother's death, would now leave them. It would be, 'a natural end to her remaining'.[18]

Another more troubling situation was the continuing illness of Aunt Vicky's husband, Uncle Fritz – he could barely speak after several operations on his throat. Although the doctors said they removed all the cancer, the family was worried. Irène felt this particularly as she was planning her wedding for that May and hoped that her grandmother would attend. As it happened, the queen did not attend her wedding, nor did she attend Alix's confirmation.

Christmas in Malta that year was a chance to celebrate. Victoria went around the decks of the *Dreadnought* for services and afterwards, they went to the Edinburghs for Christmas dinner and the opening of presents. One special present was from Aunt Julie. It was a leather-bound book with a catch on it in which Victoria used for her lists of books. Some examples that year were *Principles of Constitutional Law, Life of George Washington* as well as several novels. She was very methodical in her book lists, distinguishing between those books she was reading for the first time and others. She noted whether she read them when travelling, read them aloud and whether someone had lent them to her.

When they were stationed in Malta, Victoria read hundreds of books. As in her girlhood, she would read anything she could get her hands on. Some she read for research, for example for their book on ships' names, and some for absolute pleasure, such as the novels of H.G. Wells or Rudyard Kipling. She was unquestionably what we would call and autodidact, and when she was an old lady her children and grandchildren would call her knowledge encyclopaedic.

Victoria and Louis lived in Malta until 1897, going back and forth to various other postings, but always returning to Malta. From there Victoria would travel while Louis was at sea, going to Russia, Prussia and of course to Darmstadt.

In the new year, there would be more worries about Uncle Fritz. The doctors recommended another operation, which Victoria feared was a bad sign. During that time, Louis also fell ill with Malta Fever, a disease prevalent in the Mediterranean area. Though it did not have a high mortality rate, it was annoying for its long debilitating fever and chronic relapses. It was particularly virulent in military bases and Victoria spent anxious hours taking care of Louis, as well as reading to him.

Meanwhile, Uncle Fritz had been sent to San Remo, a coastal city in the northwest of Italy for recuperation, and while there, he underwent a tracheotomy in February 1888. Irène and Grand Duke Ludwig were with Aunt Vicky during this dangerous time.

To add to these apprehensions, Uncle Fritz's father, the old Kaiser, was extremely ill after a series of strokes. The old man died 9 March 1888, and because it was perceived that Fritz was also mortally ill, he was seen as only an interim ruler. Aunt Vicky was 'brave' according to Irène, who had now gone back to Berlin for the funeral of the emperor.

What was certain was that Irène's wedding plans would be moved up so that the new emperor could attend. By spring Louis was well, but all were now anxious about the wedding and the state of Uncle Fritz's health. Alix's confirmation, which had been scheduled for May, was now moved up to April and Irène's wedding was scheduled for 24 May at Charlottenburg. Victoria left Malta, made a slight detour to visit Queen Victoria who was in Italy at the time, and then returned to Malta, missing the confirmation.

Now sadness was put aside for a day for Irène's wedding. In attendance were both the Prussian and Hessian relations with Uncle Bertie of Wales representing the queen. Though Fritz was bedridden at this point, he valiantly dressed and, with the assistance of a cane, went to the wedding. He rose 'without difficulty at the usual points in the service'.[19] The end came for the Kaiser just a few weeks later, on 15 June.

The entire family, apart from his heir, was distraught. And indeed, it would have to be said that the accession of Kaiser Wilhelm II was not met with unfettered joy in his family. Most had no confidence that he would treat his mother and younger sisters well, certainly Queen Victoria was particularly incensed. She wrote to Victoria: 'It is too dreadful for us all to think of Willy & Bismarck & Dona – being the supreme head of all now! Two so unfit & one so wicked. He spoke so shamefully about dear Auntie Vicky To Uncle Bertie & Aunt Alix.'[20]

She was enlisting family members to make Willy see reason in the horrible treatment she envisioned for her widowed daughter. Again, she wrote to Victoria:

> I beg you to entreat him to let bygones be bygones … Tell him that the more respect he shows to her & his father & the more consideration for her wishes, the more he will be liked by his Country & all of us. – The reverse w[ou]ld do him immense harm.[21]

Irène did her best to be a peacemaker. However, she, too, found Dona and Willy difficult to get along with, so it is no wonder that there were problems.

More interesting for Victoria was that Ella and Serge were going on a pilgrimage to Jerusalem. Ella particularly wanted to go there to pray for her sister, whom she hoped would eventually come to Russia. There, they dedicated a Russian Orthodox Church, the Church of St Mary Magdalen, to Serge's mother, the Empress Marie Alexandrovna. Located on the earth considered by the Russian Orthodox church to be the Garden of Gethsemane, the onion domes of the structure were incongruous amid old yeshivas and synagogues, mosques, and the Western Wall.

Victoria followed Ella's trip through her letters, and hoped in the future that she, too, would be able to travel to such an exotic destination. Ella's trip to Nazareth and Mount Tabor, and descriptions of the Holy Land fired Victoria's imagination. Ella wrote that it was a beautiful but desolate land with pockets of Jews, Christians and Muslims. Jerusalem, she said, was radiant and she was 'deeply affected by all this. How I should like to be buried here!'[22] It was a land, Mark Twain had observed, that the Ottomans had neglected for centuries without any development or progress. Victoria, with her love of the exotic, must have been wildly envious.

Ella wrote that there was nothing more beautiful than watching the sun set on the walls of the city. There was a golden glow to the indigenous stone as the sun touched the walls. A serenity overtook the city as the muezzin called the faithful to prayer. She was incredibly moved by the Church of the Holy Sepulchre and had walked the Stations of the Cross. As noted earlier, although Serge was in many ways a strange and cruel man, he was also a very religious one. It meant a great deal to him that Ella eventually decided to convert to Russian Orthodoxy several years after this dedication.

For the time being, Victoria spent much of the autumn at Wolfsgarten and was back to Malta by November. But death dogged her once again. Louis' father, Prince Alexander of Hesse, had been diagnosed with inoperable stomach cancer and died in Darmstadt on 15 December 1888 at the age of 65. Louis and Victoria had been recalled from Malta and were there in his last days.

It was a sad blow for all, since Prince Alexander had been the stalwart of his family. He worked closely with his sons their entire lives and was there for Louis during his first difficult days as a cadet in the Royal Navy; he had been with Sandro during his frustrating tenure in Bulgaria; and, for his younger sons, though their paths might not have been so difficult, he was a prop for Liko when he was ridiculed in the press before his marriage to Beatrice. Victoria wrote to her grandmother that 'Louis is terribly unhappy, he always got on so very well with his father.'[23] As the oldest son, Louis inherited Heiligenberg and there, throughout all her time as a navy wife in rented houses, would be Victoria's true home. That winter, to settle his father's estate, Louis and Victoria stayed in Hesse.

It was also around this time that Victoria's mother-in-law noticed that there was something amiss with Alice's hearing. She brought this to Victoria's attention, who took Alice to an ear specialist in Darmstadt. It was found that Alice had a blockage of the Eustachian tubes in both ears — the part of the ear that links the outer and middle ear; it was determined, however, that she could hear somewhat. Victoria faced the problem headlong in the only way she knew how: she made sure that Alice knew how to lip-read – but also to never show her disability in a crowd. Though it might seem cruel to us today, Victoria never wanted Alice to feel disadvantaged or disabled in any way.

In January 1889, Ludwig and Alix visited Russia to stay with Ella. Alix had her coming out ball there on 29 January and was in great beauty, wearing white, resplendent in diamonds, and flowers in her hair. During her stay, the tsarevich was particularly attentive and their attachment was mutual. Naturally when she came home to very middle-class Darmstadt it was a terrible let down.

The Times of London reported on 10 January of an engagement between Alix and Nicholas. On 12 January, *The Times* said that Darmstadt denied such an engagement, but the author was convinced that an engagement would be announced at Easter. Then denied it same day in that same paper. As has been noted, Queen Victoria hated reading about such things in the papers, true or not. More important was her dread that this granddaughter would marry Nicholas.

However, the queen and Victoria had something more definite to discuss. At the beginning of 1889, Victoria discovered that she was pregnant once again. The pregnancy was much more difficult than her first one had been, and she found herself tired and listless and reluctant to do anything. The queen shot off letter after letter telling her to walk more, and other such sage advice.

Moreover, there was an unfortunate incident that took place in Austria-Hungary at the end of January. Though the facts remain unclear to this day, the official version was that the heir to the Imperial Throne, Crown Prince Rudolph, the son of Franz Joseph, committed suicide at his hunting lodge at Mayerling after shooting his teenaged mistress, Baroness Maria Vetsera. There was much discussion about this incident as well as commiseration with the emperor at this time. The queen examined it in a letter to Victoria:

> The death of the C[rown]. P[rin]ce of Austria is too horrible. There is no doubt whatever but that he led a very debauched life, & that this unfortunate girl said to be one of the prettiest & I hear fastest in Vienna Mlle. Marie Vetsera only 19 – was found dead, on his bed, both dead, & shot — & a pistol in his hand. She … wrote to her Mother the day before she went to Mayerling that she would be dead the next day!![24]

As a result, Franz Joseph's brother, Karl Ludwig, became heir. However, as he was approaching 60 and not in good health, the Imperial Court focused on Karl Ludwig's eldest son, Archduke Franz Ferdinand, the nephew of the emperor, becoming his heir. Franz Ferdinand wasn't popular among the Habsburg officialdom and had countless enemies at the Imperial Court. In 1900 he caused a sensation when marrying a Bohemian aristocrat, Countess Sophie Chotek, later granted the title of Duchess of Hohenberg by a resigned Franz Joseph. This luckless couple were assassinated in 1914, starting a chain of events that culminated in The Great War.

For Victoria and the queen there was another more immediate reason why they discussed this royal scandal. It turned out that Sandro Battenberg, who had been a long-time friend of Rudolph's, had been invited to the hunting lodge that weekend and had had to decline as he was travelling elsewhere. It seems that he may literally have dodged a bullet. To another distant cousin, Prince Philipp of Saxe-Coburg & Gotha, fell the ghastly task of entering Rudolph's chambers and find the corpses. He never spoke a word, other than to the emperor, about what he had seen.

Both women of course knew Rudolph's wife, Stephanie, the daughter of Leopold II of the Belgians and a Coburg relative. 'I knew Stephanie, his wife, since our visits to Brussels in our childhood[,]' Victoria wrote in her memoirs many years later, 'I never considered her clever then, or after I had seen her again many years later did I find cause to reverse my opinion.'[25]

And it was the following month that Sandro took the title of Count Hartenau and married his opera singer, Johanna Loisinger.

In March 1889, Irène gave birth to her first child, Prince Waldemar. The baby was born at their home in Kiel and seemed well, until it was discovered that he suffered from haemophilia. This would be the first instance that the dreaded disease would show up in the Hessian princesses' progeny. The consequences later would be catastrophic.

It was at this time that the queen again became preoccupied with Alix's marital fortunes. She wrote to Victoria:

> Is there no hope abt. E.? She is not 19 – & she shld. be made to reflect seriously on the folly of throwing away the chance of a very good Husband, kind, affectionate & steady & of entering a united happy family & a very good position wh[ich] is second to none in the world![26]

The 'E.' in the letter was Prince Albert Victor of Wales, known in the family as Eddy. Queen Victoria thought he would make a splendid match for Alix; the position as heir to the British throne, in her mind, was unparalleled. However, Eddy's affections were fickle, and Alix's were engaged elsewhere. Her grandmother knew this with dread, but nevertheless she persisted with the project until Alix herself cried halt. She loved Eddy like a cousin, and if grandmama really wished it, she would try.

There was a feeling in the queen's letters that she was flailing in her attempts to get Alix matched with someone other than a Russian. If Eddy would not do, how about, she proposed to Victoria, his younger brother, George of Wales? Alix, the queen declared, had cared for him at some point, but she was not sure if she did now. Victoria, of course, knew where Alix's affections lay, but did not want to speak about them until it was absolutely necessary.

Soon enough, the queen realised that Eddy would not capture Alix's heart, and she worried about who would 'do' for either of them. She emphasised to Victoria that Alix was the youngest daughter in a small German Grand Duchy and though beautiful, would be lucky to capture the attention of a suitable match. She was smug in her belief that Tsar Alexander III and his wife Marie Feodorovna were uninterested in Alix for their son. She was particularly incensed because she believed:

> Ella and Serge do all they can to bring it about, encouraging and evening urging the Boy to do it.

> The state of Russia is so bad, so rotten that any moment something might happen and though it may not signify to Ella, the wife of the Thronfolger [heir to the throne] is in a most difficult and precarious position.[27]

And later, in desperation, 'tell Ella that no marriage for Ali[x] in Russia wld be allowed, then there will be an end of it[.]'[28]

Victoria had more pressing issues. She went into premature labour on 13 July 1889, and Louise Alexandra Marie, Victoria's second daughter, was born at Heiligenberg. 'Unlike Alice, who was a fine sturdy baby, Louise was rather a miserable little object, and the nickname "Shrimp" which Louis then gave her remained attached to her during her childhood.'[29] Louise's father would continue to address her as 'Shrimp' in his letters even in her adulthood. The pregnancy and labour had been difficult for Victoria, and she needed rest for several months to recover. A vigorous and active person, this must have been extremely exasperating for her.

Meanwhile, Louis continued to advance in the Royal Navy. He was appointed to his first independent command on the HMS *Scout* in autumn 1889. He was much happier with this command than he had been on the Royal Yacht. This was a more serious command and not a pleasure cruiser, as the yacht had been. Regrettably, whenever Louis was promoted in the navy there was a great deal of uproar, commencing with the word nepotism and thence to xenophobic complaints.

Victoria and Louis went back to Malta, this time without the children, who would be left with their Grandmother Julie at the *Alexanderpalais*, the Battenberg home in Darmstadt. Since Uncle Affie continued as Commander-in-Chief of the Mediterranean Fleet, the Edinburghs were still residing in Malta at the Admiralty House.

However, they would be delighted by a visit from Victoria's Hessian family while they were stationed in Malta. The German naval squadron sailed in as a special treat and with it, Irène and Henry with their new baby. Henry was the captain of the SMS *Irène*. Throughout their stay, Victoria observed her sister and husband. She was able to assure her grandmother that Henry was completely devoted to Irène and that they were happy. Irène stayed on after the departure of the squadron, and Grand Duke Ludwig and Alix joined them for a visit.[30]

As with her previous stays on the island, Victoria would be charmed with all she saw and did. She was often left alone while Louis was out to sea, but she coped, just as she had during her own father's constant absences. Her myriad interests from gardening to exploring the curious rock formations on the island kept her from repining, and by spring, she was back in Darmstadt with her children.

Victoria's peripatetic existence continued through the late 1880s and into the 1890s. She visited the family and lived the life of a naval wife. It was simple for her to decamp with whatever children were available and make those visits and travel wherever her whim took her. This assuaged her insatiable curiosity for life and people – whatever Victoria learned in books, she was keen to observe in human nature. When she wasn't travelling, she was working at whatever cause called out to her. In London, for example, with Louise and later in the 1890s Nona Kerr, her lady-in-waiting, travelling companion and close friend, she worked with the poor in the East End.

Victoria continued to be the recipient of the queen's ruminations about Alix and her love life.

> We have just a faint lingering hope that Ali[x] might in time look to see what a pleasant home, and what a useful position she will lose if she ultimately persists in not yielding to Eddy's really earnest wishes.
>
> There are so few for her to marry and Eddie is very good! However if after he returns [from India] – improved and developed as we must hope he will be – who could he marry? Do tell me.[31]

Alix had visited Queen Victoria that spring but had not shown the slightest interest in either of the Wales princes. Victoria continued to placate the queen writing: 'I think it would perhaps be best not to disturb Ali[x]'s mind about Eddie just at present – but will try & speak with her about him in spring, when I get home.'[32]

The queen was dogged about this, but so was Victoria and ultimately, so was Alix.

<h1 align="center">Chapter 6</h1>

<h1 align="center">Malta</h1>

Despite what Queen Victoria thought, the Darmstadt family were close with their Russian relatives and in summer 1890, the grand duke took his family to see Ella at their lovely country home Illinskoje. The house had charm, serenity, and none of the opulence of the gargantuan palaces in St Petersburg. They spent an idyllic time, playing lawn tennis and visiting their neighbours. In addition, there was plenty of other company in the house besides friends and family, since many officers of Serge's regiment, the Preobrajensky guard, also stayed there.

It now became apparent that Ella was going to convert to Russian Orthodoxy. She had several reasons for the conversion. First, she wanted to show her sister, Alix, that converting to Orthodoxy wasn't as difficult as she might imagine. Should she wish to do so in the future, she would have Ella's full support. Ella also wanted to do it for her husband, though Serge had never required her to do so. Victoria, who throughout her life would change her views on religion, spirituality and even in the way she believed in God, supported Ella in this as well. Her family wasn't so sanguine – Irène wrote that she was depressed about it and grieved, as was their father, the grand duke. Nonetheless, Ella converted in March 1891.

In autumn 1890, Victoria returned to Malta with Alice and Louise. Alice was now 5 years old, and Victoria continued to work with her on her lip-reading and speech. Victoria said if she'd had to have a vocation, she would have liked to have been a teacher, and so teaching Alice, and later her other children, was extremely rewarding.

While in Malta, Victoria kept up her voracious reading and furthered her education with a series of lectures on geology with a certain Professor Lepsius. She continued with her love of archaeology as well as drawing and painting. Victoria continued to be unmindful of her appearance and Louis found this very trying since he was always debonair and well put-together. One imagines him checking her for lose threads or cigarette ash before they went anywhere.

The queen also had some optimistic matchmaking in the works for Alix. She had hoped that Alix might become attracted to the handsome Prince Max of Baden. Many princesses had been captivated by him because of his good looks, but again, there was little to no interest from either party. The queen was daunted but never discouraged until she was sure that she was beaten. Meanwhile, she was content that Eddy had finally found a bride – Princess Victoria Mary of Teck (known as 'May'). Victoria wrote to her about this saying that she thought it would be a 'great load off'.[1]

Certainly, it was a great load off Alix's mind, and she wrote 'Yes, darling Grandmama, I was glad to hear of Eddy's engagement.'[2] One can't help feeling

60

that there was a little exasperation in her tone. But, for now, the pressure was minimised.

Good news came at the end of that year when Louis was appointed a Captain in the Royal Navy. This necessitated a move to London which disappointed Victoria, but she was consoled by the fact that she would be living near her grandmother. Louis had invented a navigating instrument which was subsequently called the Battenberg Course Indicator. The Admiralty soon adopted his invention, as well as the Air Force during the Great War. It was also used by the navies of several other nations, including Imperial Russia. As a matter of fact, Victoria was aboard one of the Tsar's men-of-war when the Captain showed Tsar Nicholas his Course Indicator. Victoria was heard to exclaim: '"Why, that is Louis's invention." The Emperor then said to the Captain: "That is the instrument which my brother-in-law, Prince Louis of Battenberg, invented", and the Captain replied that it was found to be so good and useful that the Navy Department were going to order it for all ships.'[3]

That winter, Victoria helped Louis research and assemble a book called *Men-of-War Names,* which provided information about the way ships were given their names. Published in 1897, it was meant to be a reference. Notably, he wrote in the preface that 'but for the devoted assistance of my wife, this little book would certainly not have seen the light of day'.[4] But, he did not mention Victoria's name.

Several deaths marred the beginning of 1892.

In January, just a month shy of his wedding to Princess Victoria Mary of Teck, Prince Eddy died of influenza. He had caught a chill that quickly developed into a major infection and tragically, within a month, Eddy was dead.

There were also worries during this time about the health of Grand Duke Ludwig. He had become ill during the winter 1891, but was thought to have recovered by the new year. However, he had an enlarged heart and soon began to worsen again. Victoria and Louis had left Malta and were now living in Darmstadt, so the entire family were present when he passed away from heart disease and stroke. As would be her role many times in the future, Victoria, now pregnant with her next child, was a stalwart for her siblings: 'Victoria … is the one to whom we go for everything, & is the one to keep us all up, & the most practical for everything – I cannot imagine what it would have been without her.'[5]

The grand duke had been lonely up until the end, not reconciling himself to losing his daughters to marriage, or his one chance of happiness with Alexandrine de Kolemine (who was still getting money from the Hessian Civil List). Victoria wrote that he was the kindest, most just man she had ever known – liberal and fair-minded.[6]

Victoria's brother Ernie inherited the Grand Ducal title. He was an attractive young man of 24 with a sensitive and artistic temperament. He was hardly ready for the duties of a Grand Duke. Alix wrote to her grandmother, 'Poor dear Ernie to suddenly be placed in such a position & with such responsibilities on his young shoulders. He is so brave & good, the dear Boy.'[7] Ernie was overwhelmed by the job and the work it would entail, and Alix was broken-hearted without her father and other siblings. She was 19 and knew little of how to proceed.

Unfortunately, Alix was unpopular in the Duchy because she seemed snobbish and hostile, though in reality she was just painfully shy. Most importantly, there was no one to teach her how to be a first lady of anything, never mind a grand duchy or, later, an empire. Consequently, she had no idea of how to make herself seem appealing or charming.

The other siblings did what they could to help. Victoria continued to reside in Darmstadt. Alix did her limited best, writing to her grandmother that she would do all she could but wished that she was 'as clever as Victoria, as then I could be of far more use to him [Ernie]'.[8] Victoria did her bit by taking over the presidency of the group founded by her mother, the Alice *Fraüenverein*. But her own nomadic ways eventually made it necessary to give this office to someone who resided in the grand duchy full-time.

The queen rushed to Darmstadt the following month to give Ernie a crash course on ruling. She dreaded the trip and wrote: 'How one missed darling L[udwig], who always used to jump into carriage and welcome us with such joy. Dear Ernie, in plain clothes, and the three poor dear girls, Victoria, Irène, and Ali[x], in deepest mourning with long veils, were standing on the platform.'[9]

Queen Victoria, like his sisters, coddled Ernie, and she wrote how she pitied him deeply. He would eventually turn out to be a beloved and extremely progressive figure in the grand duchy. In his youth, he was greatly influenced by artists of the day, particularly enjoying Art Nouveau. He set aside one of the parks, the Mathildenhöhe,

> to promising architects and artists, where they were given complete freedom to design and build first their own houses, and then small modern houses for other families on the estate. This became known as the Darmstadt Artists' Colony …. made possible not only because of the Grand Duke's financial support, but also his initiative and enthusiasm.[10]

But this was in the future; for now, the queen fretted about her grandson. After just a few weeks, she concluded that the best course for him was to marry. She determined that having a grand duchess would be just as important as having the new grand duke.

She looked for likely candidates with zeal. Like an earnest matchmaker, the queen tried to think of a young woman who might be a help to him, who might feed his artistic soul and would understand his sensitivity. Cousins were thought of, including Uncle Affie's eldest daughter Marie, however, word came that at the age 17 she was engaged to Crown Prince Ferdinand, the heir to the Romanian throne. The queen found Missy's engagement extremely disappointing and was eager to secure another eligible princess before she was snapped up. The next candidate was Affie's second daughter, Victoria Melita of Edinburgh. The queen's rationale was that they had the same birthdays (though several years apart) and the same sense of humour.

They were first cousins, and with haemophilia apparent in Irène's new baby, there were solid reasons not to champion the match. The queen thought it sensible to consult her physician, Sir William Jenner. Sir William put her mind at ease, telling her that such a marriage would not be unwise. With his blessing, the queen went ahead and pushed for the match.

Meanwhile, Victoria paid little attention to the queen's machinations. She was at Heiligenberg waiting for her next confinement and more absorbed in appointing Alice's first governess, Miss Robson, who had been governess to her cousin, Margaret of Connaught. She had several visitors that autumn before the birth. One was her cousin, George of Wales, who remarked in his diary:

> Louis met us at the station & drove us to his pretty place in Jugenheim,
> where we found Victoria & her two dear little girls Alice & Louise.
> We had tea & they showed me all over the house ... They showed
> me their collection of Naval medals which was most interesting.[11]

Cousin George stayed for several days. More important to Victoria, however, was that Ella would be visiting her. Though Ella had promised to visit Darmstadt often, her visits had been very rare.

On 6 November, Prince George was born at the Old Palace in Darmstadt. Coming just a little more than six months after the death of her father, it was especially emotional for Victoria to have her first son. He was named for his cousin, George of Wales, as well as for Victoria's father and her two brother's-in-law, Serge and Henry. He would be Queen Victoria's thirteenth great-grandchild.

Victoria wrote to her grandmother:

> The baby seems a strong, healthy child & is a source of the greatest
> pleasure & interest to his sisters. Louis left us yesterday & hopes to
> see you soon, when he will be able to tell you all about me & the
> child. I am so pleased and proud he got this appointment.[12]

Indeed, Louis was now Naval Advisor to the War Office, Chief Secretary to the joint Naval and Military Committee of Defence as well as Naval Advisor to Inspector-General of Fortifications.

Louis made several trips to Germany and to his cousin-by-marriage, Kaiser Wilhelm. Willy was inordinately proud of the German Navy and boasted about it so much as to be completely indiscreet. Willy showed him drawings of battleships and Louis was invited to inspect the German Manoeuvre Squadron of the North Sea. Louis dutifully reported everything Willy said back to his superiors at the Admiralty.

Victoria and her family would now be based in London for a time. They rented a house at 37 Eccleston Square, Pimlico, which – as she told her grandmother – was cheap and very unfashionable. That it was within walking distance of Buckingham Palace, however, was a big advantage, and Victoria looked forward to popping in and visiting her grandmother whenever she fancied. Christmas that year was with the queen at Osborne House on the Isle of Wight.

As the new year rang in, the queen was plotting with Victoria again:

> [O]n Saturday I think Uncle Alfred A[un]t. Marie & the girls &
> Alfred will be coming & I am very anxious that you sh[ou]ld hint
> to Ernie to be very kind & posé [sedate] & not tease Ducky or make
> silly jokes, wh[ich]. Might destroy our hopes & wishes.[13]

Victoria, however, was of a much more practical bent. She was not necessarily sanguine about Dr Jenner's theories that there would be no harm in close cousins marrying. She wanted more explanation. She also felt that the queen was being far too pushy about the situation, and she wrote to Ernie that she was most anxious that he should not feel pressured. She finished by saying: 'please seriously think the question of relationship over once more so that if in the end you do marry Ducky you may not later have to reproach yourself at having done so without careful consideration.'[14]

With all the wedding talk for Ernie, the queen made one last ditch effort with Alix, putting George of Wales in front of her as a prospect. But he proved as unappealing to her as Eddy had, and in the end, George took another bride: Princess Victoria Mary of Teck. Fate and propinquity seemed to have brought them together after the death of Eddy and the wedding was to take place on 6 July 1893.

Victoria was thrilled that Alice would be one of the little bridesmaids along with the Wales, Connaught, Albany and Edinburgh girls. It would take place at the Chapel Royal at St James's Palace and would be a comparatively quiet affair since George's mother, Alexandra of Wales, who continued to mourn her first son Eddy, couldn't face a large gathering .

Louis and Victoria now rented Undercliff House in Folkestone and had to travel up and down to London to participate in all the lunches, dinners and festivities leading up to the royal wedding. Of the various royalty attending the wedding, Tsar Alexander III's son, Nicholas, was coming as a representative of his father. Alix had elected not to attend the wedding itself, though she went to a pre-wedding ball and saw Nicholas. She wanted to avoid him as she knew that there would be grave difficulties if a proposal did come. Of immediate interest, however, was that Ducky and Ernie were provided with a chance to meet again.

After the wedding, there were further treats. The highlight of which took place a week later when *L'Amico Fritz* and *Cavalleria Rusticana* were conducted by the composer, Pietro Mascagni.

Later that summer there was another sad death; Prince Albert's older brother, Ernst II, Duke of Saxe-Coburg & Gotha died at Reinhardsbrunn. Two brothers could not be more dissimilar; whereas Prince Albert had possessed a virtuous and moral character, his elder brother had possessed a dissolute one, but Victoria was sensitive to the fact that it was another member of the queen's generation now gone. She wrote: 'I am sure that the death of dear Grandpapa's brother will have much grieved you ... The change will be a great one to Uncle Affie & Aunt Marie.'[15] The change to which she is referring is that Uncle Affie would now be the Duke of Saxe-Coburg & Gotha, since Ernst had no legitimate children of his own. They would have to leave and take residence in Coburg.

Victoria returned to Darmstadt in the autumn of that year and spent a great deal of time with Ernie and Alix. Unquestionably, they talked long and hard over the matrimonial prospects of both young people. The queen wrote to Victoria: 'I have written twice to Ernie abt. the necessity of his showing some attention & interest. Pray tell it him & say he must answer me – Aunt Marie fears he no longer wishes it, wh[ich] I am sure is not the case.'[16]

As it was, Alix, who knew how much Nicholas desired her for a bride, continued to be in an agony of indecision about changing her religion. In addition, she was not able to manage as a 'first lady' of the grand duchy, and Victoria was forced to take a lot of the responsibility upon herself.

As the year ended, Victoria and Louis had more personal worries. Louise, who was now a delicate 4-year-old, had developed a glandular problem in her throat and had to have an operation. Sir Frederick Treves, who had operated on Uncle Bertie for appendicitis, would perform the procedure. Louise recovered easily. However, another family member was not so lucky.

It was at this time that Prince Alexander of Bulgaria, now Count Hartenau, became ill with sepsis from a ruptured appendix. Since there were no cures, the family waited anxiously for news; when it came, it was the worst they could have expected. He had died on 17 November. The queen wrote, feelingly: 'Dear, noble, charming, splendid Sandro to be snatched away like this at thirty-six, just when there was every reason to expect he would rise very high and play a great part in the future.'[17]

The queen was being slightly fanciful here. It is unclear what role she thought Sandro would play and in whose future. However, Victoria wrote with some satisfaction that '[t]he Bulgarian Government speaking for the people, asked that their first prince should be buried at Sofia, to which with his usual political wisdom King Ferdinand [of Bulgaria] cordially agreed.'[18]

A memorial service was held for him several days later and Sandro's children were given a pension by the Bulgarian government.

There was some regret expressed of the way he was treated by the Russians. Ella wrote to Louis: 'Poor boy his was not a happy life I fear & it would give you pleasure to hear with what sympathy all speak of him here – [.]'[19] That was cold comfort to Louis. And one last word from Victoria, 'it is sad that poor Sandro now can never know that his many trials & difficulties during his troubled reign served to so greatly endear him to his people.'[20]

As the year went out, there were further conversations about an engagement between Ducky and Ernie. At last, in January 1894, Ernie visited Ducky and popped the question. The two were devoted friends and cousins and appeared to enjoy each other's company but beyond that, it could only be hoped that the match was a good one. Alix was not thrilled about her brother's engagement; she thought that Ducky was too self-assured and high-spirited for him. But she put on a brave face when writing to her grandmother, saying that it was wonderful for Ernie to be engaged, but now she was feeling decidedly 'de trop'.[21]

Victoria, who never felt 'de trop', wrote to her brother dispensing a little sage matrimonial advice:

> [I]n marriage, if it is to be a really happy one – both people must learn to understand each other – and when the wife is still so young, she will continue to develop very much as the husband influences her – and that will not happen suddenly but by imperceptible degrees as each grows to know the other better and to see and tolerate lovingly the faults that every human being naturally has.[22]

The engagement was announced on 10 January, and all were encouraged to see it as a great celebration. The wedding was planned for April 1894, and many of the extended family would be invited.

Victoria and her sisters were excited to once again be together. Never mind that the match the queen had so energetically promoted would be her last attempt at such a pursuit. Level-headed and sensible as she was, Victoria was in two minds regarding this engagement. On the one hand, she was happy to see that her brother had found a life companion to assuage his loneliness. On the other, she saw it as a bad omen that both parties needed to be pushed and prodded to come to the point. Knowing the personalities, tastes and dispositions of both the young people as she did, she had pause – and not just for health reasons.

The long-awaited nuptials in April 1894 would be the first big celebration with Uncle Affie and Aunt Marie as the Duke and Duchess of Saxe-Coburg & Gotha, and they pulled out all the stops to make it the 'wedding of the decade'. Most of the family – the Romanovs, the Hohenzollerns and various Germans, Uncle Bertie of Wales and of course, Queen Victoria – were delighted with the match and they came from all over to celebrate. They gathered in Coburg, a quaint German town, surrounded by hills and a fortress called the Veste.

Louis and Victoria arrived three days before the ceremonies were to begin and were lodged at the Villa Coburg, which was in the park near the principal town residence of the Coburgs – Schloss Ehrenberg. In the beautiful nearby forest was Rosenau, where Prince Albert, the prince consort was born and where he spent his youth.

The evening after Louis and Victoria's arrival there was a torchlight serenade at the Schloss, and afterward the company attended a candlelight dinner at the palace. Overshadowing the wedding, another spectacle was brewing: the drama of Alix of Hesse and the Tsarevich Nicholas of Russia.

Nicholas had written in his diary some years before '[m]y dream – one day to marry Alix H. I have loved her for a long time, but more deeply and strongly since 1889 when she spent six weeks in St Petersburg.'[23] He indicated in this diary entry that his religious struggle had been similar to Alix's. Though they were both Christians, they were of vastly different sects.

Ella had converted to Russian Orthodoxy, but for Alix it was still a great conflict. Nicholas tried his best to entreat her, and her resolve began to weaken. Ella, too, talked to her sister. She did her best to persuade her that the religions were not as different as might first appear. She argued that the faiths had similarities with which her sister could live. Kaiser Wilhelm entered the fray, when he tried to coax Alix with political arguments, observing that it would be a great alliance for a German Princess. Between the three, Alix was able to make her decision. She and Nicholas became engaged 20 April.

Now the problem was to tell grandmama.

The queen reacted much more philosophically than her granddaughter might have expected:

> Ella came in, much agitated, to say that Alicky and Nicky were engaged, and begging they might come in. I was quite thunderstruck,... Alicky had tears in her eyes, but looked very bright and I kissed them both ... I told [Nicky] he must make the religious difficulties as easy as he could for her, which he promised to do. People generally seem pleased at the engagement, which as the drawback that Russia is so far away, the position a difficult one.[24]

Perhaps she thought such a marriage would improve the relations between Russia and Britain.

Making the best of the situation, Queen Victoria set her mind on instructing Alix in statecraft and the art of being an empress. In what had been traditional for the other Hesse princesses, Alix went to her grandmother at Windsor after Ernie and Ducky's wedding to spend her last weeks as a single woman. The queen tried to ready Alix for a very public life, health, family and even the security issues she would have to face.

Victoria and Louis were renting a charming house in Walton-on-Thames, and Alix spent time with them as well. Besides enjoying the time she had with her little sister, she and Louis wanted to take some of the burdens of the affianced couple off the queen's shoulders. Victoria joined Alix in Harrogate. Alix, who was troubled with sciatica which caused stiffness and swelling in her legs, went to Harrogate for the cures. The two stayed together in a small boarding house and had a marvellous time dunking in the waters of the spa.

Victoria saw that her sister was happier than she had been since the death of their mother. Alix felt that her future was now settled with the man that she loved. Victoria wrote to her grandmother:

> If you could see, as I do, what a great difference Alicky's engagement to the man she has so long been devoted to, has made in her – how much brighter & happier she really is, you would feel that there is one great good in this engagement, which must counterbalance many of those disadvantages you mention – & that is the deep & sincere love that Alix & Nicky will begin their married life with.[25]

As perspicacious as Victoria was, this was likely wishful thinking. What is more, her grandmother knew this as well and faced Alix's wedding with the dread.

She later wrote to Victoria: '[A]ll my fears about her future marriage now show themselves so strongly & my blood runs cold when I think of her so young most likely placed on that very unsafe Throne, her dear life & above all her Husband's constantly threatened.'[26]

Now that Alix was going to be in such an important position, she was much sought after in the family. The wife of the future heir to the Imperial Russian throne was inundated with invitations from all the family for balls, dinners and parties. The queen, however, was adamant that this was to be a quiet time for Alix and not a raucous celebratory one. Alix was to stay quietly with Victoria, convalesce, and learn about Russia. She was especially insistent that Alix *not* go to Uncle Bertie and Aunt Alix at Marlborough House, a place which the queen thought corrupting and dissipated.

Alix stayed on with Victoria and Louis, and near the end of June, Nicky arrived on the Imperial Yacht, the *Polar Star.* It was an idyllic time, and the engaged couple were mostly unchaperoned. Those quiet, private days ended too soon when the two couples were 'fetched by a Royal carriage with an outrider to go to Windsor much to the surprise of the Waltonians, who never realised who the important people stopping with us had been.'[27]

From Windsor, the entire party went to Osborne, and at the end of July, Victoria and her family went back to Darmstadt for the rest of the summer. Irène came to visit, so there was much of the family around for Alix's last months as a single woman. The queen had the last word about Alix when she wrote to Victoria that Alix would get too grand. She was convinced that she would never meet her again as Alix, but only as Alexandra Feodorovna, Empress of all the Russias.

As for Ernie and Ducky, their marriage soon became troubled. The bride was 17 and too immature to be the first lady of anywhere, and the groom was initially too bewildered by his bride and his position to be of any use. The two were capricious, irresponsible, and heedless of their duties to the grand duchy. The queen would write pages and pages instructing them in their responsibilities, even to the point of pressing them to write 'thank you' notes for their wedding gifts, but to no avail.

While Alix lived in Darmstadt, it was clear that she and Ducky were not kindred spirits. Ducky harboured some resentment that Alix and Nicky's engagement absorbed all the attention, when the focus should have been on her wedding. Their personalities clearly clashed. Victoria would often be called in to intercede by the queen and to be something of a mediator between the two. She was loved by both young women for her good advice and impartiality. For Victoria, however, it was a painful position to be in.

As autumn approached, there was ominous news from Russia. Alexander III, only in his late forties, was seriously ill. He suffered from nephritis, which could lead to kidney failure at any time. In early October, Nicky summoned Alix to be with him at his father's deathbed.

This necessitated a 'mad dash' to the Crimea. Victoria and Orchie accompanied Alix to Poland, where Ella waited to escort the young princess the rest of the way. As usual, Victoria was the stalwart upon whom everyone depended. Irène wrote to her grandmother that she 'had never seen anyone have such a way of cheering & helping one in distress like Victoria'.[28] From there, Victoria returned to Darmstadt, and then later joined Louis in Malta where he was now captain of the HMS *Cambrian*.

Meanwhile, Nicky's father died on 2 November 1894, with Alix just in time to be with the family by his bedside. It was said afterward that Nicky was terrified of the responsibility of being tsar and that he was unready for such a task. According to his brother-in-law, Grand Duke Alexander Mikhailovich, he exclaimed, 'Sandro, what am I going to do…?'[29] The Grand Duke's assertions, as troubling as they were, remained unproven; they were found in a book of memoirs he wrote years after the fall of the Russian empire. This book manages to place Alexander Mikhailovich at the center of the story, the protagonist, not a witness. Alix and Nicky were married a few weeks later.

Victoria and Alix kept in constant touch, though Victoria was unable to attend the wedding in St Petersburg. Alix was blissfully happy with her new husband and over that winter Victoria received many letters from her sister attesting to this fact. So much was different, yet Alix never 'thought one could be as happy as I am now, life is so different to what it was in the past.'[30]

Nevertheless, Victoria, who had much of her grandmother's sagacity, was frightened for her little sister. She also was aware that neither Nicky nor Alix was prepared to rule, and Nicky especially had not been prepared by his father. Queen Victoria wrote to Nicholas and stated her fervent wish to be as much help as she could to the couple. She also prayed that the two countries would be able to coexist in friendship and how happy she was that Alix was with him at this emotional and very difficult time.

Between 1895–1901, Alix had four daughters and lived in constant fear of not producing the necessary male heir for Russia. Unlike her sister Ella, who had learned to get along with the Romanovs and was a favourite, Alix was completely different. Because of her extreme shyness, she made a negative impression on her 'in-laws'. She hated parties and Russian society and loved the quiet of family life. She felt strongly that it was necessary to keep her husband and children away from the other Romanovs who were, in her opinion, completely degenerate and, worse, undutiful. This attitude did not endear her to the Imperial Family.

The queen probably said it best when she wrote, 'How impossible it seems that gentle little simple Ali[x] should be the great Empress of Russia.'[31]

Chapter 7

Coronation in Moscow

Those waning years of the century were peppered with monumental events. There would be an Imperial Coronation, Queen Victoria's Diamond Jubilee, and several devastating deaths. Meanwhile, Victoria's three children were growing up.

Alice was growing into an extraordinary beauty. She coped well with her deafness and was bright and determined. She also was showing signs of the love of exoticism and mysticism that other women of the family had felt.

Louise, though not classically pretty, nevertheless had the Battenberg bone structure: the long high-bridged nose, the intense eyes, and the moulded cheekbones. She would be tall and thin and had the Hessian elegance. Hers was a face of great character, and some preferred her look to Alice's more classic prettiness.[1] She, like Alice, was bright and determined, but quiet. She had grown out of her sickliness but would always have a delicate and fragile appearance.

As for young Georgie, he was an active child, getting into everything and wanting to do what the older children did. He exhibited a precocious curiosity and wanted to know how everything worked. He, like his father, and later his younger brother, was destined for the Royal Navy. Unlike some children, far from resenting the idea, he embraced it and was interested in everything naval.

The three children followed Victoria in all her wanderings and travels when Louis was at sea. There were whispers from some that she neglected her children, but that was not the case. Their lives were scarcely normal, since they moved around a great deal in various residences and travelled so much, but they were all close to their mother.

As the coronation of Nicholas and Alexandra approached in May 1896, Alix had been a wife for over a year, and had given birth to her first daughter, Olga, in December 1895. There were two deaths that would absorb Victoria and her family before that historic occasion.

In September 1895, Victoria's mother-in-law, Aunt Julie, Princess Battenberg, died at Heiligenberg. Ella was making a rare visit to Darmstadt and was there with her sisters when the bad news arrived. Louis could not get back from his cruise on the *Cambrian* until some days later.

The Battenbergs had been a very close family, though their mother had not been particularly warm or tender to her children. Nevertheless, Julie was a woman who always put her sons and daughter first and was tremendously ambitious for them. Oddly, Chancellor von Bismarck thought she was a dangerous woman who wanted to put one of her sons on any vacant throne, and this was the real reason for his animosity toward the family.[2] While hardly dangerous, Julie did everything that she could to make sure that their unequal birth did not hinder them. She never put herself forward and was ever tactful and aware that her less than royal origins might cause discomfort. Because of her modesty, Queen Victoria respected her tremendously.

Later, due to high running costs, Victoria and Louis sold the *Alexanderpalais* which had been their town residence. It would later become a prosaic post office. Alix sent a letter of sympathy: 'What a homecoming! Words are too poor to express all I feel for you in this great sorrow, & I can only pray for God to give you strength and comfort – … And that you should have been too far away when that woeful news came!.'[3]

Prince Henry Battenberg (Liko) was getting increasingly restless with the living arrangement imposed by his mother-in-law and wanted some adventure. In 1895, after a great deal of persuasion, Henry was permitted to participate in the expedition to the Ashanti Coast. The situation was King Prempeh of the Kumasi was engaged in raiding the Gold Coast for slaves. The queen was worried that Liko would get some kind of exotic disease, and Princess Beatrice simply didn't want him to leave. The two had been barely separated in their ten years of marriage.

The prince appealed directly to the war office for permission to go. On 6 December 1895, he left England. He was acting as military secretary to the commander-in-chief of the forces. On 27 December, he joined a column of men marching inland, and while there he caught malaria. When it was thought he had improved he was put on HMS *Blonde*, heading back to Britain; he died at sea, off the coast of Sierra Leone. As there were no burial facilities at sea, his body was put in a coffin made of biscuit tins and filled with rum. His funeral service took place in St Mildred's Church, Whippingham, on the Isle of Wight. He was interred there in what became the Battenberg Chapel. Beatrice would join him nearly fifty years later. Henry's sad and untimely death left Beatrice alone with three sons and a daughter.

Of her three boys, the younger two, Maurice and Leopold, inherited the dreaded haemophilia. Leopold died during a hip operation when he was a young man, but Maurice had a somewhat more glorious fate. Although, like most haemophiliacs, he was a sickly child, he was nevertheless permitted to join the army when the Great War began. He was struck by flying shrapnel at the start of the war and had the sad distinction of being the first member of a royal family to be killed in that war. Their daughter Victoria Eugenie became Queen of Spain when she married Alfonso XIII in 1906. She, too, would carry the haemophilia gene into the next generation. Two of her sons had the dreaded disease.

Victoria, in her enormous capacity for strength, was able to move on from these tragic deaths. She was neither sentimental nor was she unfeeling, she just didn't believe in perpetual mourning. Members of her family might complain about her supposed lack of sensitivity, but it was her brisk determination to get on with life that helped others get over these setbacks.

Better to think about the coronation in May.

Irène, who was in the early stages of her second pregnancy, stayed behind in Berlin. Otherwise, many of Victoria's cousins, uncles, aunts and various relatives were in attendance. Queen Victoria's youngest surviving son, the Duke of Connaught, and his wife represented her. Nevertheless, it was Victoria who wrote copious letters to her grandmother describing the ceremonies and festivities. She started with Alix, telling the queen that she was quite changed, 'so well & happy … [T]here is nothing left of the sad & drooping look she used to have[.]'[4] While Alix disliked the massive number of festivities and ceremonies that would take place that May, she was looking forward to being with her family afterward at Illinskoje.

Victoria and Louis arrived in Moscow a week before the ceremonies and stayed with Ella and Serge. Moscow was a far more Asiatic city than St Petersburg, and all around there were buildings of the old style with onion domes and bright colours. Because of the security necessary around the Romanovs and their family during this time, Victoria could not indulge in her love of exoticism and explore the city to her heart's content.

The city had been wired with tiny electrical lights that would be illuminated the night of the coronation. Wooden bleachers lined the street, festooned with ribbons and every sort of banner. It appeared all the residents had planted beautiful flowers and plants to decorate the avenues along which the lengthy processions would wind. Above all, there were thousands of people who had come expressly to attend this lavish and momentous occasion, swelling the city to proportions it could hardly accommodate. However, for that moment in time, the joy of a new Imperial couple was deeply and spiritually felt. It was the zenith of the Romanovs – and the nadir would swiftly follow.

The festivities commenced on 25 May with a long parade of the Imperial family entering Moscow. In this parade were hundreds of security personnel, Imperial guards, Cossack guards, the nobility, and then, finally, the tsar himself, on a light dappled-grey horse. Alix rode in a stuffy carriage behind him, looking hot, tired and unsmiling. Unfortunately for her, this was the face her people saw and remembered.

Victoria had a feeling of dread, and perceived that the Russians had much less enthusiasm for their rulers, even on this day when their relationship was being renewed. That evening there was a family dinner and Victoria was able to observe Ernie and Ducky together. Her conclusions were not happy ones. Ducky and her sister Marie (Missy), were spending too much time with their cousins Boris and Kyril, the sons of Grand Duke Vladimir Alexandrovich, Serge's brother. Though they would not divorce for some years yet, it was obvious that Ducky and Ernie were unhappy.

The following day, the coronation took place at the Cathedral of the Assumption. The Imperial couple solemnly entered a church that was full with nearly 2,000 attendees, nevertheless it was quiet enough to hear a pin drop as they processed to their thrones. The choir sang old Russian chants, the heat was intense, and the air was filled with holy incense. The couple sat on diamond-encrusted thrones and received homage, then went back up the Red Staircase and showed themselves to the cheering crowd. The coronation was astonishing in its length and pomp. Each event was more exhausting and exhaustive than the one preceding.

That afternoon there was a banquet for nearly 2,000 people. The Imperial pair ate on an elevated platform as people filed by to show their respects.

In a ball several days later, Victoria was struck by a strange mixture of people standing in one of the smaller reception rooms. She was told that 'these people were all descendants of men who had saved their Sovereign's life, from old Tsarist times downwards. It was an old custom to invite these representatives to the Coronation.'[5] Victoria considered that the entire ceremony was wonderfully well-rehearsed from beginning to end, with everyone calm and unhurried.[6]

Later, she might have eaten her words because of the calamitous disaster that took place on 30 May. A special feast for the common people was set up in a parade ground just outside Moscow called Khodynka Field. There would be free meat and beer, as well as a souvenir mug of the coronation given to everyone who attended.

People had been gathering from the night before in order to partake of the Imperial largesse. By daybreak, the crowds numbered nearly half-a-million people. From this point, the story becomes slightly murky. As the crowd heard that gifts were being distributed, they pressed forward. Panic ensued and tragedy struck. Over 1,400 people were killed, falling into trenches dug on the field used for army exercise, either trampled or suffocated or both. Thousands more were wounded. It was suggested that the crush was provoked by reports of there not being enough food and gifts for all.

Alix and Nicky were immensely upset by the tragedy and wanted to skip a ball being held in their honour that evening by the French Ambassador, but Nicky's uncles, including Serge Alexandrovich, insisted they attend. After all, the French were allies, and had spent a lot of money on the ball. Most of the family were appalled, as were Alix and Nicky, but the uncles were adamant, and they were literally forced to go. Serge, who was responsible for the logistics at Khodynka, was naturally blamed for the disaster. Calls for his resignation were ultimately quieted through Alix's intervention. The investigation and results, such as they were, were largely ignored by the authorities.

The city was stunned by their attendance at the ball, even though they had been forced to do so. Nicky and Alix made their appearance and returned to the palace in complete despair. It was from then on that Alix was called the 'German Bitch' by many of her subjects, while Nicholas was called 'the Bloody'. The gilt of Imperial divinity was losing its lustre.

Grandmama, from Balmoral, certainly had something to say to Victoria about the calamity: 'How awful & dreadful is that fearful catastrophe of that Fête! Would it not have been better to have stopped the Balls etc. for it looks so unfeeling to go on just the same. It must throw a gloom over everything.'[7]

And to the British ambassador, Sir Nicholas O'Conor:

> The papers speak of a very angry feeling being evinced amongst the people in Moscow. Trust there is [no] cause for alarm or danger to the Emperor and Empress. Also fear poor Serge as Governor [of Moscow] may be blamed.
>
> There seems to have been lamentable want of proper prudence, i.e. allowing such a number of people to collect in one spot, and to keep order.[8]

Beside everything else, the queen was thinking about her Diamond Jubilee, which would take place in 1897. Though there was a great difference between Russia and Britain, she was wise enough to know that crowds were immensely changeable.

It all became part and parcel of the miscalculations that would eventually end in tragedy much later. It is a pity the queen wasn't alive during that first decade of the twentieth century to advise the young pair. Though, as the years went by, Nicky and Alix became more obdurate and isolated. It is likely they wouldn't have listened to such sage advice as the old monarch might have have provided.

A week later, Victoria and some of the family joined Ella at Illinskoje. There for some rest and relaxation after all the gruelling ceremonies were Nicky and Alix, the Edinburgh family, and Ernie and Ducky with their first baby, a girl called Elisabeth. In the relative quiet, they bathed and boated in the river that ran behind the house, and drove in the woods. As the summer began, they picnicked and visited many of their closest neighbours, including the Youssoupov family, at Archangelskoe. Victoria spent a month with her sisters and returned to Heiligenberg in July.

As the nineteenth century concluded, the royal families of Europe were at their zenith. Queen Victoria, who rightly called herself the 'Doyenne of Monarchs', was growing old.

In the autumn of 1896, Victoria and many of the family members joined Queen Victoria at Balmoral. The visit was significant for several reasons. First, because this was Alix's first visit to her grandmother as Empress Alexandra Feodorovna, and second, this was the first time a moving picture was filmed of the royal family. The film was made by photographers W. & D. Downey by the new cinematograph process. For viewers today, the film is faded and jittery, but it was done in order to commemorate the longest (at that time) British reign, and Queen Victoria was delighted with it.[9]

The queen's impression of her empress granddaughter was not so delightful. She found Alix distant and aloof. Alix's discomfort in being an empress was evident to her grandmother. Although she was enchanted with her latest great-grandchild, the Grand Duchess Olga Nikolaevna, she was not so sanguine about Alix, who she thought was getting too grand. Queen Victoria may not have recognised Alix's demeanour as profound shyness and an inability to handle her new position. In addition, the queen found it difficult to cope with Nicholas, who she found weak and wavering. Alix's last visit with her grandmother was not a happy one.

After the Balmoral visit, Victoria, along with Nicky and Alix, visited Ernie and Ducky at Wolfsgarten. Nicky made a remark that he wished he could be a constitutional monarch like Ernie. Victoria commented in her memoirs:

> Under other circumstances, Nicky would have made a remarkably good constitutional Sovereign, for he was in no way narrow minded, nor obsessed by his high position. If one could have boiled down Nicky and W[ilhelm] in one pot you would have produced an ideal Emperor of Russia. His father's dominating personality had stunted any gifts for initiative in Nicky.[10]

In November of that year, Irène and Henry's son, Sigismund was born. He was the only healthy child of the three that Irène bore.

The following spring, Victoria joined her grandmother at the Excelsior Hotel in Nice. There was much company there for that spring before the Diamond Jubilee. The Battenbergs were there along with Aunt Helena's daughter, Princess Helena Victoria (a family favourite), Grand Duke Peter Nikolaevich, who was there with his wife, the Grand Duchess Militza Nikolaevna, and her unmarried sister, Princess Anna of Montenegro.

Victoria's brother-in-law, Franzjos, was still unattached and looking around for a bride. He had considered the extraordinarily wealthy Consuelo Vanderbilt and had an interest making a play for her. Consuelo was the daughter of William K. Vanderbilt II and Alva Vanderbilt.

Alva, who was notoriously ambitious for her daughter, had brought Consuelo to Paris to auction her off to the highest bidder (not necessarily monetarily, but title-wise); she momentarily considered the prince's offer. As she wrote in her memoirs much later, for one moment '[a] royal crown glittered more brightly than a coronet [of an English Duke]'[11] It turned out that Consuelo didn't like him, and her mother thought twice and focused her attentions on Charles Spencer-Churchill, the Duke of Marlborough, which turned out disastrously for the young woman. (The pair were almost immediately unhappy. Both had extra-marital affairs and the marriage ended in divorce in 1906.)

As to Franzjos, he was introduced to Militza's sister Anna in Nice. The couple began the courting process of driving out together and dining with the queen and other family members. After several weeks, the engagement was announced. Queen Victoria was very pleased with the match and wrote to her daughter Vicky, the Dowager German Empress:

> Franzjos was engaged the night before last to the Princess Anna of Montenegro, a charming girl who is quite determined to marry him and is devoted to him. We are all most pleased as it is in every way a good match, being a near connection with Italy and also Russia.[12]

Princess Victoria was happy because she liked her prospective sister-in-law very much. She saw that there was true affection there, and later wrote to her grandmother, 'I really think he could not have found a nicer wife anywhere, nor one who could have been fonder of him.'[13] She also remarked that their finances would never be great, but beside being charming and warm-hearted, Anna was also practical which, Victoria feared, Franzjos was not.[14] Anna became a great favourite in the family. Franzjos was made a colonel in the Montenegrin Army. He was, however, more of an intellectual than a soldier and earned a PhD from the University of Leipzig.

The couple were married in May 1897 at Cetinje in Montenegro.

It was during this year that an essential member of Victoria's household was added. Louis had encouraged Victoria to engage a lady-in-waiting for herself and the ideal choice was Miss Nona Kerr. She was a Scotswoman and the daughter of Admiral Lord Frederick Kerr and the sister of Mark Kerr, a naval comrade of Louis' who would later become Louis' biographer. She was initially engaged to assist in the children's education, but she became Victoria's travelling companion and best friend for the next nineteen years, until her own marriage.

She was patient, generous, obliging and yet strong enough not to take too much manipulation from Victoria. She was neither argumentative nor was she compliant, so different to Victoria and the perfect foil. Victoria acknowledged that she became more pugnacious and impatient as she got older, but Nona stood her ground. In addition, she became a 'still point of security for Dickie [Victoria's second son and last child] in an itinerant and somewhat rackety existence'.[15]

Nona was a strong and supportive soul and Victoria would always regret any small transgression after it occurred. She would constantly find herself apologising, and often did so in writing:

> I have never managed to say to you, though I've wanted to all along, that I thank you much for doing a great deal more than just jobs for me all this time & that I should have missed you very much if you had not been there. I don't know why I am afflicted with (I fear) incurable complaint of never being able to speak out decently even

when I much want to – but perhaps you know it & so will continue
to be patient with me.[16]

Nona wasn't the only one who needed patience with Victoria. Louis, whom she had been married to for more than fifteen years, understood her reticence to show her feelings and lived with it. Victoria continued to be a great talker and it was said that only Louis, or later her son Dickie, could tell her emphatically to 'shut up'. The pair were in many ways a match of opposites, but nonetheless, during their long marriage there was not a breath of scandal. From all that has been written it seems apparent it was that happiest and rarest of royal or aristocratic marriages – a love match.

Nevertheless, Nona acted as sort of a buffer between Louis and Victoria whenever there were any issues. Letters from the couple to Nona would describe the situation that needed sorting and apparently, she had the wisdom to do it. She joined the household during the queen's Diamond Jubilee in June 1897, but was taken on officially on 9 July.

The jubilee festivities, services and general celebrations did not compete with the queen's Golden Jubilee, but there was a substantial gathering of family, distinguished personages from all over Europe and President McKinley from the United States. Victoria had read a great deal about America, her beginnings and her democracy, and was interested in seeing the plain figure of the president among all the glittering dresses, decorations and uniforms.

For Victoria it was special not only because it was her beloved grandmother, but also because Ella would be attending in one of her rare visits to England. After a thanksgiving service at Windsor, the queen travelled to London on 21 June for the celebrations. Victoria, in a carriage with Margaret of Connaught and Beatrice of Edinburgh, was part of the procession that drove through London, as was Louis, who rode on a horse behind the queen's coach as he had done during the Golden Jubilee. A film was made of the procession which was six miles long. The film is available on YouTube, but it too is shaky and it is nearly impossible to make anyone out.

The queen had decreed that no reigning sovereigns attend the ceremonies as she was just too old. And she was understandably a little nervous because of the events at Khodynka Field. Nevertheless, everything went off without a hitch and at the end of the day, she 'touched an electric button, by which I started a message which was telegraphed throughout the whole Empire. It was the following: "From my heart I thank my beloved people, May God bless them!"'[17]

After the celebrations, Victoria spent part of the summer in Heiligenberg, and later Hemmelmark, Irène and Henry's residence. Henry had gone off for a two-year cruise to China, so Irène was left alone with her two boys.

Nicky and Alix went to Darmstadt that autumn to lay the foundation stone for the Russian Chapel that was being built for her. Since Alix's conversion to Russian Orthodoxy, she had become almost fanatically pious and therefore needed a proper place to worship when they visited her natal home. The chapel, built at Nicky's expense, would be in the Mathildenhöhe, the Artist's colony established by Ernie that year. It not only encompassed the Russian Orthodox Chapel, but was also a 'centre for emerging reform movements in architecture, arts and crafts'.[18] It became a UNESCO World Heritage site in 2021.

Later that year, Victoria was back in England and spending Christmas at Osborne with her grandmother. This was not the queen's happiest birthday as her government was now sending the British Army to South Africa to what would soon erupt into the Second Boer War.

As the new year approached, Victoria was grappling with several health crisis. Louis was suffering from his first attack of gout and hobbled around painfully for several months; 8-year-old Louise was also in distress with a possible curvature of the spine. She was smaller than her sister and continued to earn the name her father had given her in babyhood – 'shrimp'. She weathered this problem after being examined by a certain Dr Vulpius at Heidelberg. He confirmed the curvature and suggested a course of exercises that proved to be successful.

More exciting was that toward the end of 1898, Irène was going to join Henry in China. The trip would take six months and she would be leaving her two sons at home. Victoria saw this as an opportunity to get to know her little nephews Waldemar and Sigismund, and so volunteered to take them for some of the time in Darmstadt; they spent Christmas together in the old palace.

Chapter 8

'Grandmama seemed to be in failing health....'

Victoria's itinerant life was to slow down quite a bit when Louis was appointed to the equivalent of shore duty. He assumed his new position as Assistant Director of Naval Intelligence in June 1899. He established his 'claim to rise to the highest ranks … [He was] a new broom that swept clean … [and] a constructive and thoughtful architect for the future.'[1] As ever, there was the usual carping and xenophobia, but for the moment, his abilities were appreciated.

Their lives became more stable, rather than the constant wanderings and separations. They rented a house at 40 Grosvenor Gardens, London. Once again, that would mean that Victoria could spend more time with her grandmother, which, as the queen grew older and more frail, was a pleasure for the younger woman. There were clear indications this year that the queen was failing. Her vision was practically gone, as well as the usual infirmities of old age such as arthritis, indigestion and rheumatism. The Boer War began in earnest, and Victoria often saw troops leaving Victoria Station for South Africa.

The Russian Orthodox chapel in Darmstadt was completed in 1899. Nicky and Alix had arrived in September that year with their three daughters, Olga, Tatiana and Maria. Alix continued to worry about providing a male heir to the Russian Throne, and this anxiety contributed to her delicate physical condition. In photographs around this time, it is possible to see that her lips are drawn in a very thin line, and the first signs of premature ageing. Victoria and her three children joined the imperial couple during this visit and the chapel, the Church of St Mary Magdalen, was consecrated in October.

Meanwhile, Ernie and Ducky were trying to make a final effort at reconciliation by having another child. Ernie was pleased about this and wrote to Victoria: 'Ducky expects the baby next June … You can well think [of] our joy and how happy we are together sometimes I can hardly realise it, it seems too good for words. Ducky is very well.[2]

So much of this last attempt smacks of wishful thinking and sadly, the child was still-born. However, it shows a great devotion between Victoria and Ernie. 'Don't we two really understand each other the best?'[3]

Ducky was not the only one to be expecting a child at this time. Victoria and her sister, Irène were carrying their last children. Irène's son Heinrich was born at Kiel in January, and Victoria's was born in June. She was nearing her thirty-seventh birthday and was urged by the queen to move to Frogmore, Windsor, a far more peaceful and healthful place than London. It was also a place where Victoria could walk and exercise, the way the queen always prescribed. The queen and Victoria visited one another during this time, lunching, chatting and stopping by whenever the fancy took them. Later, Victoria was grateful for this last small interlude with her grandmother.

Irène's son Heinrich was christened in May of that year. Unfortunately, he would soon show signs of haemophilia. It was a sad twist of fate that two of Irène's three boys would be haemophiliacs, and that when Alix at last had a son and heir, this boy too would suffer from the disease.

On June 25, the queen wrote in her journal for that day, 'I heard on waking that dear Victoria had got a little boy, born at 6 this morning, … it was a great pleasure … saw the pretty little Baby & also dear Victoria, just for a moment. She was very well.'[4] Victoria's second son was christened Louis Francis Victor Albert Nicholas, named for his father, uncles – and naturally for both the queen and Prince Albert.

There were consultations with the other three children about what his nickname should be in order not to mix him up with other family members. Someone suggested 'Nicky', but it was thought that that would confuse the little boy with the tsar. Then someone suggested 'Dickie', not knowing that 'Dickie-bird' was Victoria's pet nickname for Louis. After some further discussion, 'Dickie' won out and Dickie he remained for his entire life.

He would have the distinction of being the last great-grandchild photographed with Queen Victoria. She observed him to be a strong and vigorous child during their photographic session, when the queen was aided in holding the child by an unseen maid. During his christening ceremony in July, the infant knocked off her spectacles and got his hand stuck in her cap-veil. She found this all highly amusing. It is interesting to note that both of Victoria's boys escaped the curse of haemophilia. Whether this was simply luck, or that Victoria did not carry the gene is not known.

Dickie was a sunny and happy child with a great love for small animals. His mother educated him the first ten years of his life and he had a slightly artistic bent and a true calling for the Royal Navy. He inherited the Battenberg tendency of wanting to constantly prove he was as royal as everyone else. He also inherited his Uncle Liko's vanity, being always concerned about his appearance and loving ornate uniforms. Certainly, that was one attribute he didn't inherit from his mother.

To cloud the joy of the year's birth was a significant death in the family. Uncle Affie, the Duke of Saxe-Coburg & Gotha and Edinburgh, died. He was the third of Queen Victoria's children to die during her lifetime. It was he, along with Victoria's mother, Alice, who had encouraged Louis to join the Royal Navy. Moreover, he and his family, including his wife Aunt Marie, had been beloved companions to Victoria and Louis and their family in Malta. The duke had lost his battle with cancer of the throat, and also with alcoholism. Uncle Affie and Aunt Marie's son, Alfred Jr., had died the year before after a short life of dissipation.

This latest blow certainly had a lowering effect on the queen, who was failing in earnest as the year progressed. The last letter she wrote to Victoria was dated 9 August 1900 and discussed the giving of some charity to a worthy cause. It was the close of a correspondence that lasted over thirty years from little 'thank you' notes from a 7-year-old, to an interesting and adult conversation over the years on myriad topics.

As the year ended, Victoria noted that the queen attended the usual service for the death-day of Prince Albert, but also wrote that 'Grandmama seemed to be in failing health.'[5]

Victoria was with her family in London for Christmas that year. At the last night of the year, the queen appointed Louis, who was her naval aide-de-camp (an office he would continue with Edward VII and George V), a trustee for her private money. About the middle of January the queen took to her bed, and on 22 January, Victoria, Louis and family members were summoned to Osborne.

Queen Victoria died at Osborne House at 6.30pm; unfortunately, Victoria and Louis arrived a quarter-of-an hour later. Victoria lost the woman who, for nearly twenty-three years, was like a mother, and one of her closest confidants; she was heartbroken. Everyone in the family and the Empire agreed that nothing would ever be the same. Ironically, it was Willy, the grandchild who may have caused her the most grief, who held her up during the last two hours of her life.

Victoria wrote a lovely summation of her grandmother in her memoirs:

> On account of our having lost our mother when we were so young, Grandmama had taken a special interest in her beloved daughter's children. Her affection for us was very warm and sincere and she proved it on every occasion. As the one of us, who was the most in England, I was the one who was in closest touch with her. After my marriage she became very fond of Louis and relied on his judgment, tact and discretion, so that she discussed not only many private, but also public matters with him – and she nominated him as one of the Executors of her Will.
>
> My understanding of Grandmama grew with the years. In childhood, I had known her as a middle aged woman, and as I was approaching middle age, she had become a very old lady … In my early youth, Grandmama was a very formidable person in my mind, someone whom my mother regarded with respect and awe … She herself, tho' very gracious to her grandchildren, expected perfect manners and immediate obedience from them and would look and speak severely to any offender … My mother's death broke through many of these outward barriers and the constant signs of affectionate pity and interest, gave to our intercourse a more natural ease.[6]

Queen Victoria's last journey from Osborne to Windsor was one the entire nation took with her. The family followed her casket to the harbour where it would be conveyed to the mainland. They, like most of the country, had an overwhelming feeling of numbness and incredulity. Alice, who was now 16 years old, was one of the few great-grandchildren who had been privileged to know the queen well, and because of that was a great comfort to Victoria.

Louis and Victoria returned to London and, along with other family members, did what they could to make sure all the visiting dignitaries were suitably quartered and comfortable. As with all such occasions, London swelled to many thousands more than its usual population.

Alix, who was pregnant with her fourth child, was in despair not to be able to come to London for the funeral. She wrote to Victoria:

> How I envy you being able to see beloved Grandmama being taken to her last rest. I cannot believe she is really gone, that we shall never see her any more. It seems impossible. Since one can remember, she was in our life, and a dearer kinder being never was. The whole world sorrows over her. England without the Queen seems impossible.[7]

Ella did not make the journey either, for reasons – according to her biographer Christopher Warwick – that were unclear. The other Hesse children, Irène and Ernie, for whom the queen was like a second mother, attended.

The queen's coffin was brought from Osborne on 1 February and made its sad and slow procession through London the following day. There were many people – family members and other royalty, following the coffin through the streets, a spectacle, according to the *New York Times* 'never to be forgotten'. It processed in virtual silence, through a grieving, black-draped capital. The cortège, two hours long, eventually ended at Paddington Station from where the coffin would be taken to Windsor. Then, the flag-draped coffin would take a much smaller journey to Frogmore, where Queen Victoria would be laid next to her beloved consort, Prince Albert in eternal rest.

It was when the funeral train arrived at Windsor that an unexpected event occurred. When the coffin arrived at the station, there was a gun carriage with two pairs of horses waiting to bear her up to the mausoleum. Because the horses had been waiting for several hours, they were cold and evidently no longer inclined to move. When the coffin was placed on the caisson, the forward horses balked, while one of the back horses reared up and collapsed in a heap, hopelessly entangling all the horses in the harnesses and lines.

Everyone stood aghast having no idea what to do. It was only Prince Louis who saw what must be done. He suggested that the lines be cut, and a whole group of his sailors pull the entire carriage up to Windsor. After that and other alternate plans were discussed, it was decided to convey this singular honour upon Louis' men of the Royal Navy. It made for an impressively moving procession to the chapel.

The queen lay in the Albert Memorial Chapel until 4 February, after which she was taken to the mausoleum where she would be placed next to Prince Albert. The family were all present for the last service at St George's Chapel at Windsor, which was redolent with the queen's favourite fragrance, orange blossom. All except the queen's eldest daughter, Victoria's Aunt Vicky, who was herself on her deathbed. She was dying of cancer but conveyed her thoughts eloquently when she wrote 'the best of mothers, and the greatest of Queens, our centre and help and support – all seems a blank, a terrible awful dream. Realise it one cannot.' She died eight months later.

For Victoria, her extended family, and for the world, nothing would ever be the same.

❁ ❁ ❁

After the death of the queen, cracks within the core of the family became apparent. The Empress Friedrich, Aunt Vicky, was lying on her deathbed, while Ernie and Ducky's marriage approached a crisis. The impact of these things would spill over into Victoria and her immediate family's lives.

That February, for the first time in long memory, parliament opened without Queen Victoria. Prince Louis became naval aide-de-camp to the new king, Edward VII. Once all the formalities were over, Victoria began her wandering once again. She went to visit her dying Aunt Vicky at the beautiful Friedrichshof. She helped where she could, sitting with the empress, reading to her, walking with her, and helping her daughters take care of her. The dowager empress was in tremendous pain and suffered greatly.

After that difficult visit, Victoria went to visit Ella at Illinskoje. While she was in Russia, Vicky died. Victoria felt the loss of a beloved aunt acutely; one of the 'caregivers' who, in early days, had helped the Hesse family through the grievous loss of their own mother.

In the autumn after the queen's death, Ducky and Ernie's marriage crumbled. It's entirely possible that Ernie had never had much interest in women in general. Ducky made allegations that he was sleeping with the stable boys, but this must be taken with a grain of salt. There are only her letters to her niece to substantiate this, and possibly she was trying to convince others that she had been right to leave. What was key, however, was that Ducky was deeply in love with her cousin, Grand Duke Kyril Vladimirovich. The couple did little to hide their attraction. The queen knew this was happening and said that she would never try to match anyone again. However, divorce during her lifetime was unthinkable.

In October 1901, Ducky left Darmstadt and went back to Coburg to live with her mother, Aunt Marie. When she left Ernie, she also left her 6-year-old daughter, Elisabeth. She was roundly criticised for this. The truth was Ducky loved her daughter passionately, but she also knew that as a princess of Hesse, the child had to remain in Darmstadt.

Ernie and Ducky were divorced in December of that year, and Alix emphatically took sides with Ernie against the cousin she'd never liked, and made it clear that she would never be welcome at the Russian Court. Victoria was not so set against Ducky, out of respect for Uncle Affie, but was acutely aware of how much she had hurt Ernie. Although Ernie certainly hadn't been much in love, despite his comments to the contrary, his pride was hurt. Victoria was the right sister to console him. As always, her advice was sensible and unclouded with useless emotion, and

Ernie was grateful for her calm. He wrote a heartfelt letter full of love for his eldest sister:

> I had felt very near on the verge of madness & those words of love comforted me & consoled me … Every word you say is true & now that I am calmer I see the absolute impossibility of going on leading a life which was killing her & driving me nearly mad … If I had not loved her so, I would have given it up long ago…. Don't worry yourself darling you have been a sister to me like there are few … One inexplicable feeling has come over me, I feel that I am given back to you my sisters … God bless you for all your love my own darling, darling Victoria.[8]

Because of Victoria's sense of fairness, she also became Ducky's confidant during this difficult period. During one of their discussions, Victoria confessed that it was better for them to part. Ducky and Kyril would eventually marry in 1905. The marriage only occurred after Alix had finally delivered a boy, Alexei, in 1904, and Kyril was sure that he would no longer be the heir to the Imperial Throne. Alix was furious about this, and Nicky quickly exiled Kyril, struck him off the Imperial rolls while stripping him of his titles, decorations and allowances. Although Alix never warmed to Ducky, the couple were eventually reinstated.

About Ducky's decision to divorce, Victoria wrote:

> I was really less surprised and startled by her decision than he … Their characters and temperaments were quite unsuited to each other and I had noticed how they were gradually drifting apart. As I had known Ducky well from a child, since the time that she lived with her parents at San Antonio, she had often spoken freely to me on the subject of her married life. She had confidence, that I hope was not misplaced, in my fairness of judgment, and in spite of my being devoted to my brother.[9]

Meanwhile, Louis was appointed to the HMS *Implacable* at the end of the year, and the family was once again installed in Malta.

The repercussions from Ducky and Ernie's divorce continued in the following year. Not surprisingly, it was the couple's child Elisabeth who suffered the most. One of the agreements put in place was that the child would live with each parent half of the year. Little Elisabeth began the sad limbo of being shuttled from parent to parent. When she went to her mother in Coburg, Ernie wrote to Victoria that it was 'terrible to see her misery at leaving, for she has such a pronounced feeling for her home. I did everything I could to make it easy for her but alas that child feels herself such a Hessian.'[10]

On a slightly happier note, at what was to be Edward VII's coronation in June 1902, Victoria's daughter Alice, now 16 years old, met Prince Andrew of Greece and Denmark. He was a tall bespectacled fellow and a younger son of King George I of the Hellenes. Uncle Bertie's coronation was cancelled due to his developing appendicitis; it was held instead in August of that year. The young people continued to see each other in Darmstadt where she and Louise attended finishing school, and he was serving in the Hessian 23rd Dragoon Guards. They quickly fell in love.

Greece had only become a monarchy in the 1830s, and King George, who had been Prince William of Denmark, and Queen Alexandra's brother, had ruled since 1863. The Greeks seemed a bellicose people with expansionist ideas. Victoria wasn't pleased to think of her daughter in a volatile Balkan state. In this they were undoubtedly right, as events would later prove. As the decades rolled along, Alice and Andrew were in and out of exile, as was the entire Greek Royal Family. More important, both Victoria and Louis thought that she was too young at the time and counselled the couple to wait.

Victoria and her family returned to Heiligenberg that July before the new date of the coronation. At that time, she celebrated Nona Kerr's fifth year as her companion. With a self-deprecating sense of humour, Victoria wrote that Nona deserved a statue struck in her honour in the stable grounds for sticking it out with her, Louis and the children. To Victoria's credit, she was well capable of self-analysis and knew how difficult she was.

The following month, those who could, hurried back to London for the postponed coronation. That included Victoria, Louis, Irène and Ernie. Alice's new fiancé, Andrew, also returned to attend the festivities. Their engagement would not become official until May 1903, when it was announced by the new Prince of Wales, Uncle Bertie's son Georgie, when Alice was 17 and Andrew, 20.

Victoria now planned what would be termed another 'wedding of the decade', to take place in October 1903. This was one of the last gatherings of Queen Victoria's extended family before the Great War. Victoria spent her time writing letters and making arrangements. Though Hesse and by Rhine was considered a minor grand duchy, it was nevertheless easily able to accommodate a full complement of family members and other royalty coming from Europe and of course, whichever members of the Imperial Family in Russia who chose to attend.

It was also toward the end of 1902 that Louis was appointed Director of Naval Intelligence. Victoria, as was her wont, travelled back and forth visiting sisters with her little entourage. The family met in Darmstadt in October of that year, and afterwards Victoria went to Irène at her house in Kiel to spend Christmas.

In the beginning of 1903, Victoria joined Louis in London and they took their eldest son to Cheam for preparatory school. Georgie, she said, loved the school and many military and naval families sent their sons there. While he was at Cheam, his sister Alice was having lessons at home with the Hessian Princesses' old governess, Miss Hardcastle, while Louise was having her lessons with another tutor. Young Dickie, was just a toddler at the time, and Victoria took him for walks to the zoo and the museum of natural history.

Andrew arrived toward the end of spring for the announcement of their official engagement. The announcement came at a family dinner given by the Prince and Princess of Wales at Marlborough House. There was also a service at a Greek church to honour the occasion.

Toward the end of the summer, Victoria was back at Heiligenberg. There was a visit to Frankfurt to meet the 'in-laws' King George and Queen Olga, a Romanov grand duchess by birth. Given the many family connections shared between Victoria and the Greeks, they were well-acquainted. Her own first cousin, Sophie of Prussia, was the wife of Crown Prince Constantine, George's eldest son. By September, Victoria and her children were back in Darmstadt at the Old Palace where they would remain until after the wedding.

Louis returned to Darmstadt at the beginning of October and other royalty followed including Aunt Alix, Queen Alexandra. She was accompanied by her son, George. All the Hessians were there including Ella and Serge, Nicky and Alix with their four girls – including Anastasia who was a toddler at that time, and Henry and Irène. The Greeks were present of course, making up a very large party. So soon after the death of Queen Victoria, there is little doubt that she was missed.

The Edinburghs, with the troubles between Ducky and Ernie, were tactfully not present. It was just as well, since Alix's hostility toward Ducky, and by extension the rest of that family, was palpable – and Alix was now by no means just a shy and difficult young sister. Furthermore, Marie Alexandrovna was critical of her nephew Nicholas' performance as tsar, as well as Alix's morose aloofness and inability to play the role expected of a Russian empress.

Louise, aged 14, was one of her sister's bridesmaids. She looked slim, elegant, and quite grown-up. She began to lose some of her reticence as she overcame her childhood maladies and Victoria thought of her as an excellent companion. Louis had hoped this would happen, writing to her that:

> In years to come I will probably be much at sea, and there must always be these long & bitter separations, which one feels more & more, the older one gets. It will always be a comfort to me to know that Mama has a helpful companion in you especially since Alice found her happiness, & thus left us so early![11]

Was Louise destined to become one of those 'Victorian' useful daughters who stayed home, unpicked their mother's knitting, and hunted for spectacles?

On the evening of 6 October there was a banquet and a reception at the Kaisersaal of the Old Palace. That day Andrew and Alice had their civil wedding, and the religious ceremonies took place the following day, first at the Protestant Schlosskirche, and second at the Russian Orthodox Church at the Mathildenhöhe.

As part of the Orthodox service there were four crown-bearers, Prince Andrew's brothers the Princes George and Christopher of Greece, Prince Albert of Schleswig-Holstein, a grandson of Queen Victoria, and Prince Victor of Erbach-Schönberg, Princess Marie Battenberg's son. The crowns had been brought from St Petersburg and were the wedding-crowns of Catherine II.[12]

After the second service there was a wedding banquet, which was a rather raucous affair. A lot of it had to do with there being so many family members, and being able to behave naturally. No less a factor was a great sufficiency of champagne and other wines and liquors.

When Alice and Andrew left in their new motorcar, a gift from Nicky and Alix, some members of the family began chasing the car, to the dismay of the ever-present detectives. There were cheering crowds determined to get a look at the newlyweds, as well as others just out to get a glimpse of all the royalty that had converged on their town. Nicky, evidently feeling secure in Darmstadt, was the ringleader of this gang chasing the car. They caught up to the car and flung a slipper at Alice along with more rice. Alice laughingly flung the slipper back at her Uncle Nicky, whom she apparently called a 'silly ass'.

Victoria returned to London where, barely two weeks later, she received some heart-breaking news. Ernie's daughter, Elisabeth, had sickened with typhoid while she was with Alix, Nicky and their children. After the wedding, they stayed at their hunting lodge at Spala, near Skierniewice in Poland. The Imperial couple invited Ernie and his daughter to join them as a playmate for their elder daughters, Olga, and Tatiana. There she caught a rare form of ambulatory typhoid and died shortly after, on 16 November. The entire grand duchy was grief-stricken since this little girl was a very great favourite.

Her parents were devastated by the loss. Her nurse Wilson had told Victoria: 'the child was very unhappy at the separation of her parents as she loved them both. Happy as she was with her mother, she always longed for Hesse which she considered her real home.'[13]

Victoria comforted Ernie as best she could, rushing back to Darmstadt to help him with the funeral arrangements. Victoria, as his confidant, was especially concerned, though she was optimistic about his recuperative powers. She wrote to Nona: 'He will continue missing his dear little child terribly but there is no reason to fear he will brood & mope over his loss.'[14] There was, however, reason for concern. Ernie was alone in the palace with no sisters or wife to cheer him. The death date of his mother, 14 December, was coming around and Victoria further consoled her brother hoping to lift him from his deep grief. She wrote a long letter of sympathy which shows the depth of their relationship. She said that he:

> so lately learnt to understand how greatly dear Mama suffered at the loss of her little ones, by the bitter loss that has come into your life ... Always I have remembered those last words I ever heard her speak ... 'Ich bin so müde' [I'm so tired] she said; & I felt it even at the moment, that she was not only tired in her body, but weary in her heart of all the anxiety & grief she had gone through – She was but as old as you are now, & she has been at rest since then.[15]

As the new year of 1904 came, Victoria's sister Irène was not spared. In February, her youngest child had an accident. Ernie wrote to Victoria to apprise her of the situation. '[Heinrich] had fallen from a chair two days ago & suffers from headaches & sickness, they hear it may be a haemorrhage to the brain & return to Kiel today.'[16] The condition was grave, and the child died at the age of 4. Victoria rushed to Kiel to be with her sister for the funeral. Irène's other two sons, Sigismund and Waldemar, would survive to adulthood. Sigismund was disease-free, but his older brother Waldemar was not.

In contrast to the sadness of that year, there was good news for Louis. He was promoted to Rear-Admiral and went back to sea. There were objections from the Admiralty from the likes of Lords Beresford and Lambton, who – for all the usual reasons, or simply jealousy – did not like the prince. Nevertheless, he continued to advance.

That summer an important birth took place. After having four girls, Alix, at last gave birth to the long-awaited heir. He was christened Alexei Nikolaevich and was now the tsarevich. Louis was honoured with the task of going to Russia as Uncle Bertie's representative. It was a great misfortune that very soon after his birth, Alexei was diagnosed with haemophilia. It was not particularly surprising, since two of Irène's three sons had suffered from the disease, but it must have made Victoria wonder even more why her sons had been spared.

Another positive that year was Ernie finding happiness with a new bride. The New Palace had been particularly lonely with no sisters and only Ernie clattering around. Naturally, Victoria continued to worry for him, so it was a great sense of relief when Ernie finally found another princess to marry. His depressions, his fear of abandonment and his wish not to die alone had never abated since he lost his little brother, Frittie, and his mother.

Victoria was elated when Eleonore of Solms-Hohensolms-Lich consented to be her brother's wife. She was a sweet, serious and mature woman – nothing like Ducky and therefore far more suited to Ernie. The Solms-Hohensolms-Lich family had been friends of the Hesse and by Rhine family since Victoria's childhood. Eleonore was born on 17 September 1871, the daughter of Hermann Adolf of Solms-Hohensolms-Lich and Agnes of Stolberg-Wernigerode, who, like Alice, taught their children to work for the good of the poor and humanity in general. She had spent time in Darmstadt the previous winter of 1904 when her mother, Princess Agnes, was ill and receiving medical treatment.

Ernie and 'Onor', as she was called in the family, became friends that winter and in February 1905, Louis and Victoria went to Darmstadt to be present at their wedding. They married in the chapel of the Old Schloss and their marriage was smooth and serene. Ernie finally got what he really wanted – two beautiful boys, George Donatus ('Don'), and Ludwig, who was called Lu. Victoria wrote: 'Ernie's second marriage was a great success. She understood him perfectly, thanks to her unselfish but very intelligent nature and they were deeply devoted to each other. There are few people whom I have learned so to respect, love and admire, as my sister-in-law Onor.'[17]

Chapter 9

Planning the Convent

In February 1905, Victoria found herself rushing through Europe and on to Moscow once again. Grand Duke Serge Alexandrovich, Ella's husband, had been blown to bits by an assassin's bomb.

The year before, Russia had declared war on Japan, and instead of a glorious victory, the Russo-Japanese war saw Imperial Russia go down in ignominious defeat. The war incited domestic unrest and reforms were proposed that were completely at odds with Serge's policies since he had taken the office of governor general of Moscow. To that end, after thirteen years in office, Serge resigned.

It was unfortunate for him that his stern and implacable visage – and some would say cruel reputation – made him the face of oppression as the twentieth century began, and he was object of every kind of degenerate and depraved rumours. Ella's cousin wrote in her memoirs that, '[d]uring the war with Japan she collected funds to equip a hospital train, but this humane project never materialised, because someone embezzled the large sums subscribed in response to Ella's appeal, and it was said in some quarters that Serge himself was implicated in the fraud.'[1]

And embezzlement was the kindest thing of which Serge was accused.

The beginning of 1905 marked a watershed in Russian history. On 22 January, workers under the leadership of a priest organised a strike and went on a peaceful march to the Winter Palace. They wanted to present the tsar with a list of grievances and call for a constituent assembly. They walked in an orderly manner to the palace.

Serge's Preobrajensky Guard was set up and waiting for them in the snowy square of the palace – a long line of soldiers with their swords drawn. Their orders were to disperse them by any means necessary, and that is what happened as the crowd walked into the square. There was sheer panic, and the guard began firing on the demonstrators, killing many of them. What was a stupidly handled fiasco henceforth became known as 'Bloody Sunday'. Although the tsar was not present, but at Tsarskoye Selo, south of St Petersburg, the sobriquet, 'Nicholas the Bloody' really stuck.

Serge was at least intelligent enough to know that his life was in danger. 'He wore a haggard, haunted, frightened look which seemed to betray a premonition of the tragic fate in store for him.'[2] To that end, he would not allow Ella to appear or travel with him. The assassins constantly shadowed the grand duke hoping to have the opportunity to murder him. It was learned later that on one occasion, they were planning to go through with their plot but saw Ella in the coach with Serge and desisted.

On 17 February they carried their plans through. At 3.00pm, when his carriage was inside the Kremlin walls, a bomb was thrown, and Serge and his coachman were killed. It was said that Ella gathered the parts of the body which were strewn everywhere, saying 'Hurry, hurry, Serge hates blood and mess.'[3] She gave directions as his body was put on stretcher.

The following day, Victoria, with Nona and Louise, hurried to Ella's side. They were able to make the trip quickly with the minimum of fuss. Louis was unable to go since he was obliged to leave for his new commission on the HMS *Drake* as well as getting on with his new appointment as rear admiral. He could hardly have been comfortable about Victoria and her party going into that anti-monarchist environment; nevertheless, Victoria went.

Henry and Irène were unable to go to Moscow for the funeral but travelled with Victoria and her party for several hours. Even Willy, who had not talked to Ella since she had married Serge, was extremely kind and helpful. She wrote that 'William met me at the Berlin station and gave me supper. He was very kind and thoughtful and much worried about Ella.'[4] Louis' sister Marie was at that supper and wrote that it was:

> [a] painful meeting. At table Victoria sat between the Kaiser and me; we talked about many things, not only about the unfortunate Serg[e]. When it was time for her to leave we went with Victoria to the carriage in which she would have to continue her journey for another forty-eight hours.[5]

Victoria arrived on the 20 February and Ernie and Onor arrived the following day. Victoria observed Russia closely, as she always did whenever she travelled there. She saw the turmoil and unrest and wrote to Onor: 'If only the bloody shadows of revolution would not spoil and darken everything. Not every hour and every second, no one could stand that, but it lurks in the background and the life for thinking people here has become very serious.'[6]

When she reached Ella, she found a woman undoubtedly in shock, but calmly writing telegrams informing people and making arrangements. Though Ella seemed very brave and collected, she moved around as though in a trance and could neither sleep nor eat. She moved her bed downstairs to sleep with her niece, Marie Pavlovna.

Marie and her brother Dimitri were the children of Serge's youngest brother, Paul, and his first wife, Princess Alexandra of Greece, who had died in childbirth. Paul had made an unequal second marriage and it was deemed unsuitable that the children should live with him. Serge loved them deeply and was extremely demonstrative towards them. Ella comforted Marie, who collapsed into her arms when she heard the news. Later, in her memoirs, Marie would insist that Ella had been cold to her throughout the time they had lived together. Memory is a strange thing.

For years, there were rumours about Ella and Serge's marriage. Serge had been accused of many different perversions, which led many to suppose their marriage was not a happy one. Queen Victoria had also felt that Ella's constant reassurances of her contentment were suspect. Her grandmother opined that if people are happy, they don't need to talk about it so much. Whatever the truth was, Victoria felt the need to say:

> Contrary to the general belief she and Serge had led a happy married life, tho' it was he who was completely the head and master of the house. Ella was very willing that he should be it and he was full of affectionate attentions to her … Both Ella and Serge were very fond of children and it was sad that they never had had any of their own.[7]

Writing the memoirs so many decades later, Victoria hardly had to cover-up for her sister with so many of the players dead. Conversely, Victoria would never write or say anything that would put Ella or those she loved in a negative light. Serge's name has been somewhat rehabilitated in recent times, and he has been declared a saint in the Russian Orthodox church.

Though Nicky and Alix were warned to stay away, Victoria, Ernie, Onor and other family members attended the funeral service. As with most Russian ceremonies, this one was long and laborious. There was much standing, lots of chanting, and prayers and incense. A mystical serenity and comfort appeared to settle on Ella's face – even joy. Victoria observed this, but not being the mystical type, she struggled to understand it. Later, she would struggle to understand this streak in her daughter, Alice.

When it was finally over, the family marched slowly and mournfully out of the Kremlin. Serge was buried in a crypt of the Chudov Monastery in the Kremlin.

Ella loved Moscow and wished to stay there. She and Victoria had endless discussions about what she would do with her life after the murder. Remarriage was never part of the picture, though for a time there was gossip about it. Because of the great interest newspapers took in the lives of royalty, they often printed pieces of gossip – true or not. Nona Kerr sent Victoria a newspaper article about Ella and Ernie: 'The gossip about Ella, which you sent me a cutting of, has appeared with yet more untrue details in some papers I hear, which say that she was secretly married last year … – & that I went to Illyinskoje for the christening of their child.'[8]

The papers also added that Ernie was headed to a second divorce.

The reality was very different. Ella, who had said as a child that she wanted to be a nun, began the process of becoming one, and dreamed of founding a nursing order. The church's hierarchy initially refused to implement her ideas. Nevertheless, she continued sending them proposal after proposal and eventually her determination paid off. Her order, the Convent of SS Martha and Mary, was founded in 1910, Ella became a nun and its abbess and was known as 'Mother Elisabeth'.

On a broader level, the political events of 1905 absorbed the entire family, and the violence of the twentieth century was just beginning.

Victoria spent nearly a month with Ella and then went to Tsarskoye Selo to visit Nicky and Alix and then back home to England. Georgie had graduated from Cheam and was now going to be a naval cadet at the Royal Naval College at Osborne.

The following month, Victoria made her way to Greece for the birth of Alice's first child. She arrived at the seaport city of Patras on 7 April and attended the First International Archaeological Congress at the Parthenon. As an aficionado of archaeology, she delighted in attending lectures. Prince Andrew, knowing his mother-in-law, took her on sightseeing excursions in his car. Together they drove to the bridges of Pentelikon, famous for its marble quarries, and then further to Elensis. But being the perceptive person she was, she could also see that Greece wasn't just an archaeological wonder for tourists, but a country that was struggling with other Balkan countries, trying to regain what it thought was its historic borders.

Some days after Victoria's arrival, on 18 April 1905, Alice presented her with her first grandchild: Princess Margarita of Greece, and Denmark. Victoria was just 42 years old and by 1914, Alice and Andrew would have three more daughters, Theodora, Cecile, and Sophie. The christening took place in May 1905 with Victoria and King George I of the Hellenes and Andrew's father acting as godparents. The occasion took on a little more importance with the attendance of Queen Alexandra, who was already there visiting her brother, the king.

Victoria spent the rest of the summer at Heiligenberg. Louise was confirmed that June, however, Louis, back on his ship the *Drake*, was not able to attend. Louise, in an introspective mood, wrote to her father and reassured him on a point that was extremely close to his heart. 'I will always try and be a helpful companion, now that I am getting older to dear Mama.'[9]

In those lazy summer days after the traumatic events of February, the world, historians said, for one moment seemed to get back to the idyllic and nostalgic time before the carnage of the twentieth century began. Victoria recalled that summer as hot and languid. She wrote in her memoirs about buying a new gramophone and making their own recordings. There were other interesting inventions to talk about from the installation of telephones to the cinema.

She loved telephones and made it a point to answer calls before servants or anyone else in the house could get to it. The obvious reason was that she adored talking. Since she couldn't talk back to the wireless radio, she was less enchanted with it.

In its infancy, she disliked the cinema since the incessant flickering bothered her eyes. She recalled her first movie being the film made of Queen Victoria in 1896. However, Dickie loved the cinema and wanted Victoria to be more, as he termed it, 'film minded'.[10] As part of his honeymoon much later, Dickie and his bride would go to Hollywood and make a private film with Charlie Chaplin called 'Nice and Friendly', which Chaplin would give to Dickie as a wedding present.[11]

Onor had a miscarriage in September, and the following month, a charming memorial to little Princess Elisabeth of Hesse was unveiled. Victoria, who had been the president of the Alice *Fraüenverein* was able to relinquish the reins to Onor. Victoria told her, 'On Thursday the General Meeting of the … Institute is taking place … I am sending you the invitation …. Of course you would give the institute great pleasure if you appear.'[12]

That autumn Louis, in his capacity as Rear Admiral, Commander of the Second Cruiser Squadron and the HMS *Drake*, made a goodwill trip to North America and the United States. Louis and his squadron were shown gracious hospitality when they arrived in Baltimore Harbour. The Americans treated the British Officers with friendliness and consideration. Nevertheless, *The Times* of London couldn't resist a slight dig when they observed that an 'exhibition of naval smartness will be fully appreciated by the people of the United States'.[13]

Louis was received by the President, the energetic and often exhausting Theodore Roosevelt. Having been Secretary of the Navy before becoming Vice-President under William McKinley, he was extremely knowledgeable about naval matters. Both he and Prince Louis were admirers of the famous Admiral Alfred Thayer Mahan who wrote *The Importance of Sea Power in History*, a primer of naval imperialism, and consequently there was much for the two to discuss. They talked of their concern about the Kaiser and his build-up of what was becoming a formidable navy. Louis' only complaint was that he left the official White House dinner hungry – he and the President were so deeply in conversation that he had waved away dishes and touched little on his plate.

After leaving Washington, Prince Louis and his party went to New York. There they attended a reception with the current Secretary of the Navy, Charles J. Bonaparte (a grand-nephew of Emperor Napoleon I from the Baltimore branch of the Bonaparte family – which Napoleon never recognised). They spent eleven days in the city and one evening there was a banquet at a Chinese restaurant with singing waiters, one of whom was the future popular composer, Irving Berlin.

Later, Berlin had occasion to be in London during the Second World War, and told Victoria the following, which she in turn told her son Dickie.

> [T]he first time [Berlin's]name ever appeared in the paper, was on the occasion of Papa's visit … Berlin was then a waiter in China Town & one of the numerous extra hands (& singing waiters), employed at a dinner for our fleet. He seems to have been given the job to attend upon the drinks & serve Papa & one of the newspapers mentioned him by name.[14]

The German community of New York as well as the Irish American community saw fit to protest the presence of officers of the Royal Navy. The reasons that the Irish protested were obvious. However, the Germans felt that his visit was 'part of a cunningly contrived plan to create an impression abroad that a secret alliance exists between England and the United States, and this alliance is specially directed towards intimidating Germany'.[15] This was ironic, in view of the treachery of which Louis was accused later during the First World War.

The prince left with a great love of the United States which he passed along to his children. When he returned, Victoria was anxious to hear his accounts of the United States. The British and, indeed many Europeans, had a very strange view of America in the early twentieth century. Many pictured the inhabitants wearing buckskins with raccoon-skin caps and chewing tobacco. Reporters from *The Times* of London maintained this antiquated view.[16]

The following spring, members of the family spent a holiday together in Venice. Ernie and Onor were there and keen to go antiquing, while Louis' sister Marie came and was particularly excited to visit one of Louis' commands. Marie wrote that Venice was 'the city of crumbling dreams, it suited us all, but me particularly, who am always listening to the slowly dying tones that sound from the dream-like past.'[17] And indeed, the end of the dream-like past was coming.

There was family excitement that spring when another royal wedding came to pass. Aunt Beatrice's only daughter, Victoria Eugenie (called Ena in the family) a tall, blonde, beautiful girl, was to be married to Alfonso XIII of Spain. Alfonso was a small fellow who stood up rather poorly to the Junoesque Ena; moreover, she was not his first choice.

Alfonso had already made the rounds with some of Victoria's other cousins, first setting his sights on Princess Margaret of Connaught. Then, when Crown Prince Gustav Adolf of Sweden won her heart, he cheerfully shifted the photographs in his wallet, and his attentions, to her sister, Patricia. She, too, was uninterested.

Although the granddaughter of a morganatic marriage, something that mattered to the Spaniards, and a Protestant (which mattered even more), Alfonso chose to overlook these obstacles and settled upon Ena, a very popular princess in England, who accepted him.

After converting to Catholicism, Ena married Alfonso in a solemn ceremony in Madrid in May of that year. It was one of those events that many of the extended family as well as other royalty attended. As was often true, this wedding took place under threats of violence. The church was crowded with family and press, and after their vows were said, the couple rode in a procession to the royal palace. En-route, an assassin threw a bouquet of flowers concealing a bomb at the couple's carriage.

Pandemonium ensued as the horse guards scrambled around the crowds looking for the murderer. Twenty-four people were killed and dozens injured, while the newlyweds tried to change carriages and proceed to the palace. Luckily, Victoria and her immediate family had elected not to attend. Like the tragedy at Khodynka Field in Russia, many felt that this boded ill for the couple. Unlike Nicky and Alix, they lacked the solid relationship that would see them through the hardships ahead.

For the next few years, Victoria spent her summers with Ella in Russia. She travelled with Dickie – who she was teaching herself – Louise, when she wasn't having lessons at Fraulein Textor's Pension for English Girls in Darmstadt, and of course, her companion, Nona Kerr.

By Summer 1906, the Russo-Japanese War was lost. Ella, who was still reeling from the violent death of her husband at this time, was nursing wounded soldiers at Illinskoje. There was so much unrest at this point and threats of assassination were endemic. So much so, that when Victoria reached Russia in July, the Governor General who received her at the station did so at risk of his life.

The two sisters spent most of their time together at the comparative safety of Illinskoje. Ella had been diagnosed with a non-malignant tumour, and undoubtedly the stress she had been under since the assassination contributed to her illness. In a letter to Ernie and Onor, Victoria reassured them about Ella's mental and physical health. Further, she went on to say that Ella looked pale and thin but no longer had that 'staring' look and can 'laugh quite naturally about something funny'.[18]

By the end of the year there was good news from Darmstadt. As noted earlier, Onor had been safely delivered of a boy. He would be christened Georg Donatus, the latter name 'in a sense of gratitude for the long-wished for heir being given them'.[19] A brother was born for 'Don' in November 1908, christened Ludwig, and known in the family as 'Lu'.

During Summer 1907, Marie Pavlovna, Ella and Serge's ward and niece, became engaged to Prince William of Sweden, Duke of Södermanland. In her memoirs Marie complained that she had given consent to the lukewarm union while she was ill. She intimated that it was under pressure from both Ella and Victoria, who was there at the time. It's hard to believe that Victoria forced her to marry anyone since she never coerced her children, and she herself was never coerced.

Marie's father, the Grand Duke Paul, was incensed that he had never had the opportunity to confer with Marie on this matter. He disapproved of the marriage as did many at the Imperial court. Some thought that the precipitous nature of this engagement, since Marie was barely 17 at the time, was in preparation for Ella's new life and the founding of the convent. Some felt that she wanted to get rid of the encumbrance.

Although she complained later in her memoirs, at the time, Marie had looked forward to her marriage, writing to her betrothed that she could hardly wait until they could live as they pleased. It was obvious that the young girl just wanted to get out of the house. The marriage took place in 1908 and was not a success. The couple were divorced in 1913.

During the summer of 1908, Victoria converted a barn in Heiligenberg into a young men's club. It was for boys who were at a 'loose end' between the end of school and induction into the army. She had a fight on her hands with some of the elders of the village to set the club up. She saw it as a place where the boys could spend the evening, play games, read books independent of the schoolmaster or the local deacon. The elders finally relented and the barn was adapted for that purpose, but it was stipulated that it also had to be used for church services once a week.[20]

Meanwhile, Victoria and Ella were absorbed with the details of the convent, such as what the nuns would wear – grey habits, not the usual black ones. Later she would write her impressions to Onor about what Ella was trying to accomplish:

> There is something extraordinary about a person who has high ideals and tries to live in accordance with them – something shaming and refreshing for us ordinary people – … and I am very sorry that Alix is so full of doubt, mistrust and envy about Ella and her undertakings; she doesn't really know Ella's art of living and I fear sometimes does not want to know. Ella and I are totally different in character and opinions, and still I feel I understand her.[21]

Alix would eventually come around and help Ella get the permissions she needed from the Metropolitans of the Russian Orthodox Church. It is telling, however, that she doubted her own sister in this, and later, when things came to a crisis in Russia, would doubt her even more.

During those years before the Great War, Victoria continued her visits to her sisters and brother and spent time with Louis, who was at this point back in Malta. By 1908, Louis was appointed a Vice Admiral, and later that year Commander-in-Chief of the Atlantic Fleet. Georgie flourished in the Royal Navy, and Alice continued to present her with grandchildren. During the first decades of their marriage, Alice seemed to be happy with Andrew. Their times in Greece were the happiest, but their many exiles as time went on would serve to erode their relationship, nor did great adversity strengthen their bond.

When Louis became Commander-in-Chief of the Atlantic Fleet, the Battenbergs were housed in the beautiful Mall House at the Admiralty in London. Louis, who was a progressive man, wanted more than anything to institute needed reforms which would bring the Royal Navy into the twentieth century. Not surprisingly, he made enemies among the conservatives and those who harboured jealousy. At that point, even Louis' friends were concerned.

His biggest champion, First Sea Lord Admiral Fisher, was worried each time Victoria and Louis went to Germany and Greece for family events. Many in the Admiralty and in the press made much of the couple's constant junkets to the Continent. Even when they went to the funeral of Louis' brother-in-law, Prince Gustav of Erbach-Schönberg's, there were insulting remarks.

There were constant snide comments issued forth about the possibility of having a German in the office of First Sea Lord. The newspapers, always eager for slander, published these innuendos. Louis, however, never answered these calumnies. He continued his work, hoping that it might speak for itself.

He was strongly supported by Winston Churchill, the head of the Admiralty. When Churchill came into that office, there was great consternation in the camp of Louis' enemies. Churchill was a great admirer of Admiral Fisher, and therefore extremely well disposed toward Louis. Victoria and Louis dined a great deal with Churchill and his wife, Clementine. Victoria, who so loved books herself, remarked upon 'his ingenious arrangement for lodging his large number of books. On deep shelves the books stood in two lines, the rear-most sufficiently raised for one to be able to read their titles over the backs of the front row.'[22]

Churchill and others at the Admiralty thought that it was an advantage that Louis had such close contacts with the various royal and imperial houses of Europe. Willy lost no opportunity to engage Louis in discussion about his navy. Most of the time, his pride and conceit usually overpowered his discretion. He was heard to remark, in a patronising fashion , that Louis, with his 'intelligent comprehension of the state of affairs'[23] could be most useful to Germany. The reality was that Louis was most useful to the British Admiralty and made detailed reports to his superiors about all his talks with his imperial cousin.

A much bigger worry for Victoria was Alix.

After the Revolution of 1905 and the birth of her son, the empress was becoming more insular, and more reliant on faith-healers and holy men. Much had to do with her self-deception. Many were aware at this time of the hatred that the tsarina had engendered, and how far from the truth her perception of her role in Russia was. However, they discovered that Alix would stubbornly refuse to speak about anything to do with Russia, or her eventual reliance on Rasputin to obviate Alexei's bleeding episodes. The *Starets* [elder, a holy man] had come on the scene, and Alix's family knew that anyone who tried to reason, or address any of these issues with her, risked expulsion from court.

It seemed as if most of the letters and discussions between Victoria, Ella, Ernie and Irène concerned how to 'handle' Alix. They spoke of trying to talk to Nicky when she was not in the room, or about Ella trying to talk sense into Alix. However, there was always the real risk that Ella would be dismissed and possibly not be able to enter her presence again.

In March 1908 Ernie and Onor planned to go to Russia to see the family. Victoria advised Onor that:

> It is also good for Nicky … if Ernie can talk freely about things with
> him … But one has to force out Nicky as well – due to circumstances
> both of them have shut themselves off so much and therefore the
> push for freer speech will have to come from Ernie.[24]

Nicky spoke more easily when Alix was not there. And it looked like he might see sense; in the end, however, he listened to Alix. If Victoria and Ella tried, which they did, the attempts came ultimately to naught. Victoria had to 'walk on eggshells' with Alix, which made her visits to her less and less congenial as the years passed.

Victoria continued to enjoy her visits to Ella and Illinskoje; however, even from the relative safety of the country, there was still a need for tight security and the sisters were not permitted to leave the grounds. Threats continued against the lives of the Imperial Family, and by association their relatives from outside the country.

Nevertheless, summers at Illinskoje still provided moments of happiness. There were teas and breakfasts on the back verandas, where many young cousins including

Alix's four girls, Olga, Tatiana, Maria and Anastasia, played with Victoria's two youngsters (Georgie was a cadet by this point). And, of course, the opportunity for the sisters to be together.

The cornerstone for Ella's Convent of SS Martha and Mary would be laid in June 1908. Ella had chosen land on the banks of the Moskva River, and the convent would eventually encompass a convent house, a home for consumptive women, the onion-domed Church of St Mary Magdalen, as well as a hospital, an old age home, and lushly planted gardens.

Ella and Victoria spent many happy hours discussing the way in which the nuns should set up their days, when they should be required to say prayers and when not, and even what they should eat. Because this was the first of such liberal institutions in Russia, they would often have to improvise answers as problems and issues arose. By the following summer 1909, Ella was living there.

Victoria returned to Heiligenberg near the end of August and had an interesting reunion – a visit from Sandro's young son.

> Assen, Louis' nephew, the son of Sandro and Countess Hartenau, who was stopping at Schoenberg [*sic*] came over for a few nights – a nice youth, but hampered in his movements by a paralysis of his right arm and leg, which he had from birth. I only met him again years afterwards when he was a grey haired man, and had come to London with an Austrian Mission.[25]

Little else was said about Sandro's children by his opera-singer wife.

In 1909, Victoria and Louis celebrated their Silver Anniversary very quietly and with no fanfare at the seaside town of Margate 'in a very empty hotel'.[26] Louis was now in command of the HMS *Prince of Wales*, and the couple had just had the good news that Georgie had passed fourth in his class from Dartmouth. In June, Georgie started his cadet training on the HMS *Cornwall;* during his tenure on the ship, he often made requests to visit relations at the ports at which they called, so much so that the commander began to be suspicious of his having so many relatives in so many different places.

The next few years, the last before the war, unfolded gently with very few ripples. Victoria and her sisters visited back and forth, and their children played together. The controversies between Alix and her extended family and, indeed, her country, continued, and the others sought in some way to mitigate these storms. It was a losing battle, but it was fought earnestly. The end of that pre-war world, however, was coming. Many marked the time in different events, but certainly one of the most significant was the death of King Edward VII on 6 May 1910, after a short reign of nine years.

Louis and Victoria, as well as the rest of the family, truly mourned this man who had played such an important part in their lives: 'His loss cast a sad gloom over all those who had known and loved him. Louis, personally felt it very much, for ever since he had been a cadet in the Ariadne in 1869, Uncle Bertie had been the kindest of friends to him.'[27]

It was Uncle Bertie who befriended Louis during his young and difficult years in the navy; it was Uncle Bertie who insisted on Louis' staying with him whenever Louis was on shore leave, so that Louis actually had his own bedroom at Marlborough House; and it was Uncle Bertie who had insisted on Louis being his Naval aide-de-camp, as he had been for Queen Victoria, and as he would now be for Bertie's son, Cousin George. Victoria wrote in a heart-felt letter to the now Queen Mary, that 'Uncle Bertie was always so kind & good to us, his sister's children … that we mourn his loss as a personal one to ourselves.'[28]

The king's funeral was a grand affair, attended by many royal families. There was the 'March of Kings', in which nine sovereigns took part in the funeral procession. The monarchs followed the coffin as it wound slowly through London. Among those included in the procession were: Alfonso of Spain; Willy; Manoel of Portugal; Haakon of Norway; George of the Hellenes; Frederick of Denmark; Albert of the Belgians; and Ferdinand of Bulgaria – all related to Bertie by blood or by marriage.[29] In addition to the monarchs, Theodore Roosevelt, now the former President of the United States, and his wife also attended. On 17 May, the actual funeral service took place at Windsor. Louis, on foot, personally escorted the gun carriage carrying the king's body.

Autumn 1910 was one of the last meetings of the family of sisters and brother, with all their available children and spouses in Hesse. Alix continued to be sickly and was suffering from sciatica and possible heart problems. The symptoms were exacerbated by anxiety over her son and the worsening political situation in Russia. Because of this, she wished to take the waters at Bad Nauheim. Naturally, with so many members of the family coming at once, it was necessary to organise and Victoria, with her usual efficiency, was up to the task. Letters flew between her and Ernie, trying to set up accommodations and amusements for the Imperial visitors:

> There must be somebody to help in occupying Nicky although he is so touchingly kind never expecting anything. Irene's idea of the hotel is quite out of the question. Firstly the season is not over, so they would be mobbed the moment anyone of them put their nose out of the house. Then as to guarding the house & all the surrounding streets, that also is not favourable. The quiet which Alix wants she would never get. In Friedberg that is all possible.[30]

Ernie was not only concerned with domestic matters however, but more urgently with security matters, since the Imperial Family could never be without their massive protection apparatus. The towns that they might visit were swept not only by the Okhrana agents, but the local constabularies were on full alert.[31]

The Imperial Family arrived in August and stayed in the Schloss in Friedberg until the latter half of October, while Alix went to the spa in Bad Nauheim. During the visit, Henry and Irène arrived with their children as well as Victoria, Louis along with Louise, Georgie and Dickie, Alice and Andrew and their children. There were luncheons and dinners, some informal and some – alas – formal, when the Kaiser showed up for several days and required everyone to dress in their uniforms. However, besides this inconvenience, it was a private and relaxing visit.

When Alix had had enough of the waters, they returned to Wolfsgarten and spent some quiet days there. There are some last group pictures of the sisters at their beloved childhood home and Ella now in her nun's habit; her cousin, Princess Marie of Erbach-Schönberg, remarked that she looked like Elisabeth in Wagner's opera *Tannhaüser*.

Victoria continued to be involved in philanthropy. Besides building a club house for youth at Heiligenberg, she was also busy while in residence in London. She, Nona and Louise did a great deal of charity work in the East End, providing entertainment and games for poor boys. They participated in the Sailors' Orphan Girls' School and the Friends of the Poor, as well as handing out prizes and purses for The National Federation of Christian Workers among Poor Children.

In March 1911, the family lived in Admiralty House at Sheerness. Louis was away at sea a great deal, but not for such long periods as before. During this time, Victoria entertained a little, giving a series of dinners and 'even a garden party'.[32]

In June, the family attended the first courts and then, on the twenty-third of that month, the coronation of King George V and Queen Mary. Victoria stayed with her Aunt Louise Lorne at Kensington Palace. Interestingly, during the winter at the end of that coronation year, May and George were the first Imperial Couple to go to India for the Coronation Durbar at Delhi. The Durbar was a time when delegations of Indian Princes and Rajas would pay homage to the representatives of the Queen-Empress or the King-Emperor. With the attendance of the Imperial Couple, this would be a far more festive event than usual. Victoria's son Georgie accompanied George and May to the Durbar and attended as their guest.

The summer at Sheerness, however, was glorious. Louis was busy training airplane pilots for the navy – his idea – and, at the time, an entirely new concept. Victoria became the first princess to fly. She described it thus: 'The planes were not made to carry passengers and for our short flight – for Louis would not allow me to be taken on a long one – we perched securely attached, on a little stool hung on to the flyer's back.'[33]

The summer may have been brilliant, but the winter was difficult. Besides suffering from circulatory problems from the cold and damp, Victoria was obliged, nevertheless, to keep the windows open because there were gunnery defences nearby who were constantly firing – it was therefore impossible to have the windows closed lest they shatter. So, besides being extremely cold, it was tremendously noisy as well. Suffice to say that Sheerness, with the noise and the cold, was not one of Victoria's favourite residences.

That year she also said goodbye to her youngest child as Dickie went to boarding school, Locker's Park, Hemel Hempstead.

Chapter 10

War

In October of 1911, the Naval War Staff was created. Prince Louis, because of his intelligence trips to Germany, knew better than anyone the necessity of preparing the Royal Navy for war. In December, along with being King George's aide-de-camp, Louis was now appointed Second Sea Lord. Churchill had wanted him as First Sea Lord, but there were the usual difficulties. Despite being a German prince, he was now one of the top men in the navy – a man well thought of and extremely capable. Victoria constantly received laudatory notes and letters from the men under his command saying what an able and fair leader he was; intelligent, organised and completely dedicated to his men.

Difficulties with Germany took a temporary backseat to the problems brewing in the Balkans. Greece continued to have troubles and conflicts that were rapidly becoming chronic. Between 1912 and 1913, she fought a series of wars called the First and Second Balkan wars, mainly, it seemed, for territorial acquisition. Macedonia, which had previously belonged to the Turks, was now coveted by many countries, including Bulgaria, as well as Serbia and Greece. The first battles in 1912 were between the Ottoman Empire and the Balkan countries. The Turks were trounced, and the loss of large areas was the consequence of their defeat. The following year, however, Greece and Serbia fought Bulgaria. The outcome after both wars was the Treaty of Bucharest. Greece was greatly expanded, adding the southern part of Macedonia, some of the Aegean Islands, and Crete.

During this troublesome period, Victoria worried constantly about Alice and her four girls. Prince Andrew joined Crown Prince Constantine as a Major at the front in Turkey. At her own request, Nona went to Greece in order to help Alice. There, Alice was working and organising hospital facilities. Nona wrote that the atmosphere in Athens was one of high exhilaration – typical of wartime exuberance. However, such high spirits could easily be quenched, and the Greeks would undoubtedly rid themselves of their current rulers if all did not go well. And, tragically, in March 1913, King George of Greece was assassinated in Salonika. Prince Andrew's brother Constantine now became King of Greece.

In summer 1912, Victoria headed off for her penultimate trip to Russia. One reason was to attend the coming out ball of her niece, Grand Duchess Olga, at Livadia Palace in the Crimea. Nicky and Alix had rebuilt the palace on the Black Sea, and it was a most beautiful and peaceful place. It was not ornate and grand like the palaces of Tsarskoye Selo, or Peterhof. Rather, it was built in the style of an Italian country villa, bright and sunny, with a friendly, and completely casual air about it that made it the perfect vacation spot. All of Russia's troubles – which were escalating – could be forgotten at that most tranquil of homes.

Victoria, Louise, Dickie and Nona then went to Ella's convent, living the lives of the ascetics. It was quite a sobering experience to a nonreligious person. Victoria always believed in the basic tenets of Christianity, celebrated holidays and went to church regularly. However, it is quite a different thing to live with religion constantly and Victoria knew she could never do it.

While she was there, she took Russian lessons and tried speaking on various occasions. However, her conversation, she wrote, was severely limited and she was 'at a complete loss,'[1] if Ella was not present. This trip, more than any others, was quite a strain since Alix was becoming more mystical, introspective, neurotic and, worst of all, dependent on Rasputin. Victoria tried hard to soothe some of the controversy between Alix and Ella as well as the ill-feelings of the other Romanovs. Alix, however, would hear nothing against Rasputin. In fact, when Ella was sent by the family to talk to Alix, she was curtly told to leave. The monk became more powerful as the years passed.

Alexei had a serious haemophiliac episode at the Imperial Family's hunting lodge in Spala, Poland, in autumn 1912. The empress enlisted the help of Rasputin, who miraculously seemed to alleviate Alexei's sufferings. Alix was used to seeing strong women rely on 'peasants', such as her grandmother did with John Brown, and later her Indian servant, the *Munshi,* Abdul Karim. She believed implicitly in their sincerity and their lack of guile and couldn't be talked out of her association. Since she was stronger but no cleverer than Nicky, she dictated, and he listened.

In the winter of 1912, despite all, Louis was appointed First Sea Lord and the Head of the Royal Navy. Victoria was happy at the Mall House and wrote to Ernie:

> our ... house is most comfortable, it has a very big dining room & study on the ground floor & above them a large drawing-room & sitting room ... On the two floors above these are the bed-rooms, amongst them two for guests, which I hope you & Onor will once inhabit.[2]

The appointment did not go without controversy. It was also possible that the man he replaced, Admiral Sir Frances Bridgeman, was bitter. The reason given publicly for his resignation was illness, but even more serious were Bridgeman's clashes with the First Lord of the Admiralty, Winston Churchill. Louis and Churchill admired one another and so, no such conflicts existed.

That Christmas, Victoria and Louis, with Louise, Georgie and Dickie, were invited by George and May to Sandringham. It had originally been bought for Uncle Bertie and Aunt Alix when they first married and served as their private country residence. Most agreed that it was far cosier than Balmoral and certainly much warmer.

Victoria's son Georgie was just 20 now, doing well in the navy, and well thought of in his own right. He was extremely intelligent and analytical. He, like Louise, inherited a lot of Victoria's family feeling, and was at Sandringham to have fun with his cousins.

Henry and Irène also visited Sandringham that Christmas as guests of the king and queen. Unquestionably, Victoria enjoyed spending the holiday season with this sister. Compared to Alix, and even Ella, she was calm, restful and peaceful, living up to her name.

The family had their usual festivities before Christmas. Tree trimming and carol singing, and all joined in with the Christmas charades and games. Inevitably, there was a lot of talk about hostilities between the Allies and the Triple Alliance of Germany, Austria-Hungary and Italy. With war a very grave and real possibility, none of the royal family with their German ancestry, wanted to fight Germany. However, they all knew that none of them would hesitate if they were called upon to do so.

While Henry was at Sandringham, he took the opportunity to talk to George and Louis about the state of relations between their two countries. Henry appeared to have been coached by Willy about precisely what to say to his cousins. He asked them, 'If Germany and Austria attacked France and Russia would England come to the aid of the latter?' It was an informal question asking whether England would act if her allies were attacked. Georgie replied, 'Undoubtedly yes – under certain circumstances.' Henry seemed happy with this answer and later took it back to his brother, who interpreted it as a stance of neutrality.[3]

Henry had this same conversation at Buckingham Palace with George a second time. In the fateful summer of 1914, he was once again sent back on the same mission. This was only days before the hostilities of the Great War began. Possibly, the Kaiser wanted confirmation of the previous talk and what he considered a policy of neutrality. When asked the same question, the king said that he did not know what 'we shall do, we have no quarrel with anyone and hope we shall remain neutral'.[4] But if Germany declared war on Russia, and France joined Russia, then the king indicated that England would most certainly be dragged in. At the close of the talks, George said that he and the government would do all they could to prevent a European war.[5]

From these declarations, the Kaiser was sure that Britain would remain neutral. He then telegraphed the American President, Woodrow Wilson, saying he had been so assured. The brothers seemed satisfied with the news that George and his government would not act. Naturally this was not at all what the king meant – nor is it what happened. We now know, due to revelations of private conversations between George and his foreign secretary, Sir Edward Grey, that the king asked for war.[6]

It is strange that Henry would have made such a misinterpretation of statements. Later, when he was implicated in all sorts of nefarious deeds, including being responsible for starting the war, these conversations were brought to light and discussed, *ad infinitum*. One can only conclude that it was absurd that Willy had not sought clarification himself. Henry admitted after the war that he'd misconstrued

George's statements, that he had interpreted an 'anxious hope as definite assurance'. He had transmitted to Willy his version of the comments, which seemed an assertion of neutrality, rather than just the hope of it. Despite the trust that the brothers had for one another, it was poor judgment to accept such important declarations without further clarification.

In May 1913, another Royal Wedding took place in the family. The engagement of Princess Viktoria-Luise of Prussia, the Kaiser's only daughter, to Prince Ernst August of Hanover was reported in *The Times*.[7] The date was set to coincide with Queen Victoria's birthday, and coincidentally, Irène and Henry's Silver Anniversary, 24 May. Unlike that sad time in 1888 when Henry's father was about to breathe his last, this was a happy occasion and a love-match between the young couple. However, the wedding would be the last gathering of Victoria's extended family before the Great War engulfed them all. It would also be one of the last times Victoria and several of her sisters were together at a family occasion.

The family gathered at the Neues Palais at Potsdam, near Berlin, for the nuptials. There was a feigned amount of camaraderie between the Emperors Nicholas and Wilhelm and George, for by now, it seemed the battlelines had been drawn and it was only a matter of time. Willy was in his element, hosting his family and feeling important. Alix did not attend, pleading illness.

They all assembled as in a dream, before the war swept away so many of the emperors, kings and princes; they interacted, danced, talked, whispered, and watched each other. On the evening of the ceremony, there was an elaborate banquet and the bride and groom participated in the traditional torch dance. With pages lining the room with torches, the bride danced with her father, her father-in-law, then with the other emperors present that evening.

Also attending were Willy's six sons. All six would survive the war, though one of the sons, Joachim, would later commit suicide in despair over the defeat of Germany and his deplorable financial situation. His mother, the Empress Auguste Viktoria, pined away; her son's death probably affected her ill-health. She died the following year in 1921.

Willy had not liked young Ernst August, nor his father the Duke of Cumberland, nor the Hanover royal family, since they had refused to bow to the suzerainty of the Hohenzollerns. Yet, as part of the marriage treaty, Willy agreed to restore the Hannoverians to the ducal throne of Brunswick-Lüneburg inherited by the groom's father in the 1880s. But chiefly, there was the bride, the new Duchess of Brunswick-Lüneburg, radiantly happy. She and her groom were the only ones to enjoy that evening with unbridled joy, for the dream would soon be over for all of them.

The years of the second decade of the twentieth century were the beginning of some of the most catastrophic and violent times that mankind has ever known. Victoria later wrote: 'The feeling of increasing political tension was very disquieting to us, especially as Louis took a rather pessimistic view of the situation in Europe.'[8] His pessimism was well founded. The peace of Europe was shattered forever by the coming juggernaut, and as if fate was mocking them, Victoria and her sisters had one last halcyon time together. The Imperial Family came to Hesse in 1913 and spent a great deal of the summer at Wolfsgarten.

Victoria was recovering from an appendectomy and Ella came to care for her and to keep her company. Once the family joined them, they spent their time playing tennis, riding and having picnics and parties. This was also when Victoria's Dickie, who was somewhat younger than his Romanov cousin, told his mother, very seriously, that he meant to marry Marie Nikolaevna when he grew up. But he was not the only one. Apparently, Louise had what Victoria termed a 'lanky admirer' that summer. Who, we do not know.

Autumn inevitably came and Victoria went back to London and the house in the Mall. Irène and Alice, with her two oldest girls, came for a visit and Victoria related an amusing anecdote in her memoirs. She introduced her two granddaughters to her own Uncle Arthur of Connaught, as the girls' great-great-uncle, 'Whereupon Uncle Arthur, in a horrified voice exclaimed "My dear, you are making an ancestor of me!"'[9]

Victoria also discovered that her Aunt Louise of Lorne was making a gift to her and Louis of Kent House on the Isle of Wight. It would serve as their family home. She was pleased with the gift and thought it would suit her, Louis and the children. The house was a lovely, gated Tudor-style building made of stone, with a bay of mullion windows overlooking the water, and a garden.

The year 1914 started quietly. There was the usual sadness over a death in the family – Aunt Louise of Argyll lost her husband, the Duke of Argyll, who died in May of inflammation of the lungs. Victoria spent some time with her aunt during that period and the king wrote to his sister: 'I am so glad that Victoria Battenberg is with you & she will be a great comfort & help to you.'[10]

Nevertheless, the round of travelling and visits continued. Victoria spent June and July with Alice in Corfu and attended the birth of her fourth granddaughter at Mon Repos. Alice, she wrote, 'is fit & well, but rather worried at the delay in the arrival of the baby'.[11] Though the birth was late, the little girl was healthy and sturdy. Dickie apparently said that it was silly for Alice to have had another girl, making now, a total of four.[12]

Victoria wrote a long and detailed letter to Ernie about the baby granddaughter and about her plans for the summer. Alice, she wrote, named her baby Sophie '(needless to say not in honour of Sophie, but because Andrea & Alice like it & because it is a name known in all countries)'[13] Alice and her sister-in-law, Sophie, who was cold and distant to her, didn't get along. She mentioned her plans to leave for Russia on 15 July, and she also began to plan for the autumn. 'Would it suit you & Onor if we came to you early in September? Alix cannot have us for long as she is going to the Crimea in that month.'[14]

Prince Louis, too, free for the moment, spent the beginning of the summer in Darmstadt. He wrote to his sister, Princess Marie: 'I shall come now every year to you, to rest. That is at last possible, now that I don't go to sea anymore, but live in London.'[15] Yet, this would be the last time he visited Darmstadt. Prince Louis was back at his post by July and the Royal Navy was in a fevered pitch, ready for a full test mobilisation. Prince Louis had wanted to do this test for many years and King George V inspected the fleet.

However, as events unfolded, Louis had the difficult decision of whether to stand down after the tests were completed, or remain mobilised. It was an issue of whether the navy appeared weak, or seemed as though it was sabre rattling. As it was, he showed excellent judgment by leaving the fleet standing in readiness.

At the end of June, with the calamitous assassination of the Archduke Franz Ferdinand of Austria-Hungary and his wife, Sophie the Duchess of Hohenberg, there was a marked exacerbation of the effects of anti-German feeling on Victoria and Louis. In an atmosphere where people were kicking dachshunds on the street and sauerkraut was called 'Liberty Cabbage', resentment against the Royal Family and anyone with a German surname was intense. Though he was hard at work for the war effort, the prince would be accused of being personally responsible for everything from sinking British ships to spying for Germany.

The summer of 1914 was Victoria's final trip to Russia. Victoria, Louise and Nona stayed at Ella's convent. Afterwards, they planned to tour Russia together during which each one would visit the places she found most interesting. They took their trip on a yacht travelling on the Volga and Kama rivers. There was much to do and see: Ella was most anxious to visit the monasteries and convents, while Victoria, Louise and Nona were engaged with the archaeological and natural sites. Victoria particularly enjoyed her visit to the Kungur Ice Caves near Perm. According to a tourist pamphlet, Victoria and Louise, like typical travellers, left their names in the caves along with the date.

As they visited towns, many would put on their finest clothes to meet Ella. While Ella visited Alapaievsk, Victoria and Louise continued from Perm and toured the Urals by special train. They visited platinum mines and the little towns that they happened upon such as Kishtyn. 'Tho' not the rose, I was near enough to it, being the Empress' sister and we were officially received there during two or three days.'[16] During their travels, they visited Ekaterinburg, and remarked that it was not a particularly welcoming place. They saw the Ipatiev House, which would later be renamed by the Bolsheviks 'The House of Special Purpose'. They also toured the various mines outside the town, and without knowing it, they may have seen the spot where, later, the bodies of the Imperial Family would be found.

It was in the beginning of August that Victoria received an anxious telegram from Louis urging her to return to England as soon as possible since it appeared that war was imminent. Both Louise and Nona became ill, and the party had to travel back to St Petersburg in slow stages. On 4 August, the day Germany violated Belgium's neutrality, they finally reached St Petersburg. Alix opened the Winter Palace, since 'we felt we could not put up at Peterhof as Alix had intended, the patients having to be kept in bed and there was a risk of spreading the infection.'[17]

Victoria described their hurried departure from Russia:

> [Alix] came to see us before we left and, with loving forethought, equipped us with thick coats and other serviceable clothing for the sea journey; we only having the lightest of summer clothing with us, also giving us smaller and lighter travelling trunks.
>
> We left St Petersburg on the afternoon of August 7th. I little dreamt that it was the last time I should ever see my sisters again. We were escorted on the journey home by Mr Wilton who belonged to the British Embassy. His brother was the Newspaper correspondent who was present at the investigation of the Ekaterinburg murders by the Russian Authorities and who wrote an account of it.
>
> We were taken by special train to the Russian Frontier at Torneo at the head of the Gulf of Bothnia. Lying at the wayside station, I caught sight of another saloon carriage on the line opposite to us in which I recognised Aunt Minnie [Dowager Empress Marie Feodorovna], her daughter Olga and party sitting at tea. We dashed across to speak to her and get the latest news. ...
>
> There is no communication by rail between the Russian frontier and Haparanda, only a high wooden bridge connecting the Russian frontier station and the Swedish town. We walked across to Haparanda and there, with infinite difficulty succeeded in getting a cart to take our luggage to the train and in obtaining a cab for ourselves.[18]

Victoria left her jewellery with Alix for safe keeping and never saw it again. They eventually got a train to Stockholm. Victoria picks up the story:

> We spent twelve hours with Gustaf and Daisy [Crown Prince and Princess Gustaf] at Drottningholm and also visited Charles (Haakon) and Maud [of Norway] at their small summer place on our way through Norway. We boarded the last steamer leaving Bergen ... The ship was crowded with the last tourists and anglers coming from distant parts of Norway and people slept on the floor of the dining saloon. We crossed the North Sea going as high up as Petershead and coasting down from Newcastle ... We arrived in London on the 17th of August, ten days after we left St Petersburg. We found Louis absorbed in his work which went on at night as well as by day.[19]

As intuitive as Victoria was, perhaps she had an idea that her world, the beautiful summer worlds of Illinskoje and Wolfsgarten, a large international extended family, the scenes of her youth and love, Heiligenberg, were all lost to her.

The bereavement was comparable to the loss of her Grandmama, for this was the world that she had made.

Victoria saw neither Ella nor Alix again.

There was now much to do since war was declared.

Victoria and Irène had had the foresight to exchange ladies' maids, Victoria sent Irène her German one, while Irène sent her English maid back to England. Irène and Henry had been in England that summer of 1914 and had hurriedly decided to leave in July when their cousin George told them that things were looking very bad.

In mid-October, Louis was admitted into the Privy Council. However, by then, the worst case was already in the works. On October 28, in the face of xenophobic pressure, Louis reluctantly resigned as First Sea Lord. This was hardly a shock to Victoria who saw with every passing day which way the wind blew, and that his resignation might ultimately be the only outcome. So much had happened before that. Now, there was only this last indignity to be revealed.

Louis was now the object of narrow-minded bias from the tabloid press, the clubs, and the public. Louis had been a member of the Royal Navy for over forty-six years and yet, at least partly because of his family connections in Germany, the tabloids clamoured for his resignation. Digs from writers who hid behind such pseudonyms as 'John Bull', and 'Bottomly', were becoming a constant. Anonymous letter writers were more specific in their charges of spying and treachery. There were accusations of sending secret signals to German ships, and other allegations of allegiance to the 'germhuns' – as the press called them. He was being blamed for every ship sunk since hostilities began and every man drowned.

In his letter of resignation, he wrote: 'at this juncture, my birth and parentage have the effect of impairing in some respects my usefulness on the Board of the Admiralty'. Besides the upper-class diehards who didn't like the influx of German royalty, there were members of the press as well as some retired officers who wanted him gone. Others felt that it was because of Victoria that he had to resign. Some feared that though she was tremendously patriotic, she was also tactless and talked too much on continental visits. However, like Louis, she was able to gather much information about the German Navy from Henry and Irène.

Not only Louis and Victoria, but their children were affected deeply by this unfortunate situation. There is a story that when young Dickie, a cadet at Osborne, heard of his father's resignation, he stood at attention in front of the Union flag with tears streaming down his face. Whether true or not, Lord Mountbatten certainly spent a great deal of time proving his Royal lineage and working out elaborate family trees. Ironically enough, the first royal casualty, a Battenberg, happened on that very same day when Aunt Beatrice's son, Prince Maurice of Battenberg, was reported killed at Mons.

On the night before Louis handed in his resignation, he arranged to see his alleged daughter by Lillie Langtry, Jeanne Marie, for the very first time. She had only learned in the last ten years that Prince Louis was her father because her mother, Lillie, had always posed as her aunt. Margot Asquith, the wife of the Prime Minister, had taken the liberty of informing Jeanne Marie at a dinner party that she was the purported daughter of Prince Louis. She was so angry that her mother had kept this from her that they never truly made up. She married a very rich young man in society, Ian Malcolm, who was incidentally a good friend of Winston Churchill.

Though the young woman was furious with her mother, she was evidently not angry with Louis, and came quite willingly that evening before the resignation. Louis' intent was to spare her the humiliation of finding out when the papers announced it. Perhaps Louis was satisfied that he was at last able to do something honourable for her after conveniently sweeping the problem under the rug after so many years.

Victoria was deeply unhappy over the need for Louis to resign. She wrote to Nona:

> What we hoped might not happen, has had to be & when you get this letter Louis will be a simple Admiral on half pay.
>
> It is the penalty of serving a Democracy, the 'man in the street' is mighty, & when the fools hour … strikes, the wise man who loves his service & the country must for their sake yield to the 'man-in-the-street' & the ignorance of the 'People'.[20]

Churchill would have stood by him, but Louis refused to have any such contention at this time of national emergency. There were others, who by way of letters to the editor of *The Times*, made their views known. From one letter he was called: 'a naval officer of very great ability, who has devoted the whole of his life to the service of England'.[21] In another missive, the entire Battenberg Family was defended: 'What proofs are the Battenberg family to afford to satisfy the country of their loyalty? The brother of Prince Louis died in the wars of West Africa, and now his nephew, Prince Maurice, has been killed in fighting the battles of Great Britain.'[22]

In any event, Victoria tried to think of it as a war sacrifice, though it was painful for her to remain in London. Therefore, they decided to sit out the war in Kent House on the Isle of Wight. They spent their time in retirement, reading, writing and gardening. Louis began his memoirs, which would cover his life up until his marriage. Victoria had much more time to brood about her family, her brother and sister in Germany and her two sisters in Russia. She wrote poignantly to Alix that: 'To-day is our Ernie's birthday, the first time in his life that three sisters can give him no news. How lonely he must be away from his dear ones, in a foreign country and hating the war.[23]

Louise joined the Voluntary Aid Detachments (VAD) and in March 1915, was sent to Nevers in France. She was, perhaps, the first and only British Princess to nurse in France during the war. Nona Kerr, too, worked at a military hospital in Rouen. She wrote a sympathetic letter to Louis which illustrated that she had become nearly as close to him as she was to Victoria. He answered, feelingly, writing: 'When the blow fell I missed you so much. Your presence would have been an additional comfort (for people have been extraordinarily kind) but you form such a real part of our small inner circle, that in any event, happily or the reverse, we miss you.'[24]

Though Nona was an integral part of their household, she now had other concerns. Besides her nursing in France she had become engaged, and married Lieutenant Colonel Richard Crichton in February 1915, a man, for those romantically inclined, that Nona had nursed.

Victoria took this in her stride, hoping that if Crichton didn't mind, she would like Nona to continue as her companion. Evidently, he did not and later offered Louis and Victoria a house on their property, Fishponds, which they gladly accepted. Nona would never attend her again as constantly as she had done prior to the war. That, however, did not stop their constant correspondence when they were apart.

During the war, different branches of the family were able to remain in contact through neutral Sweden. Crown Princess Margarethe, Victoria's cousin, Margaret (Daisy) of Connaught, would take letters from German or other relatives from the Central Powers, copy them out in her own writing, and then send them along to families who were members of the Allies and vice versa. This letter to Ernie illustrates the process:

> I enclose a letter for Onor which Victoria asked me to forward & add these few lines to say that if you or Onor want to write to her please send the letters to me & I will make sure of their getting there in much less time than the three months Victoria wrote the last one from Darmstadt had taken.[25]

Victoria wrote to Nona about a particular letter from Ernie, which had been sent through Daisy to Alix. According to its contents, Ernie hated the war and never participated in active combat; instead, he worked in an ambulance brigade and helped with rehabilitation of wounded men.

Irène was well, but Victoria felt strongly that it was depressing to get news of her German family in this way, 'knowing nothing will ever be the same again, except our personal affection for our relations'.[26] As well as these family members, there was also the plight of Franzjos and his wife Anna, who were not well off financially. Luckily, they were in neutral Switzerland.

In September of that year, Victoria was permitted a 24-hour pass, and went to Nevers to visit Louise. She spent her time helping in the hospital, assisting men to the latrines, and changing bandages. Louise stayed and nursed in various hospitals until 1919 and at no time was treated specially in any way. She cleaned and bandaged wounds, changed bedpans, and watched men die.

Meanwhile, Georgie was serving on the HMS *New Zealand* and already making a name for himself. He was said to be the cleverest and laziest cadet that his master at the Royal Naval College had ever met. He had a great deal of mechanical ability and creativity. He was able to air condition his cabin and give himself hot and cold running water before these things were commonplace aboard ship. He and Dickie were naturally a source of anxiety to Victoria, but she was philosophical, telling Nona that if it is their time to go, they would go.

However, her greatest concerns were for Alix, even though Russia was an ally. Like her grandmother, she had little reason to believe that in the circumstances, the Russian people would keep faith with their tsar and tsarina, nor did she see that changing.

Besides all that happened during the war – the tensions, the divisions, the conflicts – there were also the happy events though they could no longer freely share them with one another. Georgie had found himself a bride. She was the Countess Nadejda (Nada) de Torby, the daughter of the Grand Duke Michael Mikhailovich, a cousin of Nicky's and called by his family 'Miche-Miche'. This was the young man who, for a short time, had been a suitor of Victoria.

Besides being Victoria's suitor, Miche-Miche cut a slightly comical figure within the circle of the Imperial Family. He had contracted a morganatic union with the daughter of the Duke of Nassau, who happened to be the granddaughter of Pushkin, the great Russian poet. Even with such illustrious antecedents, she was not accepted, and therefore their marriage was spurned at the Imperial court. Miche-Miche was exiled, and he spent most of his life in Britain.

From that moment on, he made it his project to badger Nicky into making his wife an Imperial Highness, which Nicky refused to do. An amusing incident happened in the beginning of 1908 and was related by Victoria's son Dickie. Miche-Miche, it appeared:

> staggered his family by bursting into authorship in 1908 and writing a novel called 'Never Say Die' … The hero of the book is Prince Franz. The hero falls in love with Princess Margaret, but his mother, the Princess Donnerwetter, who is an imperious and jealous woman, would not hear of the marriage, although the young couple are in every way suited to one another.
>
> I was told that Princess Margaret was supposed to be my mother with whom he had been very much in love, but in fact she would not accept him.
>
> …
>
> He finally falls in love with an English girl, Ursula, and contracts a morganatic marriage with her … Nada Milford Haven told me that his brothers clubbed together and bought up the whole edition before it could be put on sale to the public, but too late to avoid the review copies being sent to the Press.[27]

Miche-Miche, from all accounts, was trying to placate Nicky with the marriage between Georgie and Nada. Since he was aware of the great esteem in which Louis was held by the tsar, he was certain that his own fortunes might improve by uniting his family to the Battenbergs. He wrote several letters to Nicky in which he took the opportunity, after describing Nada and Georgie's marriage ceremony, to ask for money. In fact, during the engagement period, both Louis and Victoria told Miche-Miche that Georgie had no money. However, Miche-Miche said not to worry about money, since he had enough – or to be more precise, would be able to acquire enough for the couple. In the end, he was the sort of relative that, when mentioned, could always illicit an exasperated response from family members.

Nada was a high-profile society figure, often photographed and mentioned in the society pages. She was an active and independent girl who loved lawn tennis, riding, shooting and dancing. She was a flamboyant creature and very sophisticated, which appealed to Georgie. She was dark, petite and pretty, and in the insecure world in which Georgie now lived, she seemed like something left of the world before:

> Georgie has just written a very happy & loving letter. He has seen his beloved Nada & they understand each other & want us to approve of a private engagement to be made public when the war is over. He says: '…that we love each other & appreciate each other for what we are'.[28]

Victoria discussed the matter very thoroughly in a letter to her cousin, the king. Georgie, she wrote:

> saw a good deal of her last autumn when she was with her mother at North Berwick & when he last had leave he told us of his affection for her & of his hopes.
>
> Unfortunately we hardly know Nada, but have always heard her well spoken of … Micha & his wife like Georgie [,] & have been most kind about the engagement which is not much of a 'partie' as worldly wealth goes, for their daughter.[29]

She ended the letter in asking, appropriately, for George's consent, which he gladly gave.

Though Alix was far away, she sent a telegram of congratulations. 'Is it possible that Georgie is getting engaged? Seems quite improbable.'[30]

Louis also got into the act, writing to his daughter Louise:

> Nada is the most attractive little thing & won our hearts completely. At any rate one feels that our dear Georgie will be really happy. Micha is an asp, but we need not mind him. His wife (whom we know called 'Sophy') is a thoroughly nice, good woman, without a trace of snobbishness or vulgarity – which seems strange when one remembers that terrible vulgarian, her mother. Nada has some delightful typical Russian ways about her.[31]

Georgie's engagement was not the only family event that spring. Dickie was now ending his school life, passing all his exams, and would be entering Dartmouth

For the purpose of this photographic section Victoria Milford Haven will be referred to as Victoria.

Above left: Princess Alice and Prince Ludwig of Hesse and by Rhine, March 1863 at the wedding of her brother the Prince of Wales (later Edward VII).

Above right: Baby Victoria, 1863.

Above left: The Hessian family with baby Victoria, 1863. Seated: Princess Alice, Prince Henry holding baby Victoria and Princess Elisabeth of Prussia, Victoria's grandmother. Back row, Prince William, Prince Ludwig, Princess Anna and Prince Karl of Hesse, Victoria grandfather.

Above right: Queen Victoria with Victoria, c.1864.

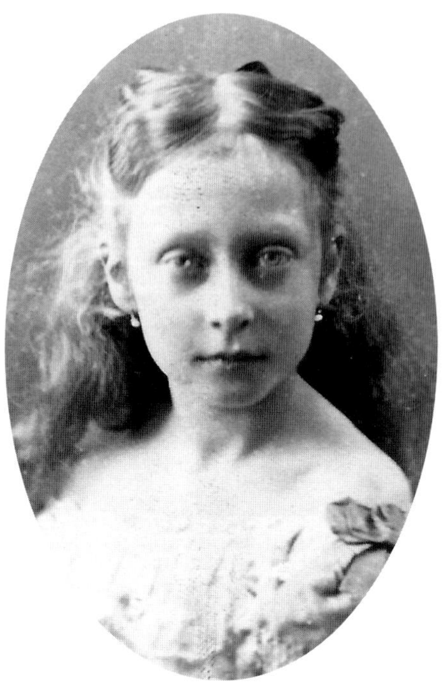

Victoria and sister Ella, the two eldest siblings c.1866.

Victoria.

Above left: 'The Three Graces', Irene, Victoria and Ella.

Above right: Alice's family (clockwise from top), Ludwig, Marie, Alix, Alice, Victoria, Irène, Ernst Ludwig, and Ella.

In mourning, 1878. Irène, Victoria,
Queen Victoria, Ella, Alix.

Victoria

Victoria about 17.

Prince Louis of Battenberg.

The engaged couple, 1883.

Above left: Wedding portrait, April 1884.

Above right: Henry of Battenberg and Princess Beatrice of Great Britain and Ireland, 1885.

Above left: Princess Victoria of Prussia (Moretta).

Above right: Queen Victoria smiling with Beatrice (standing), Victoria holding Alice.

Hessians and Battenbergs, Osborne 1885. L—standing Princess Marie of Erbach-Schönberg, Prince Alexander, Count Mensdorff-Pouilly, Prince Henry, Prince Gustaf of Erbach-Schönberg, Princess Beatrice, Prince Franz Joseph, Grand Duke Ludwig IV, Prince Louis. Seated: Irène, Alix, Princess Julie Battenberg, Hereditary Grand Duke Ernst Ludwig, Victoria holding baby Alice.

While they were stationed in Malta, Victoria, Prince Louis and Victoria's aunt, Marie Alexandrovna, Duchess of Edinburgh, and later Saxe-Coburg & Gotha.

Above left: Family group. Standing: Princess Alix, Prince Henry and Victoria. In front: Princess Beatrice with her son Prince Alexander of Battenberg, Queen Victoria with Prince Leopold of Battenberg, Grand Duke Ludwig, with Princess Victoria Eugenie of Battenberg.

Above right: When Irène became engaged, 1887. Standing: Alix and Ernst Ludwig. Sitting: Prince Henry of Prussia and Irène.

At Ernst Ludwig's wedding April 1894 in front of the Palais Edinburgh in Coburg. Back row: Prince Louis of Battenberg, Grand Duke Paul Alexandrovich, Prince Henry of Battenberg, Prince Philipp of Saxe-Coburg & Gotha, Count Mensdorff-Pouilly, Grand Duke Serge Alexandrovich, Crown Princess Marie of Romania, Crown Prince Ferdinand of Romania, Ella, Grand Duke Vladimir Alexandrovich, the Duke of Connaught, Prince Alfred, the Duke of Saxe-Coburg & Gotha. Next Row: Hereditary Prince Alfred of Saxe-Coburg & Gotha, the Prince of Wales, Tsarevich Nicholas Alexandrovich, Princess Beatrice, Alix, Princess Louise of Saxe-Coburg & Gotha, Princess Alexandra of Saxe-Coburg & Gotha, Victoria, Princess Charlotte of Saxe-Meiningen (of Prussia), Irène, the Duchess of Connaught, Grand Duchess Marie Pavlovna, the Duchess of Saxe-Coburg & Gotha. In front: Kaiser Wilhelm II, Queen Victoria, the Empress Friedrich (Vicky), and on the floor, Princess Beatrice of Saxe-Coburg & Gotha, and Princess Feodora of Saxe-Meiningen.

Wedding photo of Ernie and Ducky, April 1894.   Alix and Nicholas.

Above left: The Battenbergs in the mid-1890's: Louise, Alice, Victoria, Georgie and Louis.

Above right: The Hartenaus: Prince Alexander of Battenberg, with his wife Johanna and their son Assen.

Above left: C. 1897. Standing, Princess Mary of York (later Queen Mary), sitting: Princess Victoria Eugenie of Battenberg (later Queen of Spain), Princess Anna of Battenberg, and Queen Victoria.

Above right: Queen Victoria and baby Dickie, 1900.

In Darmstadt at Alice's wedding, 1903. The Hessian siblings and spouses: L-R, Ernst Ludwig, Alix, Nicholas, Irène, Henry, Ella, Serge, Victoria and Louis.

Above left: Alice and Prince Andrew of Greece and Denmark, wedding photograph, 1903.

Above right: A grandmother, 1905. Victoria with Margarita and Alice standing.

Above left: Victoria with her younger children: Dickie, Louise, and Georgie.

Above right: Family group c.1910. Standing, Georgie, Victoria, Dickie. Sitting, Louise with Margarita, Louis with Theodora (Dolla), Alice.

Right: Ernst Ludwig with his son Georg Donatus (Don), Grand Duchess Eleonore holding Ludwig (Lu), c.1910.

Below: The last photo of the Hessian siblings together, summer 1910. Irène, Ernst Ludwig, Ella, Victoria, and Alix.

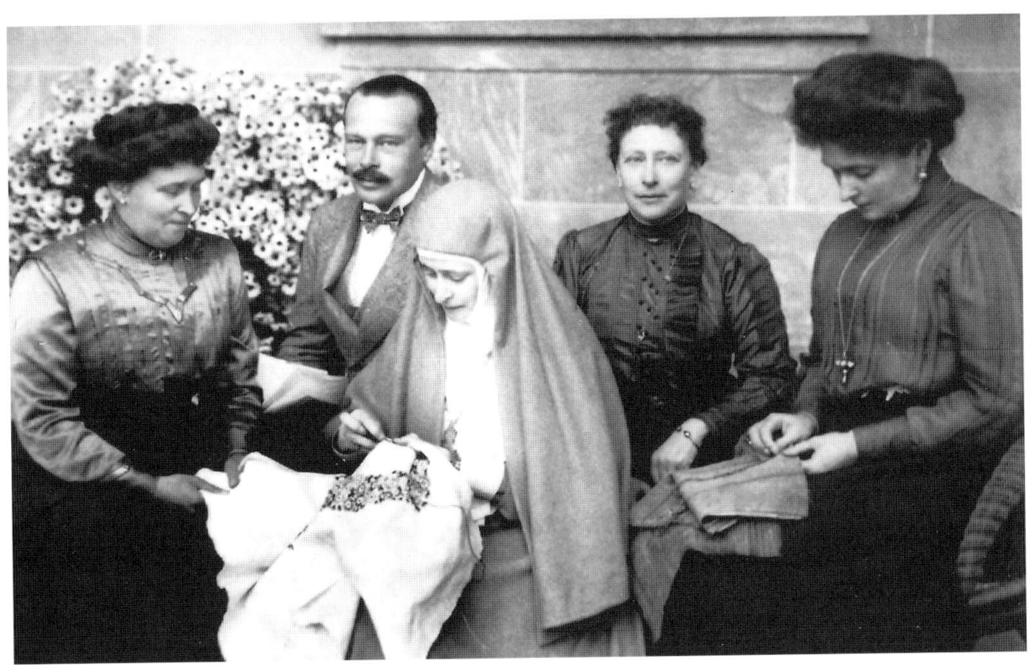

Ella at Illinskoje.

Prince Louis.

Above left: Prince Louis on a naval visit: Tsar Nicholas on the bottom rung, Grand Duke Alexis Alexandrovich and Prince Louis on top.

Above right: Alice and her daughters c. 1914: Margarita, Alice holding Sophie, Theodora and Cecile.

Dickie's Wedding, 1922. Dickie and Edwina, the bridal couple. The bridal party standing, Margarita, the Prince of Wales, Theodora. Sitting, Mary Ashley, (Edwina's sister) Joan Pakenham, Sophie, Mary Ashley-Cooper and Cecile.

Above left: Georgie and Nada's wedding, 1916. Standing: Georgie, Louise, Countess Anastasia de Torby, Princess Nina Georgievna of Russia. Sitting: the bride and on the floor Princess Xenia Georgievna of Russia.

Above right: The Milford Havens, about 1919. Victoria, Prince Louis, 1st Marquess of Milford Haven, Nada holding her son David, and Georgie sitting with Tatiana.

Above left: Louise's wedding, 1923. Georgie ready to give away the bride.

Above right: Victoria and her children with their spouses. Top: Gustaf of Sweden, Dickie, Georgie, and Prince Andrew. Second row, Edwina, and Nada. Louise and Alice flank Victoria standing in front.

Above left: Alice and Andrew at their Silver Wedding anniversary, 1928. Standing are Cecile and Sophie. Sitting are Margarita, Philip, Alice, Andrew, and Theodora.

Above right: The funeral of Countess de Torby (Nada's mother) 1927. Victoria with Nada's father, Grand Duke Michael Mikhailovich.

The funerals in Darmstadt, 1937. In his naval uniform, Dickie, next to him Philip and completely veiled, Victoria.

Victoria in the 1930's.

Victoria.

Louise and Victoria.

Philip.

Christening of King Charles III, December 1948. Standing, Patricia Mountbatten, Philip, King George VI, David Bowes-Lyon, the Earl of Athlone, Princess Margaret Rose. Front, Princess Elizabeth, and little Charles flanked by the 'grandmotherly colleagues' Victoria and Queen Mary.

Naval College. Victoria, who had taught him as a young child, was very close to him. She wrote him a truly touching and loving benediction:

> May God help & strengthen you my very dear boy, & never forget that we love you very dearly & have been young ourselves once & shall be able to understand the difficulties outside & in yourself which you may meet in your new life & if we can help by word or deed will always do so.[32]

Initially, Georgie and Nada had decided not to get married until after the war. However, a little over six months later, in November 1916, the couple did marry. The marriage seemed rather quick to Victoria and Louis. Like many men in wartime, Georgie perhaps was trying to put his life in order.

In a salute to the past, Louis gave his sons presents in honour of the occasion. Dickie described them:

> Papa has given me a lovely shirt stud, with a pearl in the centre & emeralds & diamonds round it, he gave one to Georgie yesterday for his birthday, like it and has kept the third himself so we have all 3 got one. They were given by great-grandmama [Queen Victoria] to Papa's father when he came over to attend Mama's christening.[33]

Louise, who was still nursing in France, was able to attend the wedding as a bridesmaid, which took place at Chapel Royal and Russian Embassy Chapel. King George V and Queen Mary attended, as did Queen Alexandra. Possibly not the wedding of the decade, it was, nevertheless, called the 'Wedding of the Year'.

Georgie and Nada would prove to be an unconventional couple. Nada was quite an uninhibited person and had been seen kissing Gloria Morgan Vanderbilt in a hotel room by a maid.[34] There would be trouble and scandal about this, but Victoria was very fond of her daughter-in-law, admired her strength, and always stood by her. They had two children, David and Tatiana, and settled down well enough together.

Chapter 11

Revolution

In the autumn of 1916, Ella went once more to St Petersburg to persuade Nicky to banish Rasputin. She also saw very clearly that there was a great hatred building up against the Empress, who was seen not only to be pro-German, but also to be passing secrets to her supposed confederates in Germany. Things came to such a pass that even Nicky tried to get Alix to be more discreet, but Alix would not listen. She felt that the peasants were behind her, and that she must keep Rasputin close to her as he was the only one who could comfort and help Alexei. The extended Imperial Family, who was virtually shut out of Alix and Nicky's lives now, began to think that Alix was going insane. Added to this were the spurious pro-German accusations that were hurled at Ella, who took shelter in her convent in Moscow.

Rasputin was murdered in St Petersburg in December of that year. In a letter dated 27 December 1916, by I. Hanbury Williams from the General Headquarters of the Russian Army to Lord Stamfordham, there is much speculation and worry about Alix:

> The agitation against the great lady is according to all accounts getting worse every day … The mistake they make is, in thinking that she herself is <u>pro G</u>[erman] – that is <u>not</u> so – but the mix up of influences through her special lady in waiting, who in turn is under the influence of that blackguard Rasputin – is what causes the trouble.[1]

Victoria fully realised the hopelessness of the present regime and her sister's lack of comprehension of the situation:

> I do hope that this time the news of Rasputin's death is true – though poor Alix will probably fall ill at it. What harm he has done her! I fear that among the masses in Russia she is hated, chiefly due to that vile creature & a set of people who have always tried to injure her.[2]

She commented as speculation increased about who the perpetrators of the crime were. It would later be established that Grand Duke Dmitri Pavlovich, Ella's ward, and Prince Felix Youssoupov, married to Princess Irina Alexandrovna, niece of Nicholas II, were responsible for the murder. However, Victoria pooh-poohed Youssoupov's involvement saying that '[i]f either Youssoupovs had a direct share in the killing of that brute, I feel sure it was the father, Felix is not made of stern or violent enough stuff'.[3] For Victoria, this was a rare mistake of intuition.

Greece, or at least its new king, Constantine, was insistent on remaining neutral in the war. The Greeks wanted to fight, and the Allies had promised them lands in Asia Minor in return for their support. Eleftherios Venizelos went as far as to set up a rival government to King Constantine's. During this altercation, the beloved summer home of the Royal Family, Tatoi, was burned down by arsonists. Alice and the family had all pitched in to fight the flames, but it was no use – Tatoi went up in flames, only to be rebuilt later.

By 1917, Venizelos recognised that the king was not heeding the will of the people and therefore he must go. Constantine, along with his eldest son George, who was thought to be pro-German, went into exile. Their second son, Alexander, succeeded as king – though virtually under house arrest. Alice was doing what she could, trying to protect her children, and waiting for the pieces to fall where they might. Soon enough, they had to follow Sophie and Constantine into exile in Switzerland. There, Alice and Andrew waited out the war.

As internal events heated up in Russia, it was thought by some in government that it would be a good idea for someone who knew Nicky well to make him understand the seriousness of the situation. It was suggested that Louis be sent to Russia because of his unique relationship with the Tsar. People thought that he might be able to talk some 'sense' into his brother-in-law. David Lloyd George, however, objected on the grounds of Louis' German birth and Alfred, Lord Milner, was sent instead; the mission failed completely.

The year 1917 started badly with anarchy in St Petersburg and with crowds shouting, 'Down with the German woman.' After several days of increasing civil unrest, spreading hunger, and lack of governmental control, the Romanov dynasty fell. On 15 March, Nicky abdicated in favour of his younger brother, Grand Duke Michael. King George wrote in his journal of that day: 'I fear Ali[x] is the cause of it all & Nicky has been weak … Heard from Buchanan [the British Ambassador] that the Duma had forced Nicky to sign his abdication … I am in despair.'[4]

Victoria was not unhappy at news of the abdication. She felt that it was clear that they had never been happy in their high position.

> I am very grateful that Nicky has abdicated for himself & the boy,
> for no one can tell how far the revolution may go & whether the
> socialists & anarchists may not get the upper hand before long &

then had Alix still been Empress they might have fallen on her –
this danger I hope is now averted. I hope the rumour that they
will be sent to the Crimea is true & that later on they can leave
Russia.[5]

Ella went so far as to give the new provisional government recognition. Victoria
told Nona, 'You will have seen in the papers that Ella has acknowledged the new
government & asked to be allowed to continue at the head of her sisterhood.'[6]
Louis complained to Louise that there was 'No news from Russia of our dear ones.
It is terrible & really all A[un]t Alix' fault.'[7] While this was certainly true, there was
enough blame to go around. However, no one in the family was under any illusions
about the safety of the imperial family.

In June of 1917, George V, feeling apprehensive about his own German antecedents,
renounced all his German names. The Royal Family was no longer of Saxe-Coburg
Gotha, but now, Windsor. The Tecks, of whom May, Queen Mary, was the most
illustrious member, now became the Cambridges and Athlones. And the Battenbergs,
were no longer princes, or even Serene Highnesses, but became British peers with
the name Mountbatten, and the title Milford Haven and Carisbrooke (Beatrice's
eldest son Alexander).

With all of Victoria's egalitarian notions and progressive ideas, she was
extremely conflicted by this turn of events. Possibly it was because of Louis.
They had received their title less than sixty years before, and now it was being
swept away. On the one hand, she had never been a snob about titles and so-called
bloodlines, but on the other, she muttered about how they were in the same class
of people as bankers and industrialists. She told Nona that she didn't think that
the peers would like to have the Battenbergs among them, but that may have been
a cover-up. According to Brian Connell, '[Victoria] never forgot that she was
a granddaughter of Queen Victoria and retained to the last a somewhat archaic
insistence on the personal prerogatives of royalty.'[8]

Louis became the Marquess of Milford Haven, and Victoria became the
Marchioness. Milford Haven was quite an important town and harbour on the Welsh
coast, chosen, possibly because of its naval associations. Georgie was the Earl of
Medina, a river on the Isle of Wight, near Kent House, and Viscount Alderney after
the Channel Island. Louise was plain Lady Louise Mountbatten, as was Dickie,
Lord Louis Mountbatten. As far as rank and precedence, it was determined 'that
the Marquess of Milford Haven should take rank as a Peer of Parliament before his
nephew the Marquess of Carisbrooke.'[9]

The king accepted the titles and Prince Louis wrote to the king's private secretary,
Lord Stamfordham, that he and Victoria thought a note should be appended to the
new titles that she was: 'abandoning her rank and title due to her being a Princess of
Hesse, and wishes to be known as Marchioness of Milford Haven'.[10] In the current
climate, giving up her titles seemed for the best. Though, Louis thought this was

very noble of her, undoubtedly, Victoria didn't feel noble but alienated from her sisters and brother.

For the rest of the family, she wrote to Nona, 'this would be a good occasion to settle & clarify the whole of the positions of [Cousin George's] relatives:

> It was suggested that I should continue to be Princess Victoria something or other of Nothing, but what is good enough for my husband is good enough for me – & in saying this please don't think I am insulting the British peerage, which is most honourable, it is just a touch of a princely tar-brush that I suffered from in writing like this.[11]

Louis was ambivalent and told Louise, 'Personally, I have always wanted a change of name. I am through with my career & it seems late in life to have such an upheaval.'[12]

Life, however, went on at Kent House, and Christmas that year was the first that Louis and Victoria had ever spent alone – a unique experience. However, they were delighted with the news of their newest granddaughter. In mid-December, Georgie's Nada had given birth to a girl, Lady Tatiana Elizabeth Mountbatten, in Edinburgh. Connected to Tatiana's birth is a small anecdote. According to Louis' biographer Mark Kerr, when she was born there were rumours that the Grand Duchess Tatiana Nikolaevna had escaped Russia. Prince Louis had received a telegram from his eldest son in Scotland which read: '"Tatiana has arrived", on which he said to his wife: "Then it is true that she has escaped!" but the reality suddenly occurred to the Princess who replied that it evidently was a new Tatiana who had come upon the scene.'[13] This illustrates the uncertainty of the fate of the Imperial Family.

At the beginning of 1918, another tie with the old days would be severed, when Miss Margaret Hardcastle Jackson ('Madgie') died. Miss Jackson had given Victoria and her siblings the discipline and the social conscience as well as the tools to follow in their mother's philanthropic footsteps. When Princess Alice died, she had fulfilled the needed feminine presence and given structure to their young lives.

As 1917 wore on, the revolution in Russia became more vicious. Imperial Russia seemed completely utterly fixed in the past, so no one could be surprised at the ferocity and the utter brutality that would follow from 1917 onwards. In March the Imperial Family was put under house arrest, along with those among their household who wished to remain. The Kaiser, Willy, made a lot of noise about saving the Hessian princesses, especially the love of his youth; however, this could hardly have been seen as helpful. Cousin George of England had offered asylum to the Imperial Family – offered, and then later withdrew the offer. King George thought it was bad policy to offer asylum to an autocrat, even if he was an ally and his first cousin.

Lenin, who had the Kaiser's aid in getting back into Russia after years of exile, had no truck with the Allies. In fact, in November 1917, he signed the Treaty of

Brest-Litovsk with the Kaiser to end hostilities, and with a stroke of the pen, Russia was out of the war. It had gone from monarchy, to democracy, to communism in the space of one year, and no one had any idea what had happened to Alix and her family – or Ella – and no way of finding out. As 1917 turned into 1918, Victoria tried to exert some influence, but her efforts were met with resounding silence.

Back in England, rumour and speculation were rampant. No one knew what had happened to the various members of the Imperial Family. Victoria wrote to Lenin's wife, an appeal from one woman to another, to enquire about the whereabouts of her family. She wrote to Mr Thomas Whittemore, an American working for the relief of Russian refugees after the revolution:

> Thank you so much for your letter & the trouble you have taken to talk with your minister at Stockholm about my idea of writing to Lenin's wife … I have meanwhile had a telegrame [*sic*] from the King of Spain confirming what the papers mention about the steps he has taken to have the Empress & her daughters sent to him for the duration of the war & he promises to let me know any news he gets about them. He thinks it is true that the Cesarevitch is dead – my poor sister![14]

By summer's end, she began to lose hope of seeing her brother-in-law or her nephew again. Oddly though, there were some glimmers of optimism. In August, Victoria wrote to King George:

> About 10 days ago I got a telegrame [*sic*] from Daisy asking if I had any news about Alix & the girls as Ernie had heard rumours of their death & had begged her to make enquiries. Now I have received another telegrame from Daisy which says: 'Ernie now telegraphs that has heard from two trustworthy sources that Alix & all the children are alive.'
>
> I dare not place much faith in this news, as it is likely to have been gathered from Bolshevick sources, however trustworthy the persons who passed it on may be.[15]

At nearly the same time as this news came, there was yet another desperate proposal on the horizon. King Alfonso XIII of Spain had offered to give asylum to the Imperial Family. Victoria had specifically asked her nephew-in-law to interest himself in the fate of Alix and Nicky and he had responded positively. She related his ideas to the king:

> [Alfonso] confirms what the papers say as to the steps he had already taken. He also says he thinks poor little Alexei is dead too. He says: 'My proposition is to let Alix & daughters go to neutral country on my word of honour that they would remain here till the end of the war. Hope all the different sovereigns will aid me.'

... I have just spoken to an American gentleman, recently returned from Russia, who saw Ella this spring just before she was removed from Moscow & he agrees with me in thinking she would not want to leave a country where she has created a work & interest for herself in her sisterhood, which she will hope to take up again as soon as possible – after all she has dedicated her life to this & has no family dependent on her. But for poor Alix & her girls it is different & he thinks it of the utmost importance that any steps to get them out of the country should be taken quickly before the Bolshevist rulers powers dwindle so much that their fanatical followers, & Alix's guard will be made up of such, are left without orders from their so called government to do what they like with their prisoners.

Will you, dear George, please therefore do your best that your government may be quick in its support of Alfonso.[16]

Such orders were given out by the government:

King of Spain having offered the Empress her children and the Dowager Empress his hospitality is believed to have asked the Germans to help them to leave Russia. If you have a chance of helping and saving them Mr. Balfour desires that you should do so.[17]

But by this time, it was a moot point.

Finally, in September 1918, the news of the assassination of Alix, Nicky and their five children, along with members of their household, was given to King George. As Princess Marie Louise of Schleswig-Holstein recounted events, the king told her that: 'Nicky, Alix, and their five children have all been murdered by the Bolsheviks at Ekaterinburg. I have ordered that this awful news should not be released to the Press until I have had time to let Victoria know.'[18]

Princess Marie Louise went from Windsor to the Isle of Wight with a letter from George to Victoria explaining what had happened. Marie-Louise wrote that 'I have often had to face difficult situations ... but never anything so terrible as to inform someone that their much-loved sister, brother-in-law, and their five children had all been murdered.'[19] When she reached their home, Louis met her and said that it would be better if he gave the letter to Victoria.

After receiving the news, Victoria came to Marie Louise's room to thank her for bringing the letter. They didn't talk about it much as there wasn't a lot to say about a tragedy of such extraordinary magnitude. Marie Louise felt that she couldn't even condole with Victoria in the usual way, it seemed out of place. Victoria told her, 'Let us go into the garden as there is any amount of work to be done and one gardener cannot do it all by himself.'[20]

The following day, Victoria wrote several letters. The first was to Nona, as she informed her of the awful news and her feelings:

> Almost I should be grateful if I could believe it & know that they all met their end quickly & suddenly at the same time & that poor Alicky & the girls were spared the misery I have feared for them … [T]hose poor girls. I could have wished might have been spared, they were so young they could have recovered from all the horrors & perhaps found some happiness in life still – but again evil things might have been done to them … It is quite nice having Loui[s]e here now, she is tactful & it helps me to pull myself together.[21]

And to her cousin George, she wrote:

> For my poor Alicky … one must be grateful that her sufferings are over, life would always have been a misery to her after Nicky & her boy were gone ….
>
> I shall be so grateful to hear from you any further news you may get … But however that may be God's peace is with them now & it is easier to bear the sense of their loss to me, than the thought of what they have gone through & what might have still been in store for them.[22]

Marie Louise stayed for three weeks. They gardened, picked blackberries and hunted for mushrooms, but never talked about the contents of the letter. Marie Louise realised that Victoria was working hard all day every day to lessen her pain. Together they knitted items of clothing for the troops overseas, but never ever talked of the news again. Victoria wrote her a letter afterwards saying that not talking about the tragedy helped her get a grip on events far better than discussing in detail all that had happened.

Victoria would also never allow herself to hope, as so many others did, that the stories of their demise were untrue, possibly because she continued to be haunted by the 'evil' things that might have happened to her nieces. In the face of such rumours of the horrors, escapes and some survivors, Victoria was realistic. She wrote to Cousin George:

> I thank you so much for your kind note enclosing a copy of the information supplied by the Consul at Ekaterinburg about the fate of Alix & her children.
>
> [H]e says: 'they are stated to have been burnt alive' …. & further on 'there is still the possibility of their having been taken north by the Bolshevicks [sic]' … I should fancy the more probable course of events … is that they were killed almost at the same time as Nicky & then their bodies … removed to another house which was set fire to, to remove all traces of the slaughter.[23]

Nevertheless, in the face this terror, pragmatic Victoria held out hope that Ella, the Mother Superior of the Convent of SS Mary and Martha, might have been spared.

In April 1918 Ella was handed a note by a group of soldiers informing her that Nicky needed her urgently. She and her companion, Sister Barbara, were given just minutes to get ready and were taken away from the convent by the Bolsheviks. The truth was that Lenin was jealous of, and hated, her popularity in Moscow and wanted to be rid of her by any means possible.

The nuns were first taken to Ekaterinburg, and thence to Alapaievsk, along with several other members of the Imperial Family: Grand Duke Serge Mikhailovich; three sons of Grand Duke Constantine (Ioann, George, Igor); and young Prince Vladimir Paley, the son of Grand Duke Paul Alexandrovich, and his second wife, Princess Paley. Vladimir, a promising poet, was arrested and sent away for refusing to renounce his father.

At Alapaievsk, they were incarcerated for several months in an empty schoolhouse. Besides trying to make their own daily lives as bearable as possible with a normal routine, Ella and Barbara spent much of their time looking after the men. They were able to smuggle out some letters so that others knew these bare facts, but their existence was extremely precarious.

Victoria said much of this in a letter to the king and ended with '[s]hould any news of her reach you, I am sure you will let me know & I thank you once more for your affectionate & sincere sympathy with me in my distress & sorrow'.[24]

The letter contained the facts as far as Victoria knew them. What she didn't know at that point, was that Ella was already dead.

Some months later the sad truth was confirmed to Victoria by Lord Robert Cecil. She wrote a letter to Nona that showed her deep understanding of her two sisters.

> If ever anyone has met death without fear she would have, and her deep and pure faith will have upheld and supported comforted her in all she has gone though so that the misery poor Alicky will have suffered will not have touched Ella's soul and maybe had she lived, years of solitary suffering would have been her lot, for I have recently heard that all her work in Moscow has been destroyed.[25]

Though she had no choice but to accept the ends of her sisters and families, it did not follow that she was reconciled, or thought that all had been done to save them. She knew that this was not so and was bitterly angry about it. She directed this anger towards politicians who would not save her relations, and relatives who would not or could not. Her comments about the naïve Woodrow Wilson and David Lloyd-George show that she did not mince words. They, she said, 'coquette with the Bolsheviks & think to reform them by moral suasion! The fools!!'[26] It is unsurprising that she blamed Cousin George, fairly or not, for abandoning his close family.

Cousin Willy purported to want his Hessian cousins saved, and Lenin, when the Kaiser's government had provided him with the wherewithal to travel into Russia, had promised that the two German Princesses would go free. But no one who knew them thought seriously that either Ella or Alix and her family would accept such help. There was one relative, Victoria's nephew-in-law, Alfonso XIII of Spain, who had offered to provide sanctuary for Ella, Alix and her family, though he was tragically unsuccessful. Victoria wrote him a letter of thanks.

> Now that alas there is nothing to hope for my dear Sister Alix & her children on this earth & that it is almost a positive certainty that death has released them from further suffering …, I feel I must send you a few lines to thank you with all my heart for all you tried to do to save them from their enemies.

She praised him for his efforts in trying to help the Romanovs and criticised an unnamed closer cousin, in the strongest of terms:

> the sovereign who had the most direct influence on the revolutionary government in Russia, the one who had known my sister as a child, who had the same blood as hers flowing in his veins, who formerly never failed to claim her as of his nationality deserted her, I fear I must believe, in her distress, whilst you to whom she & hers were comparative strangers thought of & strove to help them – I shall never forget the gratitude I owe you for this.[27]

The war was over, and armistice was signed in November 1918. With a stroke of the pen much of the royal world ended. Victoria knew that her grandmother, Queen Victoria, had never wanted Ella and Alix to go to Russia. The queen intuited the disaster that would come to them. She had astutely seen all the signs during her lifetime and the brutality of their eventual fates would not have surprised her. Her relations must have been glad she did not live to see how her world and many members of her family had vanished so quickly.

Willy was no longer the German Kaiser and went quietly, and almost cheerfully, into exile in Holland. The grand-nephew of the late Emperor Franz-Joseph of Austria, who, himself had died in 1916, reigned in Austria-Hungary for two years as Emperor Charles and was now also in exile, first in Switzerland and then in Madeira. As for all the Princes, Grand Dukes, Dukes, Counts and Electors in Germany – they were all, including Ernie, removed.

Ernie was allowed to stay at Wolfsgarten and keep the New Palace. He abdicated like the rest and no longer had any real power, but he was popular with the people. This may be partly due to what had happened after the Great

War, during the days of revolutionary activity in Germany. According to some of his 'closest friends', the Grand Duke faced down the revolutionary mob that broke into his residence and clamoured into the throne room. They shouted: "'Down with the Grand Duke!" "Kill the Grand Duke!"' There was a silence, which was broken when Ernie said: "'I can see no Hessian uniforms among you, but you will form a deputation and tell me what you want; in the meantime, as no one has ever been to the palace without being entertained, my wife will make you tea.'"[28]

In the face of Ernie's courageous stand, the deputation that had come to unseat him instead protected Ernie and his family. He kept his land and his title, though it carried nothing with it, and he and Onor and the children continued, for the most part, just as they always had – Ernie now working with the convalescents, and Onor continuing her role as the benevolent mother figure to the Hessians.

In early November, Irène and Henry, along with their eldest son Waldemar, fled from Kiel in their car. They were fleeing the soldiers of the German Revolution and the car was fired upon. According to *The Times*, Irène was wounded in the arm and a bullet went through Henry's coat.[29] After this hair-raising escape, the couple soon returned to their residence in Hemmelmark, almost as though nothing had happened, and all was seemingly peaceful once again.

At war's end, there was a slight bitterness in the relationship between Victoria and Irène, but it healed as well as could be expected. However, since neither travelled as they had before, they saw each other very infrequently.

Tsar Ferdinand, who had become the monarch of Bulgaria after Sandro Battenberg, abdicated in favour of his son Boris, and very quietly left the country. He settled mainly in Coburg. Of the others who retained their thrones, there was Alfonso XIII of Spain, though not for long, and also the Belgians, the Italians and the Scandinavians.

Though many lost their thrones and their lives, Prince Louis was only slightly luckier. He lost his position in the Royal Navy and much of whatever fortune he had possessed. Louis was no longer able to draw on monies he had invested in a platinum mine in Russia and various properties in Germany. This major part of his fortune was gone – and the couple seemed to be back almost where they had started, living on navy half-pay, any small inheritances, and some of Victoria's properties that remained intact. In addition, Victoria lost many of her jewels, which she had left in Russia at the beginning of the war. There was a movement to reward people who had helped in the Allied victory, and Louis' invention, the Course Indicator, was thought to be a tremendous help. Louis, however, would not accept monetary compensation for this.[30]

Added to all these financial losses, they were compelled to sell Heiligenberg, and with the devastating financial conditions in Germany, received just £30,000 – under half of what the estate was worth. From a pragmatic point of view, their son Georgie would not have the beautiful home outside Jugenheim to inherit. Their lives, which Victoria had thought sacrificed by Louis' resignation, were changed.

However, during their years at Kent House, they did war work by sheltering some of the wounded and sick men that came to the Isle of Wight. Several of these men convalesced for long periods at the cottage. It was good for Louis, for he was able to advise the men as he had advised his junior officers. They looked up to him and he began to feel useful again and kept up with several of them for some years afterwards.

The surviving members of the Hessian Family, Ernie, Victoria and Irène, continued to struggle with the rumours and misinformation that began to seep through to Germany and England about the fate of the Imperial Family and Ella. There were myriad differing accounts of the events. People came forward with new and miraculous escapes, or an even grislier version of their sad ends.

Later, between Irène, Victoria, the Dowager Empress Maria Feodorovna and her daughters, now living in exile in Denmark, they would have to contend with all the imposters parading themselves before the world. They claimed to be the Grand Duchess Anastasia, or Marie, or Olga, or Tatiana, and even the sickly Alexei. Irène and Ernie would have to deal with Anna Anderson, the most famous imposter claiming to be Grand Duchess Anastasia. It was Miss Anderson about whom movies, plays and books were written. Victoria counted herself lucky that she was not closely involved with this and would only confirm Ernie and Irène's conclusions when asked.

Victoria's Dickie finished the war as a sub-lieutenant and went off with some of his fellow officers to do courses in Cambridge and catch up on lost time. Georgie and Nada had become parents once again, when their son, David, was born in May in Edinburgh. Victoria was delighted to have a grandson at last. Though Louis was officially put on the retirement list in the beginning of 1919, he was assisting King George V as a Naval aide-de-camp. In addition, there was news of Irène. Her middle son, Sigismund, her only completely well child, was to be married to Princess Charlotte Agnes of Saxe-Altenburg and just a month afterward, Waldemar was married to Princess Calixta of Lippe.

Louise was still in France. She continued her nursing, remaining there until 1919. She had always led an independent life, especially during the war, and Victoria and Louis had felt that she should be permitted to choose her own mate. After all she had seen during her nursing, she couldn't have felt like a 'dewy-eyed' princess. Indeed, she had spurned the proposals of Manoel I of Portugal, and, it was said, Prince Christopher of Greece.

Because of the impecuniousness of the Battenbergs, Victoria and Ella had become interested in matching Louise with Felix Youssoupov. The young man came from one of the wealthiest families in Russia and would solve any money worries that would ever arise. This idea started in 1909 and went on until about 1912 when newspapers reported that he and Louise might marry. The truth was that the two young people had no interest in one another. Though Victoria would have wished it, since it would have provided a great deal of security for her daughter, she did not insist.[31]

In 1913 there had been talk of a match with Prince Friedrich Solms-Baruth. Onor and Victoria discussed it in letters, but Louise said no. Victoria explained that it was because of lack of attraction, and because the Solm-Baruth family were 'a totally Prussian family with all their distinct traditions and prejudices, loyalty to the King of Prussia, a member of his nobility, duty bound to the court'.[32] It was obvious at that late hour that such a match would be very awkward for the Battenbergs, who served in the English Navy, as well as the thoroughly English Louise.

In any event, she seemed content travelling with her mother visiting relatives in Europe and Russia, and her war work. Early in the war years she had been engaged to a man, but he was never identified and was subsequently killed in battle. Later she met a fellow nurse, a man the family called 'Shakespeare', identified as the painter, Alexander Stuart-Hill. Louise was very much in love, and they were engaged – until Louis put a halt to the attachment. Objection to the match was not because Louise's suitor was a commoner, or that he was poor, but because he was a homosexual. Louise, in her innocence, had been completely unaware of this.

Chapter 12

Jerusalem

In the summer of 1919, Victoria undertook a much scaled-down version of what had once been grand touring to visit family. In Switzerland, she was able to see Franzjos and Anna, about whom she had worried so much during the war. She also saw Ernie and his family at Thurn for the first time in six years. She approached the meeting with some trepidation, but wrote later:

> though I knew our love for each other was unchanged yet I own that I rather dreaded our first meeting, for a separation of six years – & such years as we have gone through not only must make us see many from a different point of view, but must also produce unknown effects on our respective characters. Thank God, that in all essentials I have found you the same & I hope that you have found the like in me.[1]

With Victoria and Ernie, there can be little doubt that their feelings for each other had not changed. Though Victoria had always said that Ernie was Ella's child, the closeness with this eldest sister, who had mothered him so completely, was unique. She would never direct her anger at the brother whom she had always protected and shielded from the realities of the world. Any resentment or bitterness that she cherished, which was very little, she seemed to aim at Irène, her last sister, and that did not last long. And, in turn, Irène didn't hesitate when she wrote to Victoria, to place the blame where she thought it lay: 'Europe & the World has to thank the so called Entente for the war & all its consequences. In the End Truth! Will triumph!'[2] What Victoria thought of such statements can only be imagined.

That she understood there was no hope for her sisters in Russia safeguarded her from disappointment, and she tried to impart that to Ernie. However, in her compassion, she would not stop him from hoping altogether. She wrote to Onor, that 'if he, like poor Aunt Minnie [Dowager Empress Maria Feodorovna], still has hope, then please do not rob him of this ... – time will make this hope disappear in a more gentle way.'[3] He knew even less than she did about the circumstances of their deaths and heard the same odd survival stories. The news that Ernie received from Russia was 'just as sparse & unreliable as all that one has received'.[4]

Victoria had a unique philosophy, even as her grief threatened to overwhelm her. She knew that although the worst had happened, one could still be philosophical and find happiness in life. She tried to share this viewpoint with Ernie.

> There is one great lesson the passed [sic] years have taught mankind,
> … that is not to overvalue this life on earth or to fear death as was
> the tendency before that – one learns to be really grateful for the
> small memories & to discover the value & comforts of small daily
> pleasures.[5]

This does not mean that Victoria was always stoic about the tragedies in her life.
Despite the stories about working in the garden, Victoria had many tears for her lost
sisters. Grand Duke Dmitri Pavlovich came to London in the beginning of 1919.
He felt obliged to visit Victoria and he recounted his feelings about their encounter
in his diary:

> Around 11.30 I set off for Kensington Palace to visit old Aunt Victoria
> Battenberg (now Lady the Marchioness Milford Haven). I have
> to admit that I was in an awful funk about that interview, because
> I didn't know how she would feel about me and my activities in the
> year before the revolution [The Grand Duke was one of the assassins
> of Rasputin.], which were, of course, against her poor, ill-fated
> sister Alix. But Victoria was always very observant, and so she has
> a perfectly correct view of the general state of things. Nonetheless,
> our conversation was very difficult to bear. She cried the whole time,
> and managed to draw various pictures for herself of the last moments
> of her sisters' lives.[6]

Such an emotional scene may seem unlike Victoria, but perhaps it was just too
overwhelming to see this young man again. A youth so closely associated with
both her sisters and all the lost Romanov relations, and who she had not seen since
before the war.

And as for the relationships between the cousins who had been Queen Victoria's
grandchildren? George V's biographer has an answer for that question:

> A few weeks after the Armistice, [George V's] son Prince Albert
> [later George VI] … met the Kaiser's sister, Princess Victoria
> ['Moretta']. He wrote to his father: 'She asked after you and
> the family, and hoped that we should be friends again. I told her
> politely I did not think it was possible for a great many years!!!' The
> King replied 'Your answer to Cousin Vicky (who of course I have
> known all my life) was quite correct. The sooner she knows the
> real feeling of bitterness which exists here against her country the
> better.' … Not until 1935 could [George V] write to … [Ernie]…:
> 'That horrible and unnecessary war has made no difference to my
> feelings for you.'[7]

At the end of that year, Louis, Victoria and Louise spent Christmas with Alice in Corfu. Afterwards, they travelled on to Rome. Victoria wanted Louise to 'go away from all old associations to help her restart an after war life & put the past more into the background.'[8] She noted, too, that '[Louis] is beginning to show his age rather, he stoops a bit when he walks & does not care about walking fast – well he is going to be 66, so it is not surprising.'[9] For economic reasons, they decided to give up Kent House. The reverses in the fortunes of the family took their toll on Louis, and undoubtedly he hated seeing his income severely reduced. Instead, they repaired to Fishponds at Netley Castle. Victoria was determined to make the most out of this time near her best friend and her husband.

In June 1920 there was a slight tempest about the publication in England, America and Australia of letters between Nicky and Alix. However, Princess Victoria brought forth a suit to stop the publication. They were published by Messrs. Duckworth & Co. in 1923 and called *The Letters of the Tsaritza to the Tsar 1914–16.* Victoria was sensible enough to know that it was only a matter of time before such exploitive materials became the norm in the publishing world, and that it would be impossible to sue everyone.

In early 1920, Victoria received a phone call from her Aunt Beatrice. The princess had read in a London illustrated paper that several coffins were resting in a small chapel in Beijing. The bodies, Princess Beatrice explained, were those of Ella and Sister Barbara, and others who had been murdered with her. They were in Beijing under the care of one Father Seraphim. The article explained how both the coffins were taken by wagon overland to China by the Father. He stopped in Beijing because he could literally go no further.

Victoria and Louis made inquiries to find out whether this story was true. Ella was able to inspire true faith and loyalty, and Father Seraphim was evidently inculcated with the necessary zeal to take Ella wherever she wished to be. Moreover, they would find out that he was determined that she be buried in the proper Christian manner. They were informed that many of the faithful, and most particularly the peasants, looked upon Ella as a saint. There was nothing they wouldn't do to ensure that Ella's final wish, to be buried in Jerusalem, was carried out.

Victoria slowly learned more details of the events of June and July 1918. In a report dated 24 April 1920, Father Seraphim related the story as he knew it. He had been hidden when the assassins brought the party to a mineshaft at Alapaievsk. The group was made to walk to the mouth of the shaft. Ella had begun to sing a hymn. The Bolshevik commander pronounced their sentence of death and selected Ella first – she kneeled at the edge of the shaft and was stuck unconscious by a rifle and thrown many feet down to the bottom of the shaft. The rest were dealt with in the same way, except Grand Dukes Serge Mikhailovich, who protested the outrage and was shot before being flung down.

The priest remained hidden, and the soldiers tossed down hand grenades so that although they were mostly alive when thrown down, they were mortally wounded by the grenades. When the soldiers left, those hidden could hear hymns still being sung down in the shaft. A peasant who also witnessed the murders stated in Father Seraphim's report that 'en-route to their martyrdom, the Grand Dukes and the other martyrs started religious chants'.[10] In relating the story to Ernie, Victoria added,

> I have heard that it was told by one of those who was present at her death that she prayed 'Lord forgive them for they know not what they do' – & I believe it, … The autopsy on the bodies proved that life was extinct before they were thrown into the pit, so thank God the tales of further suffering are not true.[11]

It must be concluded that Victoria was once again trying to spare Ernie great sorrow as she had always done, for it is probably not true that they were dead before they were thrown into the pit – especially if they were indeed heard singing hymns.

Later, when the White Russians were able to take over Alapaievsk, Seraphim was able to go down into the shaft with the help of the soldiers and see the state of the bodies. Ella had been trying to care for the others who had survived the fall. She had torn her nun's veil and bandaged their wounds. When she finally succumbed, her hand, he said, had stiffened into the sign of the cross.

At first, Seraphim took them to his church in Alapaievsk. The bodies were identified, washed, dressed in night-clothes, put in coffins and a funeral mass was said. The Father knew that the Grand Duchess could not stay there long. As the political situation was so unstable, there was no way of knowing if and when the Bolsheviks would return so it was imperative for Seraphim to remove the coffins as soon as possible. This he was finally able to accomplish, though it took nearly a year.

He trekked eastward with the coffins on wagons and was able to get them on the Trans-Siberian Railway. The coffins were rescued by Chinese and Japanese Troops from Russian insurgents just in the nick of time. Later, after many ordeals, he was able to put the coffins on the Chinese Eastern Railway, and they arrived at the Russian Mission in Beijing. It was here that the *London Illustrated News* ran the story and Princess Beatrice had shown it to Victoria.

With the help of Lord Curzon, Foreign Secretary at the time, as well as many others, Victoria began her mission to take Ella and her companion to Jerusalem. Having learned that the coffins reposed at an Orthodox chapel in the outskirts of Beijing, together with some of the other Imperial family members killed at Alapaievsk, she began writing letters and telegrams to make arrangements.

In correspondence with the representative of the Russian Legation in Paris, M. de Giers, Victoria learned the details of what had happened to Ella and her companions at Alapaievsk and was able to read Father Seraphim's account. Through the good offices of this same gentleman, she was able to arrange the logistics of the transfer of Ella's and Sister Barbara's coffins from Beijing to Jerusalem. The remaining coffins were left in the Orthodox chapel in Beijing and were eventually lost. To this day, the whereabouts of the other Alapaievsk victims remain unknown.

There was some obligatory haste since Victoria felt that the bodies rested in an environment hostile to Christians. Although she had been advised to leave the bodies in China, after much thought, she decided that taking the coffins to Jerusalem was most fitting. She did not arrive at this decision cavalierly – it was painful for her to remove the remains, but she was convinced it was the only way.

She wrote to M. de Giers,

> I am persuaded that, sooner or later, the day will come that the body of my sister will reenter Russia and will find definite repose in Moscow, the city that she loved so much ... but until that day comes, I so much want to know, that she is in a safe place. Or, there is only one place which it appears to me which surely the Grand Duchess, herself would have chosen, were Russia not possible, it is Jerusalem ... This city is sacred to all Christians, it is venerated by Moslems and Jews. No revolutionary group would dare to touch its churches and convents.[12]

They were able to coordinate arrangements with Father Seraphim. He and two assistants would leave China on 15 January, taking the coffins to Port Said where Louis, Victoria, Louise and their party would meet them. From there, they would board a train and travel together to Jerusalem.

It was Victoria's intention to go to Rome at the end of the year, and wait there for word that the bodies were on their journey. However, before she left, certain events occurred. In October of that year, Aunt Marie of Coburg died. Irène was able to write her details of the Duchess' last moments:

> Aunt Marie of Coburg's death [24 October 1920] will have grieved you, bringing back so many memories, just also of Malta. Quite peacefully she slumbered & neither Ducky nor Baby Bee realised when all was really over ... She is at peace too now – & for her it is also happier so, poor thing.[13]

It has been often repeated that Marie could not get over the fact that she was no longer the Duchess of Saxe-Coburg & Gotha and became nearly apoplectic when a letter with the envelope addressed to Frau Coburg was delivered to her. However, such stories are usually just that – stories. She suffered from worsening health conditions, certainly not helped by serious external factors: financial worries caused by the loss of her Russian fortune, angst about the plight of her Russian relations, and the collapse of the German Empire.

At the end of the year Irène wrote: 'God bless you dear for the thought of bringing beloved Ella's remains to Jerusalem.'[14] It appeared that the two sisters were falling back into their habits of correspondence.

The coffins arrived in Port Said on 25 January 1921, where the Milford Havens met them. For a Westerner, Egypt in January was one of the few bearable months. Usually, the weather was so hot and humid that even native Egyptians had a problem tolerating it. Their first stop was Alexandria. The British had occupied Alexandria since approximately 1880, and the city had been their chief port in the Middle East during the Great War. From there, they caught a train to Port Said. Upon reaching the port, they learned that the coffins had arrived just hours previously. Victoria described the scene at length for Ernie:

> There is a little Greek Church here & the coffins were taken there for the night, so we went to the church; they had just been placed in a small side chapel draped in black … It was very quiet & private & calm in the little chapel, only one candle burning at the head of each coffin. …
>
> [Father Seraphim] told us that when the coffins had to be hidden for some months before they were able to leave Siberia, they were in a nunnery, where they were opened, as this was necessary & our Ella's body was not decayed only dried up – The nuns cleansed it & exchanged the grave cloth for a nun's.[15]

Their train was fitted with luggage compartments that would fit the coffins and all of Father Seraphim's effects, and those of his two assistants. This was all arranged by General Allenby, a soldier famous for liberating the Ottoman region of Palestine from the Turks, and who was at this point, British High Commissioner of Egypt. They reached Jerusalem the following day and were met by representatives of the Colonial Government and the High Commissioner, Sir Herbert Samuel, as well as the Russian Orthodox clergymen. The coffins were loaded onto trucks decorated with green ribbons, and two priests in black and silver funeral vestments sat with Ella's coffin. They followed in cars provided by the High Commissioner, and eventually reached the city itself.

As the car made its way down the rocky road that led to the Mount of Olives, many of the faithful began following the cars and trucks. They were determined to participate in the funeral of the beautiful Grand Duchess and her assistant. They drove to the Church of St Mary Magdalen, the spot that General Charles Gordon had fixed as the site of the crucifixion. It had five onion domes, gleaming white in the winter sun. As the cars came to the entrance, there was a bit of a struggle. So many had come for the funeral services being held that day, as well as the two days following, that there was quite a crush.

Louis took charge and helped direct the unloading of the coffins. Victoria held on to the brass handle of one of them as they climbed the stairs to the entrance of the church. She wrote of stepping over a poor woman who had fallen on her face during the utter crush of the mourners.[16] Luckily, the group was able to get up to the church and into their seats for the service. It was long and drawn out, with a congregation that flowed out of the doorway and onto the terrace.

Victoria and her group sat through similar services for the next several days. Though the mandatory government was anxious to extend its hospitality to these most distinguished visitors, they refused all invitations. It seemed like a bad idea to have cocktails and tea dances while they were attending the funeral services of a loved one. The greatly devoted Father Seraphim had elected to stay in Jerusalem at the church with Ella and Sister Barbara, living there and praying by the coffins.

The spot was beautiful, Victoria wrote to Nona: 'The church lies beautifully on the steep slope of the Mount of Olives in its own grounds surrounded by cypress & fir trees, well back & above the high road, with a lovely view on the town.'[17]

And, to say that they found a peaceful spot in Jerusalem is to say something.

They left Jerusalem in the beginning of February and returned to Rome. From Rome, there was a great deal of letter writing back and forth between Victoria, Irène and Ernie, discussing what had happened in Jerusalem and their feelings about it. Irène was very moved by the scene at Port Said when Victoria and Louis met the coffins and thought the descriptions of the coffins resting in the little Greek Orthodox Church on a candle-lit night, beautiful. As was her inclination, she felt it necessary to close with a conciliatory remark:

> Henry beggs [*sic*] me quite especially to tell you how deeply he feels for you, & that I am to tell you & <u>dear L[ouis]</u> – that for him you both remain in his heart what you were for him before – politics are one thing but old well proved friendship another & he feels as ever that for him he is 'his old mate', & sends you both his fond love.[18]

In a letter dated the following day, Irène asked the key question:

> Has … Father Seraphim been able to tell you anything of how beloved Ella's end was? Or how it all happened? However painful his knowledge may have been one longs to know & how one would like to thank him for his faithful care of her last remains.[19]

Though Victoria told what details she knew to her sister, in a letter to Ernie she still left out some of the more distressing details:

> Our Ella's body was found quite at the bottom of the mine shaft into which the party from Alapaevsk were thrown. Her skull was fractured & the doctors who examined the body said she cannot have suffered & that most likely the rush of air of the fall sufficed to stop the heart working, as when people have fallen a great distance this has often been the case.[20]

Though she did not spare Irène, she continued to spare Ernie. That he might not have found out the harsher truth in newspapers and other publications, for some reason did not occur to her.

In the same letter, she explained to Ernie, in the kindest terms possible, the horrors that happened to Alix, Nicky and their family; the end was swift, and they would not have been fearful since the soldiers had lied to them, telling them they were to be photographed, which was why they were to wait in the cellar. They were not long kept in suspense. But, she lamented, 'Oh my dear Ernie I fear we shall not have the comfort of being able to do anything for the remains of our other dear ones shot at Ekaterinburg & whose bodies were burnt afterwards.'[21] It was only by a stroke of luck and the faithfulness of a loving monk, that they had the opportunity for Ella. Victoria was deeply cognizant of that.

Victoria moved on with her life and as she got older seemed even more philosophical and pragmatic than she had been as a young girl. After the unhappiness of the last few years, events at home provided some distractions. The Royal Navy was wearing a bit on Georgie's family life and Victoria had advice for him:

> I do so understand how you miss them & Nada & how at times you feel that life is too short to compensate for all this separation. Many a time have Papa & I felt like that in the old times, yet one must try & bear it; … When you are miserable at the thought of your days spent apart from those you love, just face the fact that you are doing so for others, because of your service.[22]

On 10 June 1921, Alice finally had her longed-for boy, Philip, born in the family villa at Mon Repos, Corfu. From the beginning, Victoria took a particular interest in this child, remarking that Philip was the image of Andrew.[23] After so many girls, she, along with the entire family, was thrilled with this latest addition.

Indeed, for a while, after the war, things in Alice's family seemed to go well. The girls were overjoyed to be in Greece again and Andrew was back with his family. Even with these positive developments, things in Greece were politically as precarious as ever. There was constant fighting with Turkey detailed in the newspapers.

They wouldn't remain in Greece for long.

In May 1921, Louis was elected President of the Royal Navy Club. There were many expressions of regret over his unfair treatment at the beginning of the war and unlike the usual outcome of such stories, there would be a satisfactory conclusion to his naval woes. Louis was invited to be the Chair of the Royal Navy Club dinner given in London in July 1921. The dinners were gala affairs given every year to honour the victory of the English Navy over the Spanish Armada, and the guest of honour that year would be the current First Lord, Arthur Lee.

After his resignation from the Royal Navy, Louis was extremely satisfied to be chairing this event. When the invitations went out, it was thought that fifty or sixty fellow navy men would be attending. However, when the evening came instead of that small number, 800 men attended, in tribute to their beloved Admiral. Victoria and Louis were amazed and gratified as the men streamed into the room. When they had heard that Louis was the chair for the evening, they came from everywhere to pay him honour.

It was a festive celebration full of uniforms and glitter and attended by a tremendous number of retired admirals and officers, as well as many who were still serving. After dinner, Admiral Lee rose, lifted his glass, and offered a toast to the chair. He expressed his sympathy at the fate that had been delivered to Lord Milford Haven and his thanks for preparing the country for war. He ended with asking the men to give three cheers for their admiral.

When he finished these words, there were loud 'hip, hip, hoorays', and a five-minute ovation. The men would not stop cheering – and it was as though he had not been gone for the last seven years. Louis was nearly overcome, as he got up to acknowledge the toast – but the men continued cheering. They would not let him speak and he was momentarily overwhelmed. As modestly as Louis took this heart-warming tribute, there's no doubt that Victoria was thinking that it was only what he deserved.

It was an excellent vindication, and it did not end there. Admiral Lee was greatly impressed by what had occurred the evening of the dinner. Afterwards, he wrote several letters urging Buckingham Palace to give Louis a further accolade.

> I am anxious to submit for His Majesty's consideration a proposal which I hope may go some way towards compensating Admiral the Marques of Milford Haven for the unmerited misfortune which fell upon him in October 1914, when circumstances over which he had no control let to his enforced resignation of the post of First Sea Lord.
>
> I need not recall the details of the unhappy controversies of that moment, embittered as they were by the unchivalrous and vindictive conduct of 'spy-hunters' who should have known better, but it would be difficult to exaggerate the personal and professional tragedy which befel [*sic*] one of the most distinguished and universally esteemed Officers in His Majesty's Service, who had just given a signal proof of his capacity and loyalty to his adopted country at the outbreak of war.[24]

Louis was promoted to Admiral of the Fleet on the retired list and given the Grand Cross of Military Division and the Order of Bath. He was only the second man in British naval history to be so honoured. George V was delighted to award this to Louis, whom he, and so many others, had thought wronged in October of 1914.

The culmination of that unforgettable summer was an invitation extended by his son Dickie and his commanding officers for a celebratory cruise on board the battle cruiser the HMS *Repulse*. The thought of being on board one of the cruisers once again boosted Louis' morale considerably. He was 67 years old now and had definitely slowed down. The great anticipation of that cruise apparently took thirty years from his face and put a little spring back into his step.

They cruised along the northern waters of Scotland, which even during the summer were icy cold. Dickie wrote to Victoria that he and Louis were having a fine time with excellent weather. Papa, he told her, was supremely happy and in his element. It was almost a fairy-tale ending for his life, receiving the honours he deserved, having one more halcyon cruise, and then dying very quietly on 11 September 1921.

After Prince Louis' summer cruise, Louise and Victoria, who were on their way to Paris, met him in London for the day. They were anxious to hear about his adventures with Dickie and had some minor concerns about his health. He was staying in the Naval and Military Club in Piccadilly, and the two women took a hotel room nearby. They met for tea and saw that Louis' face was extremely flushed. Louis had caught a chill with a fever during the cruise and was bedridden for a few days. Victoria, however, was alarmed and sent Louis straight to bed after their tea. Perhaps she ought to have known by his prompt acquiescence that something was amiss. The doctor was called for straight away but could find nothing seriously wrong.

Victoria and Louise extended their stay in London and kept the prince in bed the following day, 11 September. The doctor came once again and gave Victoria a prescription to fill. When they returned, the housekeeper, weeping told them: 'Oh dear, the Admiral is dead, ma'am.'

In answering a letter of sympathy from her cousin George, Victoria wrote what happened:

> We had some nice hours together last Saturday & even on Sunday forenoon, for though he had had a rather troubled night with acute rheumatic pains in the shoulders & remained in bed, yet felt much better ... Then while Louise & I went out to get some lunch, he must have composed himself for a snooze, as I had suggested his doing, & passed away quickly & peacefully in his sleep, for his eyes were closed & nothing disarranged in his bed. When we returned at 1.40 p.m. the housekeeper told us she had found him so about a quarter of an hour before, when she brought in his medicine, at 1.10 when she took him some soup he was still awake & asked if the medicine had come. I am so grateful he was spared any suffering.[25]

She went on to tell her cousin how devoted Louis was to him since they had been shipmates together in the old days and how grateful she was that the king promoted him to Admiral of the Fleet. The promotion had 'made him very proud & happy & he had what he called "a very good time" the last 10 days of his life, on board the Repulse – to be once more afloat in a man-of-war, with the old service life going on around him gave him real joy.'[26]

She wrote further to Queen Mary that Louis had a very real affection for her, and her children '& was always in the full sense of the words "at all your service"'.[27]

It was difficult for Victoria to realise that he was gone, but hearing from her cousin did her good as the many other tributes that poured in. She requested that Admiral Mark Kerr, Nona's brother, and a colleague very devoted to Louis and later his biographer, to come to take charge of all the details of the funeral. He would also act as one of the executors of Louis' will. Georgie and Dickie were there, though Alice was unable to reach England until after the funeral. Louis lay at the Private Chapel at Buckingham Palace for several days, and then, on 19 September, a procession was arranged. It was all quite impressive starting along The Mall, proceeding through Admiralty Arch, and thence to Westminster Abbey for the service with seven admirals and a Major-General of the Marines as pallbearers. In attendance were the Duke of Connaught, the Marquess of Carisbrooke, Aunt Beatrice's son, and the royal family sent representatives since their obligations took them elsewhere.

The coffin was taken to Portsmouth and onward to St Mildred's Chapel, Whippingham, on the Isle of Wight. There, Princess Beatrice, in her capacity as Governor of the island, Princess Marie Louise and the Marchioness of Carisbrooke, met the party. The funeral took place there, and then, along with Admiral Kerr, Victoria travelled back to Fishponds at Netley, for Alice had finally arrived.

The accolades from friends, colleagues, and common sailors continued, and Victoria was gratified and overwhelmed by the letters she received:

> I don't think I ever realised till now (nor could he with his utter want of conceit either) how many people really loved and admired Louis. In all my sorrow it was a proud moment for me as a naval man's wife, when as the coffin was taken on board the destroyer the flag of an Admiral of the Fleet was run up for him, & though it hurt I liked to hear them pipe him once more over the side. ... I am beginning to feel clearly all I have lost – but as one gets beyond the eager craving for happiness of youth, one can face sorrow more courageously I think & one learns to try & think of others more than oneself[.][28]

One friend that stepped up for Victoria was Queen Mary. The two ladies, who had always respected each other and been friendly, continued that friendship throughout the rest of their lives. Just days after Louis' death, Cousin May's consideration for Victoria was expressed in a monetary gift, which she accepted with warmth and gratitude:

I would like to tell you that ever since I knew you better as a girl when I stopped at White Lodge with your parents & later when we took a walk together soon after your marriage, I have felt more warmly towards you than just as one does to a relation because of the relationship.[29]

Cousin George was also concerned about Victoria's solvency after Louis' death and asked questions about her income and where she would live. It was during this time that the king offered Victoria a residence at Frogmore Cottage. She thanked him for his offer but decided that she would stay at Fishponds for now as the rent was paid up to January 1922. After that, she told him, she would certainly reconsider his offer.[30]

Some days after that, she sent George a cigarette case that Nicky had given Louis in remembrance of them both. She hoped that he wouldn't think her ungrateful for not accepting the cottage and asked his advice on her affairs. She also discussed with her cousin the friendship between the Prince of Wales, whom the family called David, and Dickie, who had accompanied the prince on a long tour of India in 1921.

Dickie, she told him, was loyally devoted to the prince, but Victoria, forever clear-eyed, had no allusions about her own child. 'Mistakes I fear he is bound to make still, for he is very young, eager and impulsive, but I hope David, as the elder will guide him and the boy is honest and not stupid.'[31] At the time of Louis' death, David told Dickie, who broke down and wept when he heard the news, 'I envy you a father whom you could love,' he said. 'If my father died, we should have felt nothing but relief.'[32]

A letter of heartfelt love arrived from Ernie some days after the funeral, which he naturally could not attend:

Oh darling it is you I am longing to help for I loved him also and my love to him might have comforted you a little …

Tell the boys how I feel with them and long to help them. And oh my little Louise my arms are round her and my heart bleeds with her. As to poor solitary Alice she will have a terrible time. All you darlings may God comfort – I can't.[33]

Ernie's mention of Alice brings us to the difficult road that Alice travelled for several decades. Greece had, not surprisingly, proved extremely fickle once again. They welcomed King Constantine back after his second son, Alexander, died of poisoning from a monkey bite, but it seemed as though he, like his dead son, was virtually under house arrest.

In the end, Victoria was philosophical. She wrote to Ernie on his birthday:

As the years go by & sorrows, trials & worries seem to be more one's lot, it is a comfort & joy to be able to look back to one's young days when there was so much hope & real happiness in one's life & then there always remains with us still to keep our hearts warm the love of each other one knows is able to withstand all the changes that the years have brought. And even for those that we loved & are no longer with us.

Do not think of me as too unhappy, there is an emptiness in my life & an ache in my heart that I must just bear, but I don't sit & mope for that is not my nature – ... & for the sake of the children one still can take pleasure in the things that make them happy.[34]

Later, she wrote succinctly: 'Luckily for me, I am not given to worrying over past or coming events & take the present as they come.'[35] That viewpoint would serve her well in the days and years to come.

Chapter 13

'the Aunt Heap'

The following year was more felicitous for Victoria and her remaining sister Irène. Irène's healthy son, Bobby, decided to start life over in the New World, and moved to Guatemala to found a coffee plantation. Things didn't go quite as well as he planned and he ultimately moved from there to Costa Rica, where he remained for the rest of his life.

Dickie, who had had multiple infatuations since the end of the war, was in love now. He met the Honourable Edwina Ashley, daughter of Sir Wilfred Ashley, and granddaughter of Sir Ernest Cassel, an immensely wealthy financier with close ties to Edward VII. Edwina was a great beauty, and one of the 'bright young things' of post-war society. She was also one of the wealthiest young women in England. In addition, she was very strong and determined, as well as independent, having been motherless from an early age. Victoria would always have great affection for her and would give her a ruby from Cartier for her engagement ring. As with Nada, Edwina also adored her mother-in-law and called her Aunt Victoria.

Victoria wrote to Nona that Dickie's letters were full of his love for Edwina. By the end of January, there was an engagement. Dickie had known Edwina long enough to have spoken to Louis about her, which pleased Victoria. 'Louis told him if he knew his own mind he would be pleased at this marriage, & I know he liked Edwina.' Though there is no indication that Dickie married Edwina for her wealth, marrying her made sense. She, in the future, would help with Alice's care, and Victoria figured that if anything happened to her, that 'Dickie may be able to help Louise when I am gone if necessary.'[1]

Victoria wrote to her cousin George to ask for his consent for the marriage, telling him that Louis had approved. Edwina's grandfather, with whom she had been close, died shortly after Prince Louis and Victoria thought the couple might have been drawn together by their mutual sorrow. She didn't hide her pleasure in Edwina's financial status as it relieved her of a great deal of anxiety.[2]

However, she wanted to make sure that Edwina's father knew exactly where Dickie stood and asked Georgie to speak to him. 'Be quite frank about Dickie's financial position, present & future with Colonel Ashley if you get a chance of doing so – he need not fancy Dickie is an absolute pauper, even though he will never be really rich himself.'[3]

That spring, Victoria visited Alice and her family in Greece. She remained for some time in Mon Repos and was impressed with the way that Alice had brought up her girls, telling Georgie that they were 'nice and natural'.[4] Victoria spent her first birthday without Louis with Alice, and received an extremely loving letter from Ernie saying that, 'I can't let this day pass without sending a few lines to tell you <u>how</u> I continually think of you and feel with you … This day will be hard for you.'[5]

Victoria, who was not the type to let herself be idle or unhappy, did what women in her family usually did. She made it her business to help others whether they were family or the public. Since the war, she did a great deal of charitable work on behalf of Russian refugees and the Russian Red Cross, and that, along with her work in the East End, sustained her during these difficult periods. Indeed, throughout the 20s and the 30s, she opened and spearheaded many fêtes and bazaars, and wrote letters asking for donations for such charities as the Crippled Children's Hospital. She was the honorable President of National Society for Cancer Relief, President of the Ladies Naval Luncheon Club, and Vice-Patron of the Central Committee of the Royal Naval Friendly Union of Sailors' Wives. The Court Circular of *The Times* of London is peppered with her good works.

As with her brother Ernie, she also managed her sons; but as with her brother, her sons always found her advice sensible and not irritating. This is well illustrated in a letter to Georgie:

> If they [the king and queen] are giving a garden party next month you & Nada should go, unless there is a Court you can attend – & don't forget this time to get a proper pass from the Lord Chamberlain's office for your car & to drive in where the rest of the family do & if it is a garden party arrange with Thora [Princess Helena Victoria, daughter of Victoria's Aunt Helena], who always is well informed to join up with her so as to be at the right spot when the K. & Q. come.[6]

She added that Georgie should tell his little girl, Tatiana, that baby Philip 'can stand up alone now & sits with bare legs on the hard road & crawls on it without minding the stones. He is in fact just as advanced & sturdy for his age as all the others were & has … tow-coloured hair.'[7]

Victoria returned in the beginning of the summer 1922 for Dickie's wedding which took place in July. She also made the important decision that she would accept rooms from the king and live at Kensington Palace, telling Nona that 'now I am … prepared to make a new start without [Louis]'.[8]

She and Queen Mary met at the Palace to decide what should be done with the rooms, and if they could be adapted for Victoria's use. The rooms were apartment number 7 in the western part of the palace, identified by their lofty arched windows. They had previously been the Chapel Royal, but the rooms were decommissioned in 1901. 'After Queen Victoria's death the chapel was closed and a false ceiling was inserted to allow the first-floor apartments to be enlarged.'[9] Philip and his cousin, David Milford Haven, son of Georgie, lived there for three months before Philip's wedding and it was from there that Philip went to Westminster Abbey to marry Princess Elizabeth in November 1947.

Cousin May certainly thought these rooms would do, telling Victoria that living there 'would certainly enable you to put up members of your family'. In addition, she would get the apartments on both sides as soon as they became available.[10] The king was delighted with the arrangements for his cousin writing, 'I am glad to think that you are going to join what Arthur calls the "Aunt Heap".'[11] At the time the apartment was offered to Victoria there were three of her aunts in residence, Louise, Beatrice and Helen, Duchess of Albany.[12] The rooms themselves could accommodate a lady's maid, chauffeur, cook and several others.

More important than remodelling was the wedding of Dickie and Edwina, which took place at St Margaret's, Westminster on 18 July 1922. It was reminiscent of the royal weddings of old in which there was a strong royal presence. The Prince of Wales acted as Dickie's best man, and Alice's four girls, the 'Greek Princesses' as they were called in the newspapers, were among the maids of honour. The king and queen attended as well as Cousin Minnie, the Dowager Empress Marie Feodorovna, and Aunt Alix of Wales. They were venerable now, and neither had many years left. Also attending were Prince Albert, the Duke of York, Princess Victoria of Wales, Princess Helena and her daughters, and the Duke of Connaught.

The German contingent was conspicuous by its absence. However, Dickie and Edwina paid Ernie a visit the following month at Wolfsgarten. Ernie reported back about Edwina: 'She is quite charming & won all our hearts being so natural, clever & kindhearted. I wish you could have seen them here.'[13] But Edwina was a true favourite of Victoria's. Her biographer summed up their relationship saying, 'Aunt Victoria had understood her intelligent, restless daughter-in-law; she had influenced her too. From the time of her marriage, Edwina had followed her mother-in-law's example and kept a daily diary.'[14]

That autumn, Alice's troubles once again came to the forefront. In September 1922, King Constantine abdicated again, in response to the military disaster and horrible slaughter of Greek civilians at Smyrna. In October, Andrew was first questioned and then arrested for that same debacle. He was interned in Athens, while Alice lived at Mon Repos under police surveillance. By the end of November, six ministers were executed for their part in the campaign and Andrew was reconciled to the fact that he would be next.

However, his relatives strenuously intervened, including Victoria and Georgie. King George V seemed to understand the urgency of making every attempt to get Andrew, Alice and their family out of Greece. Perhaps it was done out of guilt – because he had failed to save Nicky and Alix. But for whatever reasons, their efforts were successful. At the beginning of December, it was decided that Andrew would be exiled from Greece and suffer army degradation. Andrew was given virtually no time to get out of the country. He was escorted by an Englishman, an emissary from King George, who quickly boarded a Royal Naval vessel, the HMS *Calypso*, and made for Corfu to gather up Alice, the four girls and little Philip. They went into exile once again – though even this time, it wasn't for good.[15]

Victoria wrote in gratitude to Lord Stamfordham: 'I am indeed rejoiced at the news you send me.'[16]

Once they reached Paris, there was controversy about the family coming to London – there seemed some distaste in the Foreign Office of exiled royalty being hangers-on in London. Victoria wrote once again to Lord Stamfordham wondering what the delay was and saying that Andrew and his family had more pride than to live off Prince Christopher of Greece in Paris. However, in the end they stayed in France.[17] Alice and her family settled in St Cloud, in a house lent to them by Princess George of Greece, Marie Bonaparte. Alice decided to open a boutique called *Hellas*. She sold Greek souvenirs and embroidery, giving the proceeds to charity.

That, however, was just the beginning for Alice. Her journey, through the twenties and thirties was a sad one fraught with physical and mental illness. It was a road that denied her the pleasure of watching her young son grow up, and being present at the weddings of her daughters, who went on to marry German princes. As time went by, Alice went into a sanatorium in Switzerland; she was, in fact, in and out of it for many years. Andrew appeared to abdicate much of the responsibility for his children, possibly thinking that they would be better off with their aunts, uncles and grandmother.

The girls and Philip spent a lot of time with Victoria, and their uncles Georgie and Dickie. They were also quite close to Nada's sister Anastasia, or 'Zia', and her husband Sir Harold Wernher. In the end, it was these three men who exerted a great deal of influence over Philip, though he talked often about how much his father meant to him. Victoria gave her moral support when she could and tried to make the right decisions about Alice's health. However, it wasn't always in her power to help monetarily because of the losses she had sustained during the war. There would be others to pick up the slack, including Edwina, who was always generous when it came to her new husband's family.

Meanwhile, the remodelling continued at Victoria's apartments at Kensington Palace. Queen Mary watched their progress closely and reported to her diary that they would be 'nice when finished',[18] which they finally were in winter 1922. Victoria moved in and immediately had family members staying with her. Her granddaughters Margarita and Theodora, called 'Dolla', Alice's two eldest daughters, who would prove to be frequent visitors, were there for Christmas and Victoria reported to Ernie about how comfortable the apartment was and how much she loved the arrangement of the rooms.

There was much correspondence between the two this year and the next, mostly worrying about the state of things in Germany: the inflation, the civil war and what Ernie's place might be in a new republic. However, Victoria's letter to Ernie, written a day after Christmas, was concentrated on family news. She told him how much she liked Nada's family and especially her sister Zia Wernher, who had invited them over for Christmas and made sure that they all felt like part of the family. There was also Romanov news of Nicky's exiled sister Xenia and her family, who, 'also lives in London & has all 6 boys over here … Xenia is a dear & reminds me often of Nicky – her rotten husband [Grand Duke Alexander Mikhailovich] lives in Paris.'[19] In her last sentences, she reassured her brother that his cousins 'George and May always ask me about you, their feelings have not changed.'[20]

There were other changes to report in the New Year. Victoria's sister-in-law and Louis' only sister, Princess Marie of Erbach-Schönberg, died at Schönberg. She was 71 years old, and that left Franzjos as the only remaining Battenberg. Closer to home, another of Victoria and Irène's aunts, Princess Helena, died in June after a very short illness and the funeral took place on 15 June 1923 at St George's chapel. That only left Aunts Louise and Beatrice of Queen Victoria's daughters. Living at Kensington Palace, Victoria kept an eye on them, stopping by their doors and visiting frequently – which assuaged their loneliness as well as her own.

Also attending the funeral was Gustav Adolf, the Crown Prince of Sweden. He had been visiting England and his Connaught relatives. Gustav was extremely interested in history and archaeology and was deeply involved in excavations in Greece. He was no 'mere dilettante figure-head, but himself worked as hard and as long as any other member'[21] of the expedition.

Louise, who had had her marital tribulations in the past, had been happy in her apparent spinsterhood. She had declared to her family that she would never marry a king or a widower. At the end of June, she became engaged to Crown Prince Gustav Adolf of Sweden, who would eventually become King of Sweden. He was the widower of Louise's cousin, Prince Margaret of Connaught, whose untimely death in 1920 left five children.

Louise had been at a loose end after the war, poignantly telling her niece, Dolla, that 'all the young men she and her contemporaries had danced with in the palaces of Europe, with whom they had gone on picnics and with whom they had fallen in love, were now dead'.[22] She was described in *The Times* as 'not at all well known to the general public … She is said by those who know her to be a lady of much originality and independence of mind, as well as charm of manner.'[23] Since she was no longer interested in the society that those bygone days afforded her, she was more content to be involved with social work. She was also used to the idea that she would stay in London and be a companion to her mother, whose company she genuinely enjoyed.

However, Gustav and Louise had met that spring at a party in London and met frequently at Georgie and Nada's home. They were seen together at Ascot that year which was highly remarked upon. Beside the fact that pairings of royal persons were always highly remarked upon, Louise's being spotted with anyone, at that point, was big news.

Louise showed a great deal of reluctance at first. She didn't like the idea of uprooting herself and leaving her family and England. However, staying at Kensington Palace that summer were Alice's daughters, Margarita and Dolla, who had a close relationship with their aunt. The two young girls were enjoying the dances and social events as they frequently did. They happily aided and abetted Gustav, conspiring to leave the couple alone together. Louise had discouraged his advances, however, the more she pleaded for the girls *not* to leave them alone, the more they did so. Eventually, she succumbed to Gustav's proposal and accepted him. Their official engagement was announced in *The Times* on 1 July 1923.

Victoria would miss her travelling companion but understood that Louise could not be with her forever and had to make her own life. She was elated that Louise had found someone and wrote to George for permission, saying:

> To me it is a real joy, for I know he is a thoroughly nice man, who has been desperately lonely since dear Daisy died & I think Louise should be happy as his wife. They have both known sorrow & disappointment & have been able to speak freely & fully together before deciding on this serious step.[24]

Ernie, too, was happy for his niece, writing: 'It is the happiest news I have had since years.'[25]

Curiously, the Swedish Government, needed reassurance that Lady Louise Mountbatten was a member of the royal family. Since she was no longer a princess, it was feared that she might be a commoner. Louise didn't care about such designations any more than did her mother, but Gustav would not have been permitted to marry Louise were she a commoner. The Prime Minister of Sweden, therefore, wrote to the British government asking for confirmation. They assured him that she was, indeed, on the list of royal precedence and sent them the printed lists, which satisfied the Swedes.

During the summer, Victoria was in Romrod in Hesse, visiting Ernie and his family. She attended Ernie's sons, Don and Lu's, confirmations along with Irène and Henry. In view of Irène's remark about the Entente, it's not surprising that Victoria told her son Dickie that 'only Uncle Ernie & I can freely discuss things, as you know he has more sense & balance than average people'.[26] Their visits had become more awkward since the war, and their close sisterly camaraderie would never again exist.

In any case, neither her Aunt Irène nor Uncle Ernie were present at Louise's wedding to Gustav in November of that year. The event took place at the Chapel Royal, by permission of the king and queen. Louise, feeling embarrassed and even annoyed in her situation, felt that she was too old and too thin to be a bride. In any event, she told Dolla, she would not wear white. Instead, she wore a dress of Indian silver gauze, the sort of material used for saris, which was given to her by Uncle Ernie. Georgie gave the bride away, and all of Alice's daughters and Lady Tatiana Mountbatten were bridesmaids – David Milford Haven, the little Earl of Medina, wearing a white 'man-o-war' suit, was the only page. The royal presence for the wedding, however, was exceptional. Attending were not only King George and Queen Mary, but the Dowager Queen Alexandra, the King of Sweden, as well as Queen Olga of Greece.

When Louise and Gustav left for Sweden the following month, there was an entire family group as well as the Swedish legation to see them off. At St Pancras station, Margarita took hold of Louise's hand through the open train window as the train was pulling out. She held on to it for several moments, running alongside of the train as it left the station.[27]

Louise's marriage was an unqualified success. She and Gustav had many interests in common, such as gardening and archaeology, and she approached her position in her new country in an extremely intelligent manner. She never proposed to replace the mother that Gustav's children lost, though Gustav's only daughter, Ingrid, felt that her father had remarried too soon. She was known to them as Aunt Louise. Her only sorrow was that after one stillborn child, in May 1925, she had no more children. However, with her astuteness and good humour, she was a beloved Queen of Sweden, and step-grandmother to the current king.

Victoria, naturally, was lonely for her companion, but as was her wont, she carried on. There was an extremely pleasant distraction just a few months later. On Valentine's Day 1924, Edwina gave birth to their first child, a little girl, called Patricia Edwina Victoria, whose godmother was Princess Patricia of Connaught. She would become Dickie's adored eldest daughter and throughout his life, they shared a unique and close relationship. She was born while her father was away at sea, but he came home on leave in time for the christening.

Victoria and her new granddaughter also had a special relationship. In discussing her grandmother, Patricia Mountbatten later said that she was wonderful with children and with a penknife could construct a whole miniature tea set from acorns. She played patience and did crosswords and inculcated her love of reading to her grandchildren. She was always happy to read aloud to them when they were small and encouraged them to read to themselves when they were older. However, the most striking thing Patricia remembered was that her grandmother '[was] a walking encyclopaedia and could answer absolutely any question you asked on any subject. She was also highly intelligent and extremely knowledgeable; I once heard her correcting a Dutch Admiral during the war as to how many cruisers remained in his fleet!'[28]

However, there were tiresome things such as a gall bladder operation that Victoria had to endure right after Patricia's birth. She spent her birthday in bed, recovering from the operation, and had a note of sympathy as well as birthday wishes from Ernie. 'I write to you for your birthday with a heart full of gratitude all the way of recovery.'[29] Luckily, she improved enough to attend Patricia's christening in April of that year.

Contrasting with the birth of Dickie's first child was the sad death of Franzjos. He died in that summer in Schaffhausen, Switzerland, where he and Anna had spent the war. Victoria had been visiting Louise and wrote to Dickie from Louise's country home, Sofiero. As ever, Victoria was pragmatic and discussed with her son the need for an allowance for Franzjos' wife Princess Anna, asking him to discuss it with Edwina, whose generosity would extend to her aunt by marriage. She was more nostalgic with Georgie, commenting that this death was 'the last of Papa's brothers, whom I have known all my life & I am greatly grieved.'[30]

Gone now were the four handsome Battenberg brothers and their sister, Marie. Gone was the stunning brood who had so captivated Queen Victoria and enraged at one time or another, the Russian and German Emperors and the great Chancellor Bismarck – all of whom were gone as well.

After interceding with Edwina for an allowance for Anna, a simple task for Victoria, she decided to take upon herself a more daunting challenge. In January 1925, she wrote the following letter to King George:

> [I]n memory of dear Nicky I must write to you about his poor sister Xenia's distressing financial position. I know how fond you are of her and how generously you have already helped her, yet I appeal to you now for further assistance & an immediate one by way of a loan, repayable on the sum she must sooner or later receive from the man whom the courts last year condemned to refund her for the jewels he tried to swindle her out of.[31]

She went on to explain Xenia's situation and said that the Grand Duchess was as ignorant as a baby about money. Xenia had a kind heart and a set of 'useless' sons, 'the eldest of whom I consider to be if not half then at least three-quarter-witted with an adventurous unscrupulous wife. I won't speak of what I think of Sandro, her husband, whom she too has to support.'[32]

Victoria didn't mince words when she was passionate about something and told her cousin that Xenia had the unfortunate responsibility to support at least twenty people and then put forth, in the letter, some sensible ways that the king could help his cousin. The king responded positively to this letter and was determined to act promptly to help Xenia. Far from thinking that Victoria was a busybody, he thanked her for her intercession. 'As for her husband & her eldest son, they are wretched creatures who ought to be supporting her instead of living on her.'[33]

Baroness Sophie von Buxhoeveden, another Russian exile who had made it to England after the tragedies, often stayed with Victoria, and she remarked to Nona that 'Isa', as Alix had called her, was wonderful company. These visits, as reflected in Victoria's guest book, were usually about a month-and-a-half long and happened mostly on a yearly basis. Patricia Mountbatten later remarked that she was a charming woman who told great stories. When Victoria set out to write her memoirs in 1942, Isa gave them shape and structure and helped in the writing of them.

There have been accusations that the baroness betrayed the Romanovs, taking money and telling the Bolsheviks where the family had jewellery hidden, backed up convincingly by the archives in Ekaterinburg. It was also said that Xenia refused to receive her because of this.[34] However, if this were generally known or believed at the time, Isa would not have been as welcome at Hemmelmark as she was, nor at Kensington Palace. In fact, she became something of an unofficial lady-in-waiting to Victoria, and it hardly seems possible with Victoria's good judgment and acuity that Buxhoeveden would have been received if such things were true. A friend of Victoria's, the Countess Marika Kleinmichel, said about the Baroness that 'she was extremely loyal'.[35] The reality was that no one had a bad word to say about the Baroness, including the Grand Duchess Xenia, and that she was neither a bad nor deceitful woman.

Victoria continued that which had sustained her during her married life to a husband that was often absent – the rounds of visits she made. Now it was to

Louise in Sweden, then it might be to Ernie at Wolfsgarten, and other times to Irène at Hemmelmark. That summer in particular, Victoria noticed that Irène, understandably, was still extremely upset about Alix. Nevertheless, Victoria enjoyed the visit, despite Irène's political remarks, and the presence of Henry, she noted, with all his faults. Germany, however, was cheerless, and as the 1920s wore on there was more misery and discontent evident. Inflation, humiliation, political ineptness, and penury were the ingredients of a recipe for coming disaster.

An icon from the past was gone in the autumn of that year of 1925. In November, Aunt Alix, Queen Alexandra, died. It was another connection to that old world, and another reminder that it was lost forever. Victoria recalled that Uncle Bertie and Aunt Alix had been so kind to Louis when he was a young man in the navy. She wrote to George expressing her sympathy and heard from Ernie, who commented about the suddenness of Aunt Alix's death, as well as how much he loved her. However, Ernie and Onor were vastly cheered by the presence of Margarita and Dolla, who were visiting them at Wolfsgarten that year. 'Alice's girls [he wrote] are a great source of joy to us. I have scarcely found such cheery kind-hearted and clever little companions as them. We are all under their charms. Such humour and so absolutely unspoiled.'[36]

This seemed to be the consensus about Alice's daughters, who were constantly praised for being natural and wholesome.

Regarding Alice and her family, there were certain touchy issues that came up, at the end of that year, and into 1926. As with Xenia, Victoria had no hesitation in involving herself fully, writing to the British government and any other powers she thought might be helpful. Those sensitive issues were some questions about how the Greek government would deal with Prince Andrew's house, Mon Repos, and the contents thereof. However, during the summer, there were serious worries that the house would be confiscated by the state. Victoria did her best to legally maintain the property with her son, Dickie, the official leaseholder.

The Greek government insisted that the Mountbattens hand the villa over to them. The Mountbattens never complied, but in 1931 it was taken possession of by the Greek authorities, and the state claimed it. In 1934, Prince Andrew was legally able to win the estate back from the Greek government; he sold it the same year.

During the late 1920s, the march of the imposters who claimed to be members of the Imperial Family who had survived the terrible slaughter at Ekaterinburg began. They usually claimed to be one of the Grand Duchesses, though there was no dearth of Alexei's about. Irène, Ernie and Aunt Minnie, the dowager Empress Marie Feodorovna, now living in exile Aunt Denmark, would have to contend with the claimants, including, the most famous one, Anna Anderson, who claimed to be the Grand Duchess Anastasia. Irène saw Miss Anderson, and at some point briefly acknowledged her, though she quickly took it all back. Oddly, at the end of her life, Irène evidently thought she was mistaken for repudiating the false Anastasia. However, today it seems to have been proven that she was not a member of the

Imperial Family. Victoria never saw any of these claimants and left it to the judgment of Ernie and Irène. It was her intention to simply go along with whatever her two siblings thought in the matter.

Victoria's relationship with Ernie continued to be extremely devoted. He always showed a constant affection to his older sister. With all that happened between their two countries, Ernie marvelled at the connection they had. He wrote: 'I wonder if there are many other brothers and sister like us two. What have we not gone through and <u>nothing</u> has ever changed our love to each other.'[37]

Another meaningful relationship was with her grandson, Prince Philip. Through time, it continued to grow. He was sent to school at Cheam and Victoria's Kensington Palace apartments became a stopping off place for him for school holidays. In addition, Victoria managed him the way she managed her brother and her sons, giving him instructions on what to wear, where to stay and sending him money for various travels and events. In the meantime, Victoria divided her time between her apartments in Kensington Palace and Edwina's home, Broadlands, which the Dowager Marchioness grew to love.

At the beginning of 1929, Irène's Henry became ill and died on 21 April. There were newspaper articles asserting that Henry had throat cancer like his father, but, according to his son Waldemar, the cause was angina. *The Times* obituary printed an homage to the man they called Germany's Prince Charming and praised for what seemed like an assertion of his Englishness during the war and after the German republican revolution.[38] His grandmother, Queen Victoria, might have said that it was her influence and Irène's that led to so positive a tribute.

Chapter 14

The Thirties and Tragedy

The world continued to change as the 1930s began. Victoria and Irène were now widows, and the constant visits that had been so much a part of their lives were sharply tapering off. Victoria, who had once visited the colossal Imperial palaces and the vast expanse of Russia and her natural wonders, had now to content herself with the relative simplicity of Irène or Ernie's various homes in Germany, or to those of Louise in Stockholm. Expense, which had not seriously impeded any of them in the past, was now an issue.

Henry was laid to rest in the family vault on their Hemmelmark estate with over 4,000 people present according to *The Times*. Some of the attendees included Prince Eitel Friedrich, the second son of the Kaiser, representing him as well as several other of Willy's sons and grandsons. Ernie and Onor were there to comfort Irène, but Victoria was not. It is possible she felt that she did not want to be seen in such a public fashion, at what became quite a large event in Germany. Maybe the lessons of 1914 were crowding in on her at this volatile time.

※ ※ ※

Victoria's brood of grandchildren was rounded off with the birth of a little girl, born one day before her Great-Uncle Henry's death, 20 April 1929. Pamela Carmen Louise Mountbatten, Dickie and Edwina's daughter, was born at the Ritz Hotel in Barcelona, on 19 April, and the middle name of Carmen was, among other things, a tribute to her Spanish birth and for her godmother, the Duchess of Peñaranda. The Prince of Wales and the King of Spain were present at her christening two months later with, among others, Alfonso and Victoria serving as Godparents.

Later that year, Princess Moretta of Prussia, the highly romantic girl who had so desperately wanted to be the wife of Prince Sandro of Battenberg, and the centre of controversy involving two emperors and Chancellor von Bismarck, died. This alone was her claim to fame until several years before her death, when, still romantic as ever, she fancied herself in love. The object of her affections was a 27-year-old expatriate Russian waiter and the son of a professor of anatomy, Alexander Zoubkoff. She was 63. They married and the younger man proceeded to spend all her money and leave her when the funds were depleted. On 18 November 1929, the princess died and Irène and Prince Adalbert, another of Willy's six sons, represented the former Kaiser at the funeral. Willy had not talked to his hapless sister from the time she started on this last romance – she was, by then, estranged from most of her family.

However, as would be the trend in the '20s and '30s, Victoria's focus would be on her Greek grandchildren whose parents were separated, and whose mother, Alice, continued to be in difficulties. At the beginning of the decade the four girls all married, while Philip went to school in England.

It would be the youngest, Sophie, known as 'Tiny' in the family, who would steal the march up the aisle on her sisters. Sophie's engagement to Prince Christoph of Hesse[1] was announced in the summer of 1930. Their marriage would be celebrated in December at Friedrichshof, the old home of Victoria's Aunt Vicky. The Schloss was now in possession of Vicky's youngest daughter Margaret, the Landgravine of Hesse-Kassel. 'Cri', as Prince Christoph was called, was her son. He was killed in an air crash during the Second World War. It was said that he was an ardent Nazi, however, there were also claims that he had been murdered because he had renounced Nazism. His renouncement, if it happened, was after many long years of devoted party service.

Cecile, too, became engaged. She had become interested in her cousin, Ernie's eldest son, Don. They were in the process of getting to know one another before the beginning of the year. Victoria wrote to her brother, 'I wonder how Cecile strikes you, now you know her better, I personally think well of her character, though of course she has her faults, a good many due to her youth merely.'[2] Was this an anxious inquiry on behalf of a love-struck granddaughter, or just the usual discussions and gentle gossip that went on in the family? However, just several weeks later, the engagement of Don and Cecile was announced and Victoria, thrilled with the couple, wrote the following to her granddaughter:

> I must send you a few lines through Uncle Ernie, to tell you how pleased I am at your and Don's engagement. That one of my granddaughters should find a home in what was my first one is a joy to me and though I know Don less well than I should have done, had the years of the war not kept us apart, yet what I do personally know of him has given me the best impression as to his character and gifts.[3]

They would marry in February 1931 with Victoria, Irène, Prince Andrew and Prince Philip in attendance. *The Times* remarked upon the great interest by the inhabitants of Darmstadt, and the personal popularity that the family continued to enjoy.[4]

Alice's other daughters were married into various German Royal Families at about the same time. Margarita married Gottfried Prince of Hohenlohe-Langenburg,[5] in April 1931, and Dolla married Berthold the Margrave of Baden[6] in August 1931. All the weddings took place without their mother in attendance. It was certainly, in large measure, Victoria's strength and determination that kept her grandchildren from going adrift during these times of transition.

At that time, Victoria was able to tell Ernie that Alice felt she was being well cared for, as Victoria told Ernie: '[Alice] says I must not worry.'[7] And then added a little family news: '"the Aunts"[8] are well and so are Georgie and May, with whom I had tea yesterday and who all asked after you and when you would at last be coming here'.[9] A very different attitude than they had towards Willy's immediate family.

Promptly thereafter, Don and Cecile presented her with a little boy, and Victoria was made a great-grandmother at the age of 68.

> I am very proud of being Great Grandmother and you must give your boy a special kiss for me ... Now you will understand more and more what it is being one and that love for one's child calls out ones love light through the generations. That is why you are so dear to me and your child too.[10]

And several weeks later, apropos of tightened purse strings: 'I thank you and Don very much for asking me to be godmother to my Great-Grandson. I would have loved to be present at his christening, but in these days one's purse tyrannically prevents one's doing many things one would like.'[11]

Nevertheless, Victoria went to Darmstadt and stayed with Ernie at least once a year. As the decade began, she, like many with royal ties in Germany, watched the rise of Nazism, initially with optimism. It was hoped that the Nazi's would restore the Hohenzollerns to the German throne. In addition, the exiled Romanovs had hopes that the Communist-hating Nazis would rid Russia of Stalin. However, these budding expectations were quickly replaced with revulsion, as Hitler's plans were revealed. And, for those slow to be convinced, when the war came, the various German Princes were eventually thrown out of the German army and even, in some cases, interned in concentration camps.

The entire country was blanketed with red banners with the black swastikas. Early on, even with Hitler's Jewish policies, Victoria looked at the situation pragmatically, writing:

> I suppose people are furious at the German persecution of the Jews. I think it grossly unjust & most risky, but Anti-Semitism has always been strong in Germany, where the people are wanting in the business & political instincts, which save England & America from the dread & dislike of Jewish power & push. ... As the Germans do not mind being ordered about, & had their fill of it during the Socialist regime too, they don't seem to object to dictatorship. It remains to be seen however if Hitler is a big enough brain to become the German Mussolini.[12]

Here one can see the typical 'gentlemanly' anti-Semitism to which even Victoria was prey. However, she was also hard on the Germans, and seemed to understand their character well. Patricia Mountbatten said later that her grandmother 'would have very quickly changed her mind as soon as it became apparent what their policies were – which she absolutely abhorred of course',[13] and which she most certainly did. Her grandson, Prince Philip, echoed these sentiments when he wrote: 'I think most people at the time hoped that Hitler would give Germany some effective leadership after the fiasco of the Weimar Republic. I suspect that it was the existence and the behaviour of the uniformed SA and SS which quickly disenchanted any objective observer.'[14]

The Times, however, remarked that by March 1933, the Nazis were in control in Hesse, completely displacing the Weimar-coalition based government with a virtual dictatorship.

That year, Victoria's son Georgie did something extremely difficult – he left the navy. There was every indication that he would have gone as far as Prince Louis. He had attained the rank of commander at the time of leaving, but he had a family to support, Nada having lost all her money at the fall of Imperial Russia. He took a job as the Director of Sperry Gyroscope Company, and this was no honorary appointment. The company wanted Georgie's expertise, his mathematical brain and inventiveness. He was happy in the years he worked there and if he regretted the navy, the family never heard about it.

Georgie spent a lot of time with his nephew, Philip. Georgie's son, David Milford Haven, and Philip were, in fact, very good friends. Nada and Edwina were also very good friends and companions and travelled together to a great many exotic destinations. As Patricia Mountbatten explained, 'Aunt Nada was unconventional and Bohemian in style and she and my mother did some quite adventurous journeys together such as flying across deserts in *tiny* planes.'[15]

Victoria did her part in continuing to organise young Philip's life, writing letters to him and to others arranging for clothing and travel. In addition to clothes, Victoria was constantly telling Philip to whom he should write, giving him addresses where to write to those people, and often telling him exactly what to say. In short, she was trying to fulfil the role of a mother as she had done for her own brother, sisters and children.

Meanwhile, Alice would go to Meran in the South Tyrol for the winter, liking it well enough. She was feeling better that year, and improved in her health, but not in her mental state. She later went to a sanatorium in Martinbruhn and enjoyed that change as well. Victoria took a break from the care of her grandchildren and the wandering Alice, travelling to Dickie, who was now stationed in Malta, for Christmas. It would be like old times when Louis and Victoria had been stationed there.

In the beginning of 1933, Victoria gave herself a new project. She decided to ask Admiral Mark Kerr, Louis' close friend and colleague and Nona's brother, to write a biography of the prince. Though she spent the beginning of that year on a whirlwind of visits to Alice, who was now taking the waters at Kreuznach, to Irène and Ernie in Darmstadt, then off to Louise in Stockholm, the idea of a book about Louis was completely absorbing. Later, when she returned home to Kensington Palace in the summer, she started going through Louis' letters and notes in earnest, seeing what could be used for publication. She commented to Dickie:

> I have been looking through Papa's letters to me (rather a saddening
> job) to see if I could find anything which might be of use to Mark
> Kerr's book – there is hardly anything as your father was very

outspoken in them about people & I don't want to be controversial. You are so like him in many ways, my very dear boy & that is a great joy to me.[16]

It is difficult not to wonder what Victoria elected to withhold from the book.

When the book was published the following year, Victoria was mildly critical of the work. She said that there was too much about royalty in it, and that it was certainly not literature, but otherwise felt it was a decent portrait of Louis.[17] *The Times* review was subdued when they wrote that 'Admiral Mark Kerr, who served under him … has written an appreciative and affectionate memoir of his old chief.'[18]

Cecile had another son in April 1933. She named him Alexander, which pleased Victoria immensely. She wrote 'I am so glad the boy will be Alexander, which name has so many connections for us.'[19]

That summer, Victoria sent Philip off with his father, Prince Andrew, for a visit to Wolfsgarten, and thence to Salem. Philip's sister Dolla, now the Margravine of Baden, lived there. Meanwhile, Victoria was free to do some of her beloved reading. Some of her choices that year were: *Left Behind,* the memoirs of Princess Paley (Grand Duke Paul Alexandrovich's second wife) by Baroness Buxhoeveden, and *Always a Grand Duke* by Grand Duke Alexander Mikhailovich. One can only imagine what Victoria thought about the remarks the Grand Duke made about her brother-in-law Serge.

Though her daughter-in-law Edwina freed Victoria of worrying about the monetary burdens of taking care of Alice, the Princess still worried about her family and the handling of money. Perhaps, this came from the fact that Victoria had not grown up in the fabulous wealth that some of her relatives had enjoyed, nor had she lived her married life in that manner. However, it also could be seen to come from the privations, relative or otherwise, that many of her relations had suffered after the Great War.

In the case of Ernie's son Don, she would have no compunction in advising him to learn an occupation so that he could run his estates and understand about his private finances. As was her wont, she gave both her nephew and her granddaughter the benefit of her thoughts: 'I hope Don will be able this winter to start studying the management etc. of affairs.'[20] Besides being interested in their day-to-day finances, Victoria had something else in mind as well – the former Tsar's fortune. She wrote to Dickie:

> The proper German law authorities have now declared that the fortune (shrunk to a 10th & less) of poor Alix & Nicky's children shall fall to the heirs according to German law. Their surviving paternal & maternal nearest relations. In this case: Aunts Xenia & Olga of Russia & the widow of Uncle Nicky's brother, Countess (not Princess) Brassow [sic] & myself Aunt Irène & Uncle Ernie.[21]

Victoria made a claim for her part of the money and was determined to keep the sum in Germany. Her interest was altruistic; she wanted to help Baroness Buxhoeveden and her family, as well as Pierre Gilliard, the former tutor to the Imperial children.

That summer, Irène visited her son Sigismund in Costa Rica. She wanted him to return to Germany. However, Bobby and his family were happy where they were.[22] When she returned from Central America, Irène went first to Wolfsgarten to see Ernie and Victoria. Victoria told Georgie that:

> Poor Aunt Irène arrived a week ago thin & run down & had to go to bed, where she still is, having caught a chill on her way here, which gave her bronchitis … She did not stand either the food nor the climate at Costa Rica.[23]

Towards the end of the summer, a family event like the ones of old took place. Princess Marina of Greece – the daughter of Prince Nicholas of Greece and his wife, Grand Duchess Elena Vladimirovna of Russia – became engaged to young Prince George, Cousin George's son, who would later be the Duke of Kent. It would be a modified gathering of the extended family, the Greeks and even the Germans were invited. Louise would also be coming, and Victoria was in her element getting people organised and properly attired for the event. She wrote letters to Cecile, who was becoming something of a confidant, telling her what Don should wear for the different events of the Kent wedding. She ended this letter with a refreshing bit of humour: 'Please don't be so "respectful" when you end your letters to me, it sounds as if I were indeed an ancestress.'[24] – echoing the Duke of Connaught when Victoria had introduced her eldest granddaughters to him some years earlier.

However, as in all events, there was some controversy. She told Cecile that:

> I hear Kyril [Grand Duke Kyril Vladimirovich, Ducky's second husband] is coming with his wife and daughter – such a bore for all. He has declined meeting any of Aunt Xenia's sons, so for peace's sake they are not invited, but Aunt Xenia will go for the service at Buck[ingham] Pal[ace] only.

Victoria was upset about the Grand Duke's appearance at the event because she felt that Kyril was 'the only one of the Russian family whose conduct at the outbreak of the revolution was utterly despicable'.[25] Nevertheless, she was happy that Prince Philip would be invited to the wedding, apparently at the suggestion of Princess Marina.

The following year marked another milestone occasion in the life of Victoria and her remaining cousins, and that exclusive circle of Queen Victoria's grandchildren was growing even smaller. Though Victoria would choose to remain in Malta and not take part in the celebrations, it was King George V's Silver Jubilee on 6 May 1935. Victoria told May:

> It seems to me that the position of the King is so strong now, that if ever, which I pray may not occur, there were a conflict between him

and his government, his people would back him up through all, & prefer that the King should rule them, rather than any party dictator, to which other countries have succumbed.[26]

There was a service of Thanksgiving at St Paul's, on a lovely warm day. George V seemed like the right sort of monarch for the times – unpretentious, ordinary, trustworthy – and above all, liked. Victoria's remarks have a ring of prophecy, considering what happened just a little over a year later.

Though not present at this event, Victoria would be present at Louise's stepdaughter's wedding. Princess Ingrid would marry Frederick of Denmark in Stockholm that same month. While she was there, Victoria had an opportunity to visit Grand Duchess Olga Alexandrovna, Nicky's other surviving sister. She commented to Dickie that '[Olga] lives in a comfortable house on a farm bought with the proceeds of her inheritance from Aunt Minnie's jewellery etc. & her husband Col. Something-or-other [Colonel Nicholas Koulikovsky] runs it.' Olga enjoyed her visits to Louise and Gustav in Sweden, and regularly visited there once a year. In 1948, feeling imperilled from Soviet troops amassing on the border, she and her family left Denmark for Canada. She would live there until her death in November 1960.[27]

Victoria continued to comment on her visits to Ernie in Hesse. She was optimistic about her findings. 'Compared with last summer things seem quiet & normal here & the Party seems to be gradually subordinated by & absorbed into the service of the State.'[28] Further, she thought that:

> the mass of the people still has complete confidence in Hitler & his leadership & are working hard & cheerfully – the young Nazis are less to the fore & when they have done a year's real military service will have much of the swagger & conceit taken out of them.[29]

It is gratuitous to point out how wrong Victoria was; however, it is instructive to see that someone with normally excellent political instincts could hardly have comprehended what was to come. Meanwhile, Victoria's life in some respects resumed the pace of old. She read her colourful Cousin Missy's, Queen Marie of Romania, memoirs, the three-volume tome, *The Story of My Life*. The memoirs were beautifully written and richly illustrated with photographs and were full of the theatricality of which Missy was most certainly fond. No one could accuse Queen Marie of not believing her own publicity, since she was one of the first self-promoting royals. She even inspired Elinor Glyn, the overwrought romance writer of such classics as *His Hour*, a romance of the Russian court, to write *Three Weeks*.

This was the writer's most famous opus, also made into a silent film, about a mad and passionate affair between a Balkan queen and a young man on a continental tour. This queen, whom the young man worshipfully called 'Queen', used to loll about seductively on tiger skins. This was all very obviously patterned on Marie's exotic behaviour. Victoria's interest in her first cousin's book, far better written than La Glyn's volume, would have been her thoughts and feelings about the old days, and especially the family and the large number of grandchildren of which she was part.

That summer, Victoria visited one of her old 'haunts', the Isle of Wight and spent time with her Aunt Beatrice. She told Cecile:

> [I] came here for a week's visit to Aunt Beatrice on Friday – though the trippers swarm around us, there is a sheltered place in the garden, where we sit in the morning, which they can't overlook and in the afternoons we drive to some quiet spot in Osborne grounds, near the sea and take our tea with us and where I can stroll about.[30]

This was most likely one of the last times that they could find any place in the grounds of Osborne that was free of tourists.

There were some tragic royal deaths in 1935 and 1936 – some important to the political scheme and others more personal in nature. At the beginning of 1936 King George V died. His son, David, came to the throne as Edward VIII. Victoria attended George's funeral, along with Gustav and Louise. Then in March 1936, on the heels of the old king's demise, Ernie's first wife Victoria Melita, the passionate Ducky, died. Victoria was hardly one to dwell on the past, though it certainly occurred to her that her generation was quickly fading.

There were always distractions from the gloom. Ernie was sending his son, Ludwig (Lu), to England acting as a cultural attaché of the Third Reich. Victoria anticipated getting to know this nephew with pleasure and wrote about it to Cecile. However, she noticed something was amiss with the letters that she received back from her granddaughter. She remarked wryly, 'there is a very zealous customs official at Darmstadt apparently, for all letters nearly, from the New Palace, etc. arrive having been "gesetglich [lawful]" opened – poor man he must have a super – suspicious complex evidently.'[31]

Opening mail was hardly the worst part of the brutal regime tightening around the old Grand Duchy.

That summer, Victoria travelled to Hemmelmark for Irène's seventieth birthday. Ernie joined them along with her two granddaughters, Cecile and Sophie. In August, the infamous 1936 Olympic Games took place in Berlin, which Victoria's son Georgie attended, and apparently enjoyed.

Philip was growing up in the mid-thirties. Victoria thought him very much like Prince Andrew, with his father's height. His idea for joining the Royal Navy must have started at this time as he had written a letter to his grandmother about it. Victoria told him, 'I showed [Prince Andrew] your letter & quite agree to the plan of your getting a naval training later on – it will be useful to you in many ways.'[32]

Philip had initially expressed some preference for the Royal Air Force, but eventually went with the family tradition of sailors. In 1935, while Philip was making this decision, King George II was invited back to Greece by a nationwide plebiscite. No doubt there were those who wondered why the young prince didn't join the Greek Navy. Perhaps the family had learned their lessons about Greece, a country that continually threw them out, and thought that Philip, since he most certainly was not an heir to the throne, must join a more stable navy.

Philip was now going to school at Gordonstoun in Moray, Scotland, though he spent a great deal of time with his grandmother, stopping there for holidays and for some tender loving care when it was needed. When the reburial of King Constantine and Queen Sophie in Tatoi took place in November that year, she organised his clothes, remarking that 'I am glad to hear that there is a good tailor at Elgin, so that you can get the necessary clothes made there.'[33]

In the same letter she discussed Philip's wardrobe for funerals and what other clothes he would have needed on the Continent. Knowing something of the character of impatient young men, she told him what he should wear, whether he liked it or not. In another letter, she told him: 'Dolla has just telegraphed that the funerals at Athens are to take place on Nov. 17, … You had better inform Herr Hahn [Headmaster of Gordonstoun] of this now.'[34] In a later correspondence, she worked out the entire route of his trip to Greece.

While Philip was gone, the Abdication Crisis took place in England. Edward VIII abdicated on 11 December 1936. Cousin George had died in the beginning of the year, and by its end his son could no longer continue without Mrs Wallis Warfield Simpson, his 'inamorata', as Victoria called her. Wallis was friendly with both Nada and Edwina, and they had travelled together. However, Victoria felt that she exerted a negative influence on David – a double divorcee with two husbands still living. Victoria had never been a religious woman in the style of Ella, or even Alice, but this would have been a little much, even for her. His mother, Cousin May, would have absolutely nothing to do with the woman that he loved. It was easy to see that a woman, who cheerfully accepted the brother of her dead fiancé because she felt it was her duty to do so, would never accept Mrs Simpson.

Some thought that this spelled the end of the monarchy in England. However, the young king's abdication seemed to be met with nothing more than slight disquiet or interest. Taking his place was George's second son, now George VI ('Bertie' to the family) along with his charming wife, Elizabeth Bowes-Lyons, and their two young daughters, Elizabeth ('Lillibet'), and little Margaret Rose. This family stepped into the shoes of Bertie's father. Ultimately, most agreed that the whole sorry business turned out in the best possible way.

Victoria had a word to say to Ernie on the subject:

> Poor David in his infatuation is to be deeply pitied for he has made a sacrifice of his duty & his position for a person I feel is unworthy of it. … Bertie & Elizabeth will not have David's popularity – much of which he has lost by his selfish action, but I think the people respect them & will be loyal to them, when they find them doing their duty as George & May did.[35]

And, what Victoria did not add, and could not know at that moment, was that in doing their duty in the worst of times, Bertie and Elizabeth far eclipsed David – or even his parents, George and May – in popularity.

The coronation of King George VI and Queen Elizabeth took place in May of 1937. Victoria was pleased that Queen Mary, now the Queen Mother, had thought to invite Cecile and Don to the event:

> Cousin May says that the stand at the Abbey reserved for the family – both her's and Elizabeth's, will be very full – so she hopes you will have no lady in waiting with you and suggests either no train or a very small one, which you can drag behind you as you walk up the Abby. ... I am not going to be present for the coronation festivities except perhaps the naval review.[36]

Before the festivities, Victoria made a trip to Breibach in the North Rhine to check on Alice. She told Dickie that Alice was well and seemed cheerful. Then she moved on to Darmstadt to see Ernie and Onor. Ernie had influenza and colitis, but according to Victoria was now on the mend, though he was a bit thin and shaky.

As Don and Cecile were expected on 4 May, Victoria returned to England. They all lunched with Queen Mary at Marlborough House on the seventh, just a few days before the coronation. The festivities were overshadowed for Victoria by the knowledge that Ernie continued to be ill and was not getting much better. By June she was writing to Cecile: '[H]e really seems far from well.'[37]

Meanwhile, Ernie's younger son, Lu, continued in his post as an honourable cultural attaché for the German Embassy. A year before, he had met a Scottish girl, the Honourable Margaret Geddes, when they were both studying painting and literature in Southern Germany. She was the daughter of Sir Auckland Geddes, who was British Ambassador to the United States, among other things. Though there were some objections, the couple announced their engagement during the summer of 1937. Victoria wrote to Ernie about how difficult it might be for 'Peg', as she was called in the family, and that the couple might have a hard time ahead.[38] It was never clarified in any of the letters that flew back and forth what the objections were. It seems likely that the political climate was the reason.

Ernie continued to be ill. Victoria, who had gone to be with him at Wolfsgarten, told Nona that he was, in fact, feeling completely miserable. He had gone through an 'X-ray treatment' for his lungs. He might have a long recovery, Victoria wrote, but there was 'still hope that by the time of Lu's wedding he may be fit enough to come over for it.[39] There was some temporary improvement, and the siblings had a last visit, since Irène was there, and Dickie and Edwina came for a short visit in August. However, by the end of September, Victoria was increasingly concerned, and on 9 October 1937, Ernie died.

Ernie had continued the Hessian tradition of cultural and artistic activities, while Onor embraced the nursing and social work that Grand Duchess Alice had started. Ernie had been an avid artist and decorator who enjoyed the Art Nouveau school as well as the Surrealist one – some of the drawings he did, even the doodles in the guest book at Wolfsgarten, were reminiscent of Salvador Dali. He was lauded by *The Times*: 'Thanks to his encouragement, many eminent artists settled in Darmstadt in pre-War days, and he was patron of the Great Century Exhibition of German Art held at Darmstadt in 1914.'[40]

His funeral took place on 12 October. It was the first time that Alice was seen in public with her family for a very long time. However, Victoria took the opportunity to look back. She responded to a letter of sympathy from Cousin May saying that she feared that Ernie was one of the last of:

> our old line, who will ever rule in Hesse again & my only pride is that the last reigning Grand Duke was till the very end of his life a model of a broad minded, warm-hearted & conscientious 'father of the people'. ... [T]heir son's marriage will take place quietly on Nov. 20.[41]

Strangely enough, the death of Ernie had rather an astonishing outcome. In thanking Philip for his letter of condolences, Victoria told her grandson that his mother, Alice, had seemed to recover her health and was 'quite her old self again, like before she fell ill, ...'[42]

Peg and Lu's wedding, which had been scheduled for October, was postponed to November of that year. Victoria wrote a timely reminder to her grandson that he was expected to attend the wedding. Indeed, the entire Hessian family, the Dowager Grand Duchess Onor, Don, Cecile, their two boys and various retainers planned to fly to England from Hesse to attend the festivities.

❋ ❋ ❋

Before the wedding, fate had another truly horrific event in store for Victoria. On 16 November, en-route to Croydon, England, the entire wedding party from Hesse was killed when their plane crashed in Steene, Belgium. Besides the tragic deaths, Cecile's unborn child was also killed. Among the wreckage, the Hessian pearls, and the veil of Honiton lace which Princess Alice wore in her wedding were destroyed. Ernie's childhood wish of everyone joining hands and going to heaven together was gruesomely fulfilled.

The family in England was in extreme shock and Victoria was the one to pull everyone together. She suggested – and Sir Auckland, along with the remaining wedding party agreed – that the wedding should take place quietly and right away. Lu would need his wife beside him to withstand the ordeal to come. Therefore, Prince Ludwig, now the only remaining member of the Hesse and by Rhine family besides little Johanna, Cecile, and Don's daughter, whom they had left behind in Darmstadt, married Margaret Geddes the following day.

On 17 November 1937, strikingly reminiscent of his grandmother Alice's wedding to the Grand Duke of Hesse over seventy years before, yet another funereal wedding took place. This time the bride wore black, and they spent their honeymoon going to the scene of the tragic accident and taking the coffins back to Hesse for burial. Just two days later, the family assembled to take the coffins to the *Rosenhöhe*, the family mausoleum. Dickie's Edwina wrote in her diary, 'Too ghastly … one by one and quite endless…'[43] Queen Mary remarked to Victoria that she was 'thankful that poor Lou [*sic*] is married, anyhow his wife will be a comfort and help to him in his terrible bereavement….'[44]

The newlyweds adopted Don and Cecile's daughter, Johanna, but, unhappily, the little girl died of meningitis two years later. Again, instead of plunging Alice deeper into depression, the death of her daughter and cousin seemed to speed up her recovery, possibly due to the shock of this unbearable family catastrophe. Peg and Lu were stalwarts of the Hesse and by Rhine Family, then and during the war that was coming. During and afterwards, they housed royal refugees at Wolfsgarten. Unfortunately, they were never able to have children and the line effectively died with them.

There was more tragedy to come.

Chapter 15

Second World War

In November 1937, Victoria's son, Georgie, fell and broke his leg while dining at Brook House, the London home of Dickie and Edwina. At the time, no one thought much of it. It was mentioned in letters, and Alice wrote to Dickie that she was sorry to hear about Georgie's leg. Of more import to the family was Louise, who tended to be sickly and was having a tonsil operation at the end of the year.

For Victoria, however, major worry had set in regarding Georgie's leg. She wrote to Dickie that the 'bones are not knitting together as they should & he has frequent pain & is getting thin & pale'.[1] By the end of the month, things had taken a sombre turn. In another long letter to Dickie, Victoria detailed Georgie's condition. He had bone cancer and had gone for treatment, but there was little hope of it working. In short, Victoria told Dickie stoically that she didn't know how long he would live and that he was being given heroin for the pain.

As the months wore on, there was no improvement in Georgie's condition. Victoria wrote to Philip that '[p]oor Uncle Georgie is making no progress, ... but he keeps up his courage & is most patient'.[2] Life, however, went on during this difficult time. Victoria made necessary arrangements for Philip's school holidays. As ever, she was precise in her instructions. She thought it best that Philip travel to his sister, Dolla, at Schloss Salem, and then afterward, the Orient Express to Athens. A car would meet him there, also arranged by Victoria.

April of that year saw Victoria celebrating her seventy-fifth birthday, though with Georgie's condition deteriorating by the day, the celebration was quiet and subdued. It would be the last time she received a birthday card from all four of her children. Three days later, George Mountbatten, Second Marquess of Milford Haven, died at the age of forty-six.

Georgie was well liked by everyone who knew him. Queen Elizabeth II, who was seated next to him at a wedding when only a child, wrote, 'He was one of the most intelligent and brilliant of people. He spoke to children just as if they were grown up.'[3] In this, he was very much like his mother, of whom this was often said. Patricia Mountbatten seconded that opinion of her Uncle Georgie. Not only was he a charming and good-looking person, but he 'had a brilliant mind and had no trouble quickly solving problems which took my father much longer to do through hard work.'[4]

The Royal Family felt deeply for Victoria in this latest of a too heavy load of catastrophes endured throughout her life. Uncle Arthur, the Duke of Connaught and Victoria's only remaining uncle, wrote: 'I can hardly find words to express adequately to you how deeply I feel for you in this new great grief that has fallen upon you....'[5]

The funeral took place in the little village of Bray. Georgie and Nada's home, Lynden Manor, was located there and the procession wended its way through the village to the small, unpretentious cemetery where Georgie would later be joined by Nada. Wreaths came from everywhere, from senders as varied as the king and queen to the actress Marlene Dietrich.

This sorrow served to temporarily break Victoria's spirit as the previous ones had not managed to do. Patricia Mountbatten later said that this was the only time that she had seen her grandmother cry. The day after the funeral, Victoria wrote to May. She thanked her for her sympathy and said: 'I am strong and my health is all right only my nerves are rather strained so that I can't control my feelings as well as I would.'[6] The queen visited Victoria soon afterward. Though Victoria appreciated her family's sympathy, she remarked to Nona that she would never be her former self again.[7]

In June and with a heavy heart, Victoria once more began to take up her life. She continued her various and diverse reading, but this year, the subjects had a clear emphasis in the family tragedies and problems. She read, *The Woman who Rose Again* by Gleb Botkin and put in brackets after it, 'Story of the so-called Gr[an]d D[uchess] Anastasia', *Anastasia* by Harriet Rathlef-Keifman, *La Fausse Anastasie* by Pierre Gilliard and Constantin Savech, *The Murder of the Romanovs* by Capt. Paul Bulygin, as well as *The Road to Tragedy* by Alexander Kerensky.[8] Hers was a mind continually active, and this no doubt helped her to cope with her immense sadness.

In the early summer, the round of visits started again. They were therapeutic and presented a return to a modicum of normal life, such as it could be for her. She met Irène at Wolfsgarten, a poignant visit at best, with memories and phantoms at every turn. Irène wrote to their Aunt Louise, Duchess of Argyll:

> It was such a comfort for me & Victoria on arriving here together yesterday for the first time in our dear old home since we lost so many of our loved ones. One has the feeling that dear Ernie & Onor must step in & be there & that they are only just by chance absent – one cannot realise it – & I often feel like in a dream.[9]

Victoria also penned a letter to her Aunt Louise about their stay at Wolfsgarten, with details of the family members that remained. It was inevitable, at this vulnerable time in Victoria's life, she wrote with great nostalgia:

> My thoughts are often with you & in this dear old place now so empty & still I often think of those happy days of my youth, when you were here with us … I hope to go & visit my Louise & Gustaf, after they have got back to Sweden.

However, she also wrote some good news, which would serve to elevate her mood:

> I am glad to find that Ernie's son Lu is developing a real interest in the garden & grounds, which Ernie had done so much for with

real taste & understanding, so that everything will be well looked after…. I think Ernie would have been pleased to find his boy trying in every way to be worthy of his dear father.[10]

From Wolfsgarten, Victoria joined Irène, who had returned to her home at Hemmelmark. Writing to Peg, she thanked her for the visit, saying: 'It did me good to see how sensibly and bravely Lu is facing the loss of those he loved for I find it very hard to bear the loss of my Georgie on top of the other sorrows.'[11]

Just a few months later, Victoria felt impelled to write a postcard to her nephew and niece saying: 'Whatever befalls you will be both always in my thoughts and heart.'[12] Victoria was hardly being prescient, as the signs of war and upheaval became apparent to everyone as the thirties wore on.

By the end of the summer, Victoria was with Louise at Sofiero. She gardened with her daughter, which was always curative, and continued her correspondence with her friends and family. She confided in Nona, mentioning Alice, who she felt was living a lonely life, separated from her husband and seeing little of her children. Alice either stayed with family in England or lived alone in a small flat in Athens.

Victoria returned to London in the autumn to more sad news. Her Uncle Arthur of Connaught had lost his son, Prince Arthur,[13] to cancer. Victoria distracted herself by doing what she did best – organising people. In this case, she concentrated on Philip once again. He was finishing his time at Gordonstoun and preparing to enter the Royal Navy, exams were looming.

> You will have heard from Mr. Hahn that it is advisable you should pass your exam in March … As it means a good deal of hard work before & there is no time to waste, you will have … to study a bit even during the Xmas holidays.[14]

She also wondered what tutors she should arrange for him.

Alice was staying with her at the end of that year and would return to her flat in Athens in January 1939. Victoria arranged for Philip to visit his mother: 'I enclose your ticket for Dec 15th to here. The sleeper will cost 7/6 so I enclose a £1 note for it & for other small expenses … We won't discuss your "misdeeds", as I hope they won't occur again & they are passed [*sic*] & over.'[15]

One wonders to what schoolboy 'misdeeds' Philip's grandmother refers. However, Victoria was able, as an experienced mother of two boys to put these transgressions in perspective and to deal with them.

As the year of 1939 was ushered in, Victoria was visiting the Duke of Connaught in France and remarked that she had seen Alice's estranged husband, Andrew. She commented that he was sticking to beer and a little white wine in moderation. Andrew was living the typical exile's life on the Riviera with his mistress. Victoria was bound to Athens for Easter, hoping to see both Alice and Philip. This visit probably didn't occur because Victoria sprained her ankle at Cannes.

By April, she was back in Kensington Palace and in touch with her niece-in-law, Peg regarding some treatments that she hoped would be:

> a great success, but it may be some time before its effects show themselves … Much love to Lu who will be relieved that your treatment is over before he knew of it, though he will man-like probably reproach you for not telling him beforehand about it – I think you were wise however not to do so.[16]

This most likely refers to some sort of fertility treatments. It was not to be Peg's fate to bear children, though she wanted them. She did, however, continue to care for her niece Johanna, until the little girl's tragic death in June of that year.

Irène visited Victoria in May and the two of them visited Queen Mary at Marlborough House. Since the dowager queen liked reminiscing about the past, the three spent a great part of the visit talking about old times, as well as the dear ones from long ago.

More momentous that summer, though obviously not known at the time, was the meeting of Philip with his cousin, Princess Elizabeth. The young man was at the Naval College at Dartmouth. The princess and her family were on a cruise of the south coast on the *Victoria and Albert*. They made a private visit to the school that George VI had once attended as a young man. Philip was delegated to entertain Princesses Elizabeth and Margaret with ginger snaps and lemonade. They played croquet together and Philip had lunch on the yacht. The students then escorted the royal yacht out of the harbour. The meeting made quite an impact on Princess Elizabeth.

As the summer ended, Victoria became extremely introspective writing to Dickie about her faith and beliefs as though she knew that they would be tested once again. She clearly explained her position to her son:

> I am not an atheist or theist, but a humble agnostic i.e. one who does not pretend to know anything beyond this finite life & world …. We who come from an old stock of a privileged family, that has not had to worry over material existence, have inherited that sense of duty towards our fellow men, those especially whose nation we belong to, & who look to us instinctively for example & guidance. I know that you feel this way too, more than ever in times like these.
>
> Let us live or die honourable.
>
> …My love for you & my pride in you are too deep for selfish worries or repining –[17]

In September 1939, Hitler marched into Poland marking the beginning of the so-called 'Phony War'. These events prompted Victoria to examine her faith and recollections of the first Great War. She wrote feelingly to the Grand Duchess Xenia:

I am thinking so much & lovingly of you, to whom this new War under such altered circumstances will bring back so many recollections. ...

I should much have liked to go & see you, but I am looking after this place & my granddaughters as well as 24 evacuated school children & their 2 teachers, which are lodged in the servants quarters here. Edwina is doing many necessary jobs in London & is living in my apartment at Kens[ington] Palace as Dickie was worried at the idea of her living in her exposed flat in Brook House. I was in London a few days ago to see how my poor aunts are getting on & will try & do so weekly. ...

Alice & Philip are together in Athens, it will be a comfort to her to have him there. Louise, thank goodness, is in a completely neutral country & may be able perhaps to hear from time to time how Alice's daughters & Irène are keeping.[18]

Philip, who had been visiting his mother at her flat at 8 rue Coumbari, Athens, returned to London at the end of September. By then things were already chaotic. Alice complained that letters from England weren't arriving. Victoria told Philip:

I can't write to the sisters, but Aunt Louise has been able to & sends them my love. She can do the same for you if you ask her to & can also let them know that you are well ... I go to London once a week to look after my affairs & see Aunt Edwina & my Aunt Louise.[19]

It was especially difficult for Victoria's nephew, Lu of Hesse, who, of course, had married a Scottish girl. Victoria often wrote to Lady Isabelle Geddes, Peg's mother, anxious to transmit any information she had concerning Peg. Victoria was able to tell Peg's mother that she 'is marvellously brave, her commonsense and her kind heart and feeling come to the fore more than ever – I cannot tell you how much I admire her.'[20] She later wrote further to Lady Geddes, possibly as a reassurance, that: 'I would like to remark that the Hessian's amongst whom Peg lives, have never been like the Prussians and have remained attached to our family and have evidently included Peg in their affection, thanks to her character.'[21] And finally, and most importantly, Victoria told Lady Geddes that, 'Peg writes that Lu is so touchingly good and such a comfort, they seem the most devoted couple and I am sure she is the greatest standby to him.'[22]

In a letter to Cousin May, Victoria told her that Edwina was moving all her possessions to Broadlands. Edwina moved into Kensington Palace with her mother-in-law at the beginning of the war since it was safer there than her home. The two women got along well. In fact, Victoria approved strongly of Edwina's war work and wrote to her: 'You have grown as dear to me as if you were my own daughter by birth & I am proud of the way in which you are facing the duties & difficulties of the war & its possible consequences.'[23]

For Britain, it was a long and difficult travail, especially when they stood alone against the Nazis from 1939 to nearly 1942. King George VI and Queen Elizabeth proved to have a tremendous amount of mettle. There was much appreciative talk about the queen, clad in her floral and pastel dresses, matching coats, and hats, visiting people in the devastated East End which had been bombed out in the blitz. They were delighted to see her, attracted by her beaming countenance, and her ability to say the right thing at the right time. When Buckingham Palace was hit by bombs on 13 September, she smiled calmly, and cheerfully said that since they had been bombed, she could now look the East End in the face.

Victoria spent her time visiting and got herself a small car. Sometimes she left London and went down to Bray to look after the garden at Lynden Manor. She would often have Tatiana, Georgie and Nada's daughter, and Tatiana's lady companion for company. On one visit she observed to her son Dickie that Philip was bored at Dartmouth and that Tatiana was extremely backward. Tatiana was mentally challenged and lived her entire life, very quietly, outside the public eye. Victoria was contemplative that sad autumn that signalled another war. She observed to her confidant, Queen Mary, that as a result of the war the 'Bolsheviks' will be dominant.[24] She would remember this when the so-called 'Iron Curtain' fell across Europe after the war.

As 1939 ended, another sad death occurred. In December, Princess Louise, Duchess of Argyll, died at Kensington Palace. The aunt who had been a favourite of Victoria's and had given her the beloved Kent House on the Isle of Wight was now gone. She wrote: 'When I pass Aunt Louise's door without going in, I feel I miss her affectionate pleasure at seeing me very much.'[25]

When the shooting war at last started in 1940, Victoria was persuaded to go to Broadlands where she would be safe. However, she managed to go back and forth quite often to Kensington Palace. A widow for nearly twenty years, it was difficult for her to give up her independence and move in with the family. Eventually, good sense prevailed and she spent a good deal of her time in the country.

She filled in some of the time in the ensuing years working on her unpublished recollections. She dictated them to her friend, Baroness Buxhoeveden. She was, however, never very happy with them and told Dickie that 'Isa B. is now here with me & we have been working again on my "Recollections", if you realised how much they bore me, you would be grateful to her keeping me up to the mark.'[26] It was a shame they bored her. They remained unpublished, but they are not uninteresting.

The rest of her family was intimately involved with war work. Victoria wrote her hopeful observations to her friends:

> I still feel convinced that the Germans can't last out as long as we
> and that their spirits may break up unexpectedly, more so now that
> their idol is in command of his army and any failures of his may have
> a bad impression for him on the 'home front'.[27]

In this, Victoria wasn't entirely correct. However, her estimation of Winston Churchill, who had been at the Admiralty with Prince Louis, was more on the mark:

Winston Churchill has, from all I hear from the Admiralty, ripened in character from what he was 25 years ago – with his abilities, dash & powers of eloquence he may make the right sort of Prime Minister in war time.[28]

… and her estimation of England's chances, after Dunkirk:

I am almost relieved that now the French can't fight any longer, we shall no longer be drained of troops, and ammunition, etc. but can keep these at home. A campaign against an Island Power is none so easy to carry out as an attack on a continental country [and] our Navy and airforce are better than the enemy's.[29]

Politics aside, Victoria missed her family, spread out as it was in Europe – some on the 'other' side. She wrote to Philip:

Since the fall of the Netherlands & Belgium Aunt Louise & I can no longer write to each other, except by chance & I have had no letter from her for a long time. Mama has written a couple of times … Mama says she is well & your sisters too.[30]

Dickie and Edwina had sent Patricia and Pamela to America. Dickie had been concerned because their great-grandfather, Sir Ernest Cassel, was Jewish. Mountbatten was criticised for the move, people pointing out that the king and queen had not, and indeed would not, send the princesses away. Nevertheless, the two girls joined a group of evacuee schoolchildren being sent to the States in July of 1940, Patricia Mountbatten continued, saying:

[we] no idea when, or whether, we would ever be able to return home. We sailed in the American ship Washington's last crossing with many American families.

Our mother came over to the US on a wartime lecture tour for Red Cross and St John in late 1941 and took Pamela home with her. I stayed on till my Graduation (from Miss Hewitt's classes in NYC) in June 1942 and flew back with a plane load of GIs, to join the Women's Royal Naval Service.[31]

When Patricia returned to England, Victoria noted to Nona Crichton, that she was unchanged by the experience.

Victoria never became downhearted or discouraged. She wrote to Lady Geddes during the Nazi successes of Spring 1941: 'When I recall the critical and gloomy periods of the last war, when the enemy seemed so successful, I feel confident that this present anxious time will not cast us down too much and that he will breakdown ultimately as he did then.'[32]

In addition to spending time in Broadlands, Victoria spent much time with May at Badminton. The dowager queen wrote to her brother, Alexander, that it was 'very pleasant and agreeable, & we have long talks about everything, & family affairs as of course she gets news of her people through Louise of Sweden'.[33]

Victoria reported to the king on her 'doings' with his mother and that she found May 'in very good health. She helps clearing up the dead wood in the big avenue, as the ground is to be put under the plough. We also visited a couple of factories in Bath.'[34]

The main thrust was, as contemporaries, they had known all the same people and had witnessed together over fifty years of royal events, scandal, and family matters. However, that did not mean that they weren't very much aware of and living in the present. Victoria told May:

> As I increase in age & the circle of my contemporaries grows smaller, it is a real pleasure to me to talk over past days & acquaintances with them. You not only share these recollections with me but have also the rather rare gift of taking interest in present & future development of the world & people's trend of thought, without the strong bias against inevitable change, which so often clouds older folks judgment.[35]

May echoed these sentiments when writing to her brother Alexander: 'We are having some good talks … about old days etc. She has seen A[un]t B[eatrice] lately who she says is most alive & alert – as to brain, though feeble in body.'[36]

That spring, Victoria heard of a death out of the very distant past. In May, Madame de Kolemine died at Hotel des Trois Couronnes, Vevey, Switzerland.[37] She was the woman Victoria's father had precipitously married when Victoria had married Louis, and the marriage had just as precipitously been annulled at the insistence of Queen Victoria. No doubt it all seemed very long ago and in a radically different world.

During the autumn, while taking some courses, Philip stayed with Victoria at Kensington Palace. Philip had 'circulated pretty freely among other members of the family, in particular to [his] … sisters',[38] but had always had short visits with her. He thought her a very pivotal character in his life and observed this about her:

> She always wore ankle-length, and usually black, dresses. She smoked a good deal and as she never carried a bag, she kept her heavy silver cigarette-case, lighter and cigarette holders in a pocket at the bottom of her petticoat. There were no 'filter-tips' in her day, but she obviously appreciated that the 'raw' smoke was dirty as she had a number of glass cigarette-holders into which her maid inserted a bit of cotton-wool. When the cotton-wool became stained by the smoke, she would discard it and start on a clean one. At the end of the day her maid would then clean out the dirty cotton-wool and insert clean bits.[39]

Victoria's unique smoking ritual was well-known in the family and described often. However, she never quit the habit she picked up from her cousin Willy, who, incidentally, had died in exile in June 1941.

When Philip arrived at the palace, Victoria wrote to Cousin George that he had arrived safely from Greece and would certainly inform the king himself. In addition to that, the young man wanted to 'thank you for allowing him to continue his service in your navy, which he is so proud & keen to do'.[40] Philip went to visit the Royal Family at Windsor during this time, and Victoria wrote another letter to King George, thanking him for his hospitality and telling him how much Philip enjoyed himself and was glad that they liked her grandson. She also penned a description of Philip to her dear friend Nona: 'He has broadened out & his likeness to his father, in face, is getting very pronounced. He looks quite the man & is very independent & glad to be back.'[41]

Family sorrows continued through the war when Victoria's Uncle Arthur of Connaught died 16 January 1942. More tragically, the young Duke of Kent was killed on 25 August 1942. Victoria had just gone to the christening of the duke's younger son, Prince Michael, and had stood as his godmother.

The sad bane of Victoria's existence as she entered her eightieth year, however, was her problems with circulation and the chilblains from which she had suffered since childhood. However, now she complained and apologised in her letters that her handwriting was getting shaky due to this condition. In a letter to May, she grumbled a little about the affliction on her fingers and toes, though a new treatment seemed to improve her circulation. Nevertheless, she retained her dry sense of humour and commented that after her birthday in 1943, the Court Circular seemed to be on a countdown from then on.

That summer, Dickie was made Supreme Allied Commander of Southeast Asia. There was also some family gossip and scandal, though Victoria never subscribed to innuendo about her family. She did, however, complain to Dickie about Lady Iris Mountbatten, the granddaughter of her Aunt Beatrice. The young woman was a lady whom 'I have never managed to like, [and] is getting herself more talked about than ever.'[42]

Victoria was occasionally able to hear news about her family in the Axis countries. She told May that correspondence with Louise was difficult; however, she had heard recently from her daughter that Irène was well. Later, the news wasn't as good. Telling May that her chilblains made it difficult for her to write letters, she continued:

> You will be sorry to hear that my granddaughter Tiny's husband (Sophie) Mossy's son Christopher, has been killed in a long-distance flight.[43] You will sympathise with poor Mossy going through your own most sad experience now. This is the 3d son she has lost by war, the two eldest in the last great war & her favourite in this war.[44]

In January of 1944 more interesting news came down the 'royal pipeline' from Germany.

> They [Lu and Peg] were packing up their flat at Potsdam and both now moving for good to Wolfsgarten. My daughter says too that she

has heard that all Princes of former reigning houses and the members of prominent houses are no more at the front – I can't fathom the reason, evidently a political one, for this removal.[45]

This alludes to the edict removing the old aristocracy from Hitler's army.

That summer, while Victoria stayed at Kensington Palace, she wrote to Nona about the air raids. 'I am careful & keep as sheltered as I can in my inner corridor chiefly when the guns begin to go & I don't go further than across to my garden when the sirens go.'[46] In order to continue to ensure Victoria's safety, she was urged to go to Windsor for the duration and her daughter-in-law, Edwina, arranged the move. The best part of that time was that she became better acquainted with both Princess Elizabeth and Princess Margaret. Victoria told Nona:

> we take our meals together otherwise I am free to do what I like. Princess Elizabeth does host at meals, when her parents are away – when they are here we generally lunch amongst ourselves only. These young girls are charmingly brought up, not shy & quite natural. The younger does not come to dinner as a rule yet ... The elder is the more attractive to me.[47]

Victoria continued to be the 'gasbag' and talked ceaselessly. The princesses, however, profited from this endless chatter since she talked a great deal about her family and their history. Princess Elizabeth had a special interest in the family and loved listening to all of Victoria's stories. The young princess, like many others in Victoria's family, always noted that her mind was as sharp as ever. All in all, she enjoyed her stay as she had 'not lived in the castle for years and enjoy[ed] going about the grounds'.[48] As she had been much of her life, Victoria was never interested in fashion or appearance; she wore the same hairstyle and, especially after Louis' death, dressed frequently in black.

The year 1944 saw some further sad and significant deaths in Victoria's family. In October, the last of Queen Victoria's children and Victoria's close friend, aunt and sister-in-law, Beatrice, died at Brantridge Park in Sussex. She told her granddaughter: 'She was only 6 years older than I & we had many recollections of our youth in common. Though she became my sister-in-law ... I always thought of her as my Aunt.'[49] Several months later in December, Prince Andrew of Greece died of a heart attack at Hotel Metropole in Monte Carlo. He and Alice had been separated for many years, and not seen each other during the war – nevertheless it was another painful break with the past. Theirs had been one of the 'Weddings of the Decade' back in 1903, and one of the last times that the Romanovs had joined in family festivities. Dickie and Alice notified Philip, who was at that time serving on the HMS *Whelp*.

After the liberation of Athens in October 1944 and the entrance of the Allies by the end of the year, Alice was able to make a surprise return to England in early 1945. She spent her sixtieth birthday with Victoria at Broadlands. She returned to Athens, however, in March of that year. In a letter to Lady Geddes, Victoria remarked that Alice had been with her for two weeks, and that she was now 'safe back at Athens, it was a great pleasure having a visit from her after not having seen her since 1939.' Later in the letter, she commented that 'Peg wrote too that Wolfsgarten was filled "to last cupboard" by refugees, friends and relations mostly.'[50] Indeed, Wolfsgarten had become a kind of refuge for friends and family. No one was turned away, though the couple lived in constant fear of the Gestapo.

As the war finally wound down, news from the other side was more forthcoming. Irène's son, Waldemar, died of a haemorrhage at Tutzing, Bavaria, since there was no means of blood transfusions, and possibly because the Allies denied it to him. Though this was sad news, Victoria was worried about her own son and grandsons, as well as her nephew, Lu, and all her granddaughters and families in Germany. She wrote to May:

> I have heard ... that Peg & Lu are all right at Wolfsgarten & Tiny [Sophie] & her children are still at Friedrichshof, though no longer in the main building, which is occupied by the Americans – ... – Tiny & the youngest will remain with Mossy who has been very ill.[51]

Victoria was 82 years old and began the process of withdrawing from the world. She often joked that she would wake up in the morning and look about her thinking, *still here?* As if to punctuate the process, she did not attend the VE day service at St Paul's and would not travel again to Germany.

During the summer, Victoria began to hear more about her relations in Germany, as well as having some communication from Irène. Since the New Palace in Darmstadt was bombed and destroyed during the war, Victoria worried about many of the possessions of the Hessians, and most important, the letters, photographs and documents stored in the archives.

As news slowly began to trickle in of her German family, she was gratified to hear that a visitor there had been successful in retrieving various documents, including letters from Queen Victoria. With the New Palace gone, Heiligenberg lost to her a long time ago, and Wolfsgarten being the only Hessian residence intact after the war, Victoria surely felt a great nostalgia for the places of her youth, now living only in her memory. Characteristically, however, she interested herself with affairs in the new Germany, divided as it was between the Allies. She wrote to Lady Geddes that she believed leadership could come from some of the former ruling families. However, she was positive that 'such a movement must come of itself, not imposed by the conquerors'.[52]

Alice and Louise could now visit back and forth once again and there was much discussion about Philip's future. Dickie, who had returned from Southeast Asia in 1946, was interested in taking part in these deliberations. Victoria began travelling and paying some visits again, including to Louise in Sweden. However, she would never be as active as she had been and was certainly of an age to stay quietly at home. She was wistful as the year 1945 closed, writing to Dickie:

> I take life as it comes & have always found it easy to adapt myself to circumstances as by nature I don't cling to old ways & habits &

happiness does not consist for me in having a thousand little things
of no real importance in life. The older I get the less my everyday
needs & desires become.[53]

Luckily, bad as the war had been, it had not devastated her family in the way that
the Great War had. Outside of the death of her granddaughter Sophie's husband,
Prince Christoph, her immediate family suffered no casualties. Even though Hitler
had rejected the German aristocracy in the last years of the war, Victoria had to
write letters and avowals to clear Lu's name. She wrote a statement vouching for
his character and then sent it to King George for his comments: 'Thank you most
gratefully for so promptly returning my proposed declaration that my poor nephew
Lu was not over here in 1946 [she meant 1936] to make propaganda for the Nazis.'[54]

The family was also occupied in settling Prince Andrew's estate. Eventually, Philip
would go to the South of France to sort out his father's affairs.

Victoria was anxious to see her last living sister, and Irène tried to obtain
permission to go to Sweden where Victoria would be visiting. Unfortunately, she
was not able to get authorisation, though May tried to intercede. It would be some
time before the German relatives would be able to freely visit with their 'Allied'
counterparts. Like many of her generation, Irène, too, liked to think about those
old days before war, loss and heartache had changed her world. 'Life is full of
sadness but I like to think of old days when we were one autumn together with dear
Grandmama in Balmoral especially.' She was probably referring to the family visit
in 1896 when the film of the family was made.[55]

Chapter 16

'I'm still here? I'm not supposed to be here....'

Victoria was ever forward thinking, possibly because she had more family around her than Irène. Patricia became engaged to be married in the summer of 1947 to Captain Lord Brabourne of the Coldstream Guards, and in October, the couple were married at Romsey Abbey in the village of Romsey near Broadlands. The wedding took place in the presence of the king and queen as well as the Princesses Elizabeth and Margaret, who were bridesmaids. Victoria, Alice, and Philip also attended. It was said to be the first time that Elizabeth and Philip were photographed together.

Dickie continued to be Supreme Commander in Southeast Asia, and as such was responsible, as he put it, for 128 million people. The decisions he made during that period after he accepted the Japanese surrender in Singapore, were, he said, dictated by history, and by Victoria's excellent advice: 'My mother said, "Don't worry about what people think now. Don't ever work for popularity. Above all, don't care what the newspapers say. What is important is that your decisions should be clear and stand up to history."'[1]

Not only was Victoria prescient like her grandmother, but her advice was sound. Dickie came home a hero and was now on his way to becoming First Sea Lord, the title his father had to give up in 1914. It was a deep and personal ambition that would come to fruition in 1955.

In 1947, he and Edwina went to India as its last viceregal couple. It was flattering for Dickie to have the responsibility of what would prove to be an extremely difficult 'hand-over', but Victoria was not the least gratified for her son. She objected, thinking that if it all went wrong, he would be blamed. She was tremendously suspicious of the intentions of politicians and felt that they had ruined her husband. She feared that they would use Dickie as a scapegoat since 'Politicians are incorrigible'.[2] Patricia Mountbatten said that this was the first time she saw her grandmother swear. Luckily it went well enough under very harrowing circumstances.

Another more positive development was Alice's continued good mental health. She had successfully combated her psychological and emotional problems and wanted to start a nursing order in Greece as her Aunt Ella had done so many years before in Russia. It was not a completely successful venture. Alice never became a nun, though she always appeared in the habit.[3] She had spent the Second World War in Athens working as a lay sister and, incidentally, had bravely rescued a Jewish family by hiding them in her apartment. Her lifelong deafness came in very handily when the Gestapo would try to question her. She would pretend not to understand, though she could lip-read in five languages. They would just dismiss her as a crazy old nun. Nevertheless, she was hardly without her wits and is recognised today by Yad Va'Shem as a Righteous Gentile. Not only that, she had been able, in a normal manner, to recover from the harrowing deaths of her daughter, Cecile, and Don, as well as Sophie's husband, and her own estranged husband. She spent most of her time in Athens but would often come to England to care for her mother who was becoming increasingly arthritic and fragile.

Meanwhile, the plans for Philip were coming to fulfilment. He had taken the name of Mountbatten, though that had never been his mother or father's name. Princess Alice had been a Battenberg until she married Andrew. He renounced his Greek titles and became a naturalised British subject. Prince Philip of Greece and Denmark became Lieutenant Philip Mountbatten, RN. Victoria felt that this would be the best thing for her grandson and would give him a firm basis for his life, as well as a fixed career. It seemed in this, that he was going the way of his grandfather. There had been hints all along, and comments from many members of the family, of another reason for Philip's naturalisation. The Duchess of Kent thought it a good thing as it would be 'an asset for other matters'.[4]

Early in 1944, Victoria wrote to Dickie that as Philip 'has not touched on the subject you spoke about to me with reference to his future, I also refrain from doing so'.[5] Later that year, Alice wrote to Philip on his birthday and mentioned that she has heard he had been to Coppins for Easter and 'paid an interesting visit as well as lunching with a certain young lady & her parents before you left'.[6] That young lady was Princess Elizabeth.

The king and queen gave their consent to the engagement in January 1947; however, it remained a secret until the summer. In July, the engagement of Philip to Princess Elizabeth was officially announced by the Palace. Philip stayed at Kensington Palace that summer along with Alice. Victoria was getting ready for the wedding by having the drawing room of her apartments painted, and since the family was frequently there, the excitement was intense.

Alice wrote to Dickie, who continued in India, that Victoria was 'delighted as she is very fond of Lilibet & likes her character very much'.[7] However, there was one snag – the German sisters could not be invited. It was impolitic to invite great numbers of any German Royal Family – even sisters. Nevertheless, Victoria with her sense of history and family, was overjoyed about so many things. She wrote to May: 'How well I remember my Alice's pride at being one of your bridesmaids & now my granddaughter Pamela is to be one of the bridesmaids to your granddaughter.'[8]

The wedding took place 20 November 1947 at Westminster Abbey, and Victoria was one of the proud signatories to the marriage certificate along with Nada, Edwina, Dickie, Alice, and Lady Patricia Ramsay, formerly Princess Patricia of Connaught. Philip, who wore his grandfather Prince Louis' sword for the ceremony, probably felt slightly disappointed that his sisters could not be there. However, the king created him Duke of Edinburgh, and a host of other titles just before the wedding.

The festivities were considered relatively austere because of the post-war rationing. Indeed, the material for Princess Elizabeth's dress of pearl satin, with clouds of tulle, seed pearls and crystal, with a 15ft-long train and designed by Norman Hartnell, had all been bought with ration coupons. The couple received thousands of presents, which were all laid out at St James Palace.

Victoria was now in her late eighties and did little travelling. Mostly it was just back and forth from Kensington Palace to Broadlands. She was lucky that outside of the childhood illnesses of scarlet fever and diphtheria, and the bout of typhoid from which she suffered when a young woman, she was never seriously ill. She had an excellent constitution, though she continued to have circulatory problems and suffer with arthritis. She was exceedingly fit for a woman of her age, and walked every day with a firm stride, but effects of chain-smoking and the frailties of old age were decidedly setting in.

As her long life crept to its close, she undoubtedly felt as though she had a foot in two worlds. With her friend May, whom she considered among other things, her grandmotherly colleague,[9] and the few others still alive, she reminisced about the old days.[10] They talked of taking brownie pictures of one another, sailing on large yachts, walking through the countryside, attending Queen Victoria for tea, and sneaking cigarettes. They talked of those that were gone and how they missed grandmama and the large royal gatherings.

And then there was the much less colourful and different world of the present. Dickie was back in the Royal Navy, having returned from India in the spring of 1948. Irène was still alive, but Victoria no longer visited Germany. The two wars had the inevitable effect of distancing the sisters, even though they were the last of their immediate family's generation. They kept in touch, but it was more sporadic than before.

As the year progressed, Victoria continued to slow down considerably. There was no specific illness, but she was weakening. There were colds, problems with circulation, as well as her chilblains – nothing major, but annoyances nonetheless. Just before the birth of Prince Charles she wrote a letter to May thanking her for 'your note & your kind thought of sending me some of your excellent nourishing food to help me pick up quickly after the stupid cold I have suffered from'.[11] The dowager queen was proving to be the loving friend of Victoria's old age. May also consistently sent Victoria very welcome cheques. It was a consideration of which most people knew nothing.

On 14 November, Princess Elizabeth gave birth to Prince Charles Philip Arthur George at Buckingham Palace, Victoria's great-grandson. Charles was named for King Haakon of Norway, whose original name, before he went to Norway to be king, had been Charles. Victoria must have been thrilled to hold this baby who would one day be King of the United Kingdom of Great Britain and Northern Ireland. She attended the christening ceremony on 15 December 1948. It was probably her last major family occasion. She wore grey, pearls, and a black hat. The infant was christened by the Archbishop of Canterbury, wearing the royal christening robe of white silk and Honiton lace that had been used for Queen Victoria's children and subsequent progeny.

His godparents were the king, May, Princess Margaret, the King of Norway, Prince George of Greece, Patricia Brabourne, Princess Elizabeth's maternal great-Uncle, David Bowes-Lyon, and Victoria. According to the Archbishop, the baby was 'as quiet as a mouse' as he was bathed in water specially brought from the River Jordan, a royal tradition dating back to the Crusades.[12]

Charles' biographer Anthony Holden made the observation that 'the room contained four grand-daughters of Queen Victoria – the Dowager Marchioness of Milford Haven, Princess Marie Louise, Princess Alice, Countess of Althone, and Lady Patricia Ramsay – all of whom themselves had worn the same christening robes.'[13]

There is a photograph of the occasion, the last official one of Victoria, with the baby Prince's sponsors. Victoria is sitting on one side of Princess Elizabeth, while May is seated on the other. It is a nice symmetry.

The christening day was full of remembrances of their dear grandmother, but for Victoria, the day carried another meaning as well. She undoubtedly experienced some great satisfaction that this great-grandson would someday be the king. With the prejudice that Prince Louis had experienced during his life and the petty annoyances from relations, such as Willy of Prussia and Sasha of Russia about Louis' less than perfect pedigree, the position of this child would be vindication indeed.

❀ ❀ ❀

Victoria's last few years were quiet, but she remained just as irascible and energetic as it was possible for her to be. Though increasingly frail, she continued to talk unceasingly, and as her grandson remembered the '[c]onversation with her brother and others of her generation was pretty competitive'.[14] She was inexhaustible in her habit of smoking and when her doctors advised her to quit, or at least to halve her daily intake, she did so – cutting her cigarettes in half, and smoking as much as ever.

But her health continued to decline, worrying her ever watchful children, and she wrote her last letters in May 1950 – to Queen Mary and Dickie. As the summer came, Victoria was suffering from bronchitis, and she was endlessly frustrated by waking up every morning. Louise told May's brother, Alexander, who in turn told May that 'dear Victoria is not easy to nurse because she wants to die!'[15] She was adamant about remaining at her home in Kensington Palace, and hoped she would not linger too long. But as the summer wore on, so did her life. It didn't help that people who had come to say goodbye had to make second visits. 'She would wake up in the morning and say: "Am I still here? I'm not supposed to be here."'[16]

But longevity had at least a few added benefits. On 16 August 1950, Princess Elizabeth gave birth to her second child, Princess Anne. There was general rejoicing and Victoria was gratified that another great-grandchild was born. During that last summer, there were times when Victoria 'picked up' a little, however, those times were temporary, and she mostly declined. In August she had a heart attack and her bronchitis got much worse. By September the case was looking hopeless. Though he didn't want to distress anyone, Dickie, in a pragmatic way his mother would have endorsed, began to make the necessary arrangements.

On the morning of 24 September 1950, Victoria, Princess of Hesse and by Rhine, Princess Louis of Battenberg, the Marchioness and Dowager Marchioness of Milford-Haven, died peacefully at Kensington Palace, at the age of 87. Her remaining children were with her.

Victoria left a letter for her family in which she expressed her deep regard for them. She continued:

> The bitterest grief in my life has been the loss of Georgie. You will miss me I know, but let it be a comfort to you to realise that the best part of my life & on the whole it has been a happy one, was ended when your dear father died & that I am ready & willing to enter into my rest at any time now.[17]

On 28 September there was a small private service at the Chapel Royal. This was only for closest relatives, friends, such as the Crichton's, Baroness von Buxhoeveden, and some of Victoria's household. Irène, who was 84, did not attend.

Victoria lay at the Chapel Royal at St James Palace while the king decreed family mourning. She was subsequently conveyed from there to the Isle of Wight, where she was buried alongside Prince Louis at St Mildred's Church in Whippingham.

A chapel devoted to the Battenberg family is contained inside of St Mildred's. The sarcophagi of Prince and Princess Henry of Battenberg rest there, and along the walls are many interesting commemorative plaques and items associated with the family. The children of Prince and Princess Louis Battenberg are on one end: Prince Alice of Greece, Queen Louise of Sweden, Prince George, Second Marquess of Milford Haven, and the Earl Mountbatten of Burma. Outside in the little churchyard stand the graves of Victoria and Louis. There is a large cross surrounded by shrubbery, and some tall trees in the background. The view overlooks the River Medina.

It was most appropriate that Princess Victoria was there in the Isle of Wight, where she had had a home, Kent House, and, of course, where she had visited Queen Victoria at Osborne House on so many occasions. It was also a place with many naval associations and Dickie remarked in his diary that she would have been happy to feel that the navy had buried her.[18]

Victoria was eulogised in *The Times* as a calm presence and a woman of a retiring nature whose 'good work was done with as little fuss and publicity as possible'.[19] The papers no doubt thought this because, unlike her more famous sisters, she led such a private life. Had she not been seen often in the Court Circulars, she might have been the perfect Victorian lady who was only in the papers at her birth, marriage and death.

Irène wrote to Dickie that she was terribly grieved at being unable to see Victoria one last time. 'Mama's courage & loving heart were wonderful & her loving advice I always had from her, in so many ways.'[20] Accolades came from other relatives as well. Victoria's niece-in-law, Lady Irene Carisbrooke, who was married to her Aunt Beatrice's only surviving son, Alexander, wrote to Dickie that his mother gave 'always such wonderful sane advice, & had one of those rare things, an out-look on life which discarded the unnecessary things (which so many cling to) & kept her eyes on what really mattered'.[21] Harold Wernher, Nada's brother-in-law wrote to Dickie that she was a woman who had much sadness in her life, but that '[w]ithout doubt she was the most outstanding woman I have ever met. She did not grow mentally old, but remained alert and up to date in a changing world.'[22]

Her nephew Lu, gave an interesting, loving, and yet extremely honest assessment of her character. He wrote to Dickie that he was:

> struck again and again at her 'greatness' … her fanatical intellectual honesty and her very loving understanding for anything human. There was absolutely nothing bogus and nothing hypocritical about her, a very rare thing, I have found, amongst people of her generation. It is very sad to think that our world will now have to do without her astringent criticism and always loving, though not always forgiving understanding.[23]

On 24 October, at the decree of the king, there was a memorial service for Victoria. It was attended by the king and queen, as well as members of Victoria's family and representatives from Greek and Swedish delegations. Alice and Louise were unable to attend since both had already returned to their respective homes.

Dickie wrote his mother's epitaph:

> Then come what will and come what may!
> As long as thou dost live, 'tis day.
> And if the world through we must roam,
> where ere thou art, there is my home.
> I see thy face so dear to me,
> Shades of the future I do not see.

Victoria's death was truly the end of an era. Only nine of Queen Victoria's forty-four grandchildren remained alive, and none had been as close to their grandmother and understood her quite so well as had Victoria. Indeed, she was one of the last survivors of a generation who had felt the full attention of their illustrious grandmother.

Victoria was a woman who was endlessly curious and constantly learning. She was voracious in her desire to understand life and all its mysteries. She constantly sought out the truth no matter the consequence and once found, clung to it.

In addition, she was devoted to her extended family and loved her near ones fervently and completely. She was the enduring keystone of her family throughout their many crises and tragedies. To that end Victoria was an example of fierce loyalty and steadfastness.

Finally, she was intensely honest and had a finely honed sense of honour and loyalty. Of the utmost importance to her, however, was to live her life by the standards she had been taught, using everything she had learned from the queen as a guide. And, at last, to always do her duty.

Notes

Abbreviations

BA – Broadlands Archives, at Hartley Library, University of Southampton.

Buckle 1 – Buckle, George Earle, ed. *Letters of Queen Victoria: A Selection from Her Majesty's Correspondence and Journal Between the Years 1862-1878, Vols.1 and 2,* (Longmans, Green & Company: New York, 1926).

Buckle 2 –________, *Letters of Queen Victoria Third Series: A Selection from Her Majesty's Correspondence and Journal Between the Years 1886 and 1901.* In 3 vols., vol. 1 1886–1901. (Longmans, Green & Company: New York, 1931).

Buckle 3 –________, *Letters of Queen Victoria Third Series: A Selection from Her Majesty's Correspondence and Journal Between the Years 1886 and 1901.* In 3 vols., vol. 2 1886-1901. (Longmans, Green & Company: New York, 1931).

Buckle 4 –________, *Letters of Queen Victoria Third Series: A Selection from Her Majesty's Correspondence and Journal Between the Years 1886 and 1901.* In 3 vols., vol. 3 1886–1901. (Longmans, Green & Company: New York, 1932).

HI Hoover Institute Archives.

HS – Family Archives, Darmstadt OR Hessiches Staatarchiv Darmstadt Section D 22, 24, 26 (Grand Ducal Family Archives).

QV'sJ/QVJ – Queen Victoria's Journals.

RA – Royal Archives, Windsor Castle.

RD – Royalty Digest.

RAM – Royal Archives, Madrid.

Rec – *Recollections: Victoria Marchioness of Milford Haven Formerly Princess Louis of Battenberg.*

SA – Southampton Archives, Hartley Library, University of Southampton.

Dickie – Lord Louis, Earl Mountbatten of Burma.

Ernie – Grand Duke Ernst Ludwig of Hesse and by Rhine.

NK – Nona Kerr.

Onor – Eleonore of Solms-Hohensolms-Lich.

QV – Queen Victoria.

VMH – Victoria Milford Haven (Princess Victoria of Hesse and by Rhine, Princess Louis Battenberg).

Prologue

1. Invitation courtesy of Ian Shapiro.

Chapter 1

1. Nina Epton, p.90.
2. Princess Helena, p.18.
3. Epton, p.98.
4. Helena, p.20.
5. Buckle 1, p.40.
6. Christopher Hibbert, p.166.
7. Gerard Noel, p.96.
8. Arturo Beéche, Miller, *Royal Collections IV: The Grand Ducal House of Hesse*, p. iii.
9. *Ibid.* p.42.
10. 'Shame on him who thinks evil of it.', which also happens to be the motto of the Order of the Garter, Rec., p.35.
11. Count Egon Corti, p.63-4.
12. Rec. p.10.
13. Ilana Miller, *The Four Graces*, p.5.
14. Meriel Buchanan, *Diplomacy...*, p.18.
15. Marie, Princess of Erbach-Schönberg, pp.25-6.
16. Richard Hough, *Louis and Victoria*, p.20.
17. Rec., p.12.
18. QV to VMH 22 August 1883, RA VIC/MAIN/Z 88/12.
19. Marie, pp.25-6.
20. Zeepvat, RD, *An Ordinary...* p. 195.
21. Buckle 1, p.75.
22. 18 April 1863 QV to Vicky RA VIC/MAIN/Add U 32/12.
23. Noel, p.194.
24. 5 April 1863 Vicky to QV RA VIC/MAIN/Z 15/8.
25. RA VIC/ MAIN/ QVJ: 27 April 1863.
26. Buchanan, *Diplomacy* p.1.
27. John Van der Kist and Bee Jordaan, *Dearest Affie,* p.50.

Chapter 2

1. 10 July 1865 Alice to QV, Noel, p.103.
2. Rec., p.17.
3. David Duff, p.120.
4. Marie, pp.25-6.
5. RA VIC/MAIN/QVJ: 23 August 1866.

6. *See: Advice to My Granddaughter: Letters from Queen Victoria to Princess Victoria of Hesse.* These letters are just the queen's, and don't show Princess Victoria's replies.
7. Rec., p.18.
8. *Ibid.*
9. Jerrold Packard, quoted from QV's J, p.115.
10. Roger Fulford, Vicky to QV 22 April 1866, p.185.
11. QV to Vicky, June 27, Fulford, p.197.
12. Marie, p.118.
13. Alice to QV, Noel, p.240.
14. QV to Vicky, Fulford, p.158.
15. Alice to QV, Noel, p.213.
16. Rec., p.3.
17. Zeepvat, RD, *An Ordinary*... p.197.
18. Rec., p.5.
19. RA VIC/MAIN/Z/78/30.
20. Noel, p.280.
21. Buxhoeveden, p.127.
22. RA VIC/MAIN/Z /78/60.
23. Ernst Ludwig, *Erninertes*, p.60.
24. Noel, p.321.
25. RA VIC/MAIN/Z/78/102.
26. Hector Bothitho, QV to Empress Augusta, p.208.
27. Alice to QV, Noel, p.320.
28. Ernst Ludwig, p.58.
29. *Ibid.*
30. Alice to QV, Noel, p.348.
31. VMH to Alice, 11 June 1876, HS Abt. D 24 Nr. 26/2.
32. E.F. Benson, p.161.
33. Marion Wynn, RD.
34. Buckle 1, vol. 2, p.646.
35. *The Times* of London 13 December 1878.
36. RA VIC/MAIN/QVJ (W) 14 December 1878 (Princess Beatrice's copies). Retrieved 5 November 2021.

Chapter 3

1. Hough, *Advice to my Granddaughter* (AGD), p.9 QV/VMH Windsor Castle, December 14, 1878.
2. 29 December QV to VMH RA VIC/MAIN/Z/ 86/12.
3. Rec., p.30.
4. VMH to QV 16 December 1878 RA VIC/MAIN/Z 86/2.
5. Rec., p.31.
6. VMH to QV 16 January 1879 RA VIC/MAIN/Z /86/22.

7. VMH to QV 2 March 1879 RA VIC/MAIN/Z/86/24.

8. Rec., p.31.

9. VMH to QV 30 April 1879 RA VIC/MAIN/Z/86/41.

10. VMH to QV 30 April 1879 RA VIC/MAIN/Z/86/42.

11. Marie Louise, p.60.

12. Ella to QV 16 December 1878 RA VIC/MAIN/Z/86/3.

13. Buchanan, *Diplomacy*, p.26.

14. Rec., p.33.

15. Ernst Ludwig, p.77.

16. Rec., p.38.

17. VMH to QV 9 September 1879 RA VIC/MAIN/Z/ 86/71.

18. AGD 4 July 1879, p.15.

19. *Ibid.*, 26 October 1880, pp.28-9.

20. VMH to QV 3 October 1879 RA VIC/MAIN/Z/86/77.

21. AGD, 12 December 1879, p.21.

22. *Ibid.*, 4 April 1880, p.23.

23. *Ibid.*, 4 August 1880, p.26.

24. VMH to QV 4 December 1880 RA VIC/MAIN/Z/ 87/9.

25. AGD, p.29.

26. VMH to QV 15 January 1881 RA VIC/MAIN/Z 87/20.

27. VMH to QV 19 March 1881 RA VIC/MAIN/Z /87/29.

28. VMH to QV 22 April 1881 RA VIC/MAIN/Z/87/34.

29. VMH to QV 13 Dec 1882 RA VIC/MAIN/Z/87/121.

30. Ernst Ludwig, p.60.

31. Rec., p.40.

32. *Ibid.*, p.44.

33. GV/PRIV/AA43/10.

34. Prince Arthur of Connaught to QV 24 June 1883 RA VIC/MAIN/Add A 15/4014.

35. Packard, p.165.

36. Bothitho, 27 July 1883, QV to Empress Augusta, p.249.

37. AGD, 29 July 1883, p.49.

38. AGD, p.54

39. AGD, 28 November 1883, p.58.

40. VMH to QV 29 December 1883 RA /VIC/MAIN/Z/88/30.

41. Epton, p.166-7.

42. Ella to QV 1 March 1884 RA VIC/MAIN/Z 88/35.

43. RA VIC/MAIN/Z 88/36.

44. Cyril, *My Life in Russia's Service,* p.13.

45. ADG, p.56.

46. RA VIC/MAIN/R 12/47.

47. AGD, p.63.

48. Louis, *Bachelor Recollections...* p.90.

49. RA VIC/QVJ 30 April 1884.

50. *The Times* of London 1 May 1884.

51. Marie, p.183.

52. RA VIC/QVJ 30 April 1884.

53. Hough, *Louis and Victoria,* p.122.

Chapter 4

1. Zeepvat, RD, *An Ordinary,* p.197.

2. Rec., p.48.

3. RA VIC/MAIN QVJ (W) 2 May 1884 (Princess Beatrice's copies). Retrieved 5 November 2021.

4. *The Times* 5 May 1884.

5. HS Abt. D 24 Nr. 35/1A.

6. Rec., p.52.

7. Hough, *Louis and Victoria,* p.128.

8. Marie, Queen of Romania, p.94.

9. Louis, p109-10 letter from PL to Hon. Francis Spring-Rice a shipmate, dated 23 June 1885.

10. AGD, 29 September 1884, p.67.

11. VMH to Ernie 13 October 1884 HS Abt. D 24 Nr.35/1b.

12. VMH to Ernie 23 December 1884 HS Abt. D 24 Nr.35/1.

13. Longford, p.479.

14. VMH to Ernie 3 January 1885 HS Abt. D 24 Nr. 35/1b.

15. Hibbert, p.287.

16. VMH to Ernie 9 January 1885 HS Abt. D 24 Nr.35/1b.

17. RA VIC/QVJ: 25th February 1885.

18. RA VIC/MAIN/Z/ 88/69.

19. VMH to Ernie 15 March 1885 HS Abt. D 24 Nr.35/1b.

20. AGD, p.73.

21. VMH to QV 22 August 1885 BA S 372.

22. Marie, p.217.

23. Rec., p.54.

24. Prince Louis to QV 4 December 1886 RA VIC/MAIN/H/32/107.

25. VMH to Ernie 25 February 1889. Hs Abt. D 24 Nr. 11/7.

26. BA S 373.

27. Rec., p.55.

28. The Times of London, *Eminent…*, p.73.

Chapter 5

1. AGD, p.76.

2. Irène to QV, 25 December 1886 RA VIC/MAIN/Z 89/5.

3. VMH to Ernie 25 November 1886, HS Abt. D 24 Nr. 35/1b.

4. QV to VMH, 20 February 1886, BA S 405.

5. QV to VMH, 27 February 1887 BA S 372.

6. Ernie to VMH 26 March 1887 HS Abt. D 24 Nr. 35/3.

7. VMH to QV 6 April 1887 BA S 372.

8. Irène to QV 24 March 1887 RA VIC/MAIN/Z 89/ 11.

9. AGD, p.89.

10. Hibbert, p.301.

11. RA/VIC/MAIN/Z 89/17.

12. QV to VMH 10 June 1887 BA S 405.

13. RA VIC/MAIN/Z/189/48.

14. Hough, *Louis and Victoria,* p.160.

15. HS Abt. D 24 Nr. 35/1.

16. AGD, p.93.

17. 26 December 1887 HS Abt. D 24 35/1.

18. 3 December 1887 RA VIC/MAIN/Z 89 /32.

19. *Illustrated News of London,* 2 June 1888.

20. BA S 405.

21. AGD, p.94.

22. Millar, p.53.

23. BA S 372.

24. AGD, p.98-9.

25. Rec., p.119.

26. AGD, p.100.

27. Hibbert, p.318.

28. ADG, p.106.

29. Rec., p.122.

30. Hall, RD, p.132.

31. Hibbert, p.317.

32. BA S 373.

Chapter 6

1. 10 December 1891 RA VIC/MAIN/Z/475/117 her mind.

2. Alix to QV 12 December 1891 RA VIC/MAIN/Z/90/17.

3. Mark Kerr, p.119.

4. *Men-of-War Names,* p.vi.

5. Irène to QV 11 March 1892 RA VIC/MAIN/ Z 174/ 9.

6. Petra Kleinpenning, p.63.

7. Alix to QV RA VIC/MAIN/ Z 174/23. 18 March 1892.

8. Alix to QV, 9 May 1892 RA VIC/MAIN/Z 174/39.

9. Buckle 1, vol.2, pp.111-2.

10. Margit Fjellman, p.33.

11. RA GV/PRIV GVD/1892: 1 October 1892.

12. *Ibid.*

13. QV to VMH 11 January 1893 BA S 405.

14. HS Abt. D 24 35/1.

15. VMH to QV 30 August 1893 BA S 373.
16. QV to VMH 24 September 1893 BA S 405.
17. Buckle 1, vol.2, p.322.
18. Rec., p.91.
19. Ella to Prince Louis 8/20 November 1893 SA MB1/T95.
20. VMH to QV 23 November 1893 RA VIC/MAIN/H 36/118.
21. Alix to QV 26 December 1893 RA VIC/MAIN/Z 90/66.
22. HS Abt. D 24 Nr. 35/2. VMH to Ernie 29 December 1893.
23. Andrei Maylunas, Mironenko, p.20.
24. Buckle 3, pp.394-5.
25. VMH to QV 6 June 1894 BA S 373.
26. Hibbert, p.329.
27. Rec., pp.95-6.
28. Irène to QV RA VIC/MAIN Z 91/108.
29. Alexander, p.168.
30. Alix to Prince Louis 10/20 December 1894 SA MB1/T95.
31. Buckle 2, p.454.

Chapter 7

1. M. Eager, p.145.
2. Ernst Ludwig, p.41.
3. Alix to Louis 11/24 September 1895 SA MB1/T95.
4. VMH to QV 20 May 1896 BA S 374.
5. Rec., p.104.
6. VMH to QV RA VIC/MAIN/Z 160/2.
7. AGD, p.136.
8. Buckle 4, p.48.
9. https://youtu.be/kaCzruFqaHQ.
10. Rec., p.110.
11. Consuelo Balsan, p.28.
12. Agatha Ramm, pp.201-2.
13. VMH to QV 16 April 1897 BA S 374.
14. VMH to Ernie 24 April 1897 HS Abt. D 24 Nr. 35/2.
15. Philip Ziegler, p.25.
16. VMH to NK 7 August 1900 BA S 383.
17. Hibbert, p.335.
18. https://whc.unesco.org/en/list/1614/.

Chapter 8

1. Ziegler, p.23.
2. Ernie to VMH HS Abt. D 24 35/3.
3. Ernie to VMH 31 December 1900 HS Abt. D 24 35/3.

4. RA VIC/MAIN/QVJ: 25th June 1900.
5. Rec., p.124.
6. Rec., pp.125-6.
7. Buxhoeveden, p.90.
8. Ernie to VMH 10 November 1901 HS Abt. D 24 Nr. 35/3.
9. Rec., p.135.
10. Ernie to VMH 16 March 1902 HS Abt. D 24 Nr. 35/3.
11. Prince Louis to Louise 9 June 1903 SA MB1/T90.
12. Marie, p.294.
13. Rec., p.146.
14. VMH to NK 23 November 1902 BA S 383.
15. VMH to Ernie 13 December 1903 HS D 24 Nr. 35/2.
16. Ernie to VMH 10 February 1904, HS Abt. D 24 Nr. 35/3.
17. Rec., p.152.

Chapter 9

1. Alice Athlone, p.18.
2. E. A. Brayley Hodgetts, pp.231-3.
3. Rec., p.154.
4. Marie, p.303.
5. *Ibid.*
6. VMH to Onor 17 August 1906 HS Abt. D 24 54/1.
7. Rec., pp.154-5.
8. VMH to NK 19 October 1906 BA S 383.
9. Louise to Prince Louis 17 June 1905 BA S 261.
10. Rec., p.158.
11. https://youtu.be/-3K1R5_0qes.
12. VMH to Onor 16 October 1905 HS Abt. D 24 Nr. 45/1.
13. *The Times* of London 2 November 1905.
14. VMH to Dickie, 9 January 1944 BA S 261.
15. *The Times* of London 6 November 1905.
16. Miller, *Reports…*, p.28 and other W. H. Russell letters.
17. Mari, pp.304-5.
18. VMH to Onor, 17 August 1906, HS Abt. D24 45/1.
19. Rec., p.162.
20. *Ibid.,* p.165.
21. VMH to Onor, HS Abt. D24 45/1.
22. Rec., p.186.
23. Marie, p.374.
24. VMH to Onor 16 March 1908 HS Abt. D 24 45/1.
25. Rec., p.173.
26. *Ibid.,* p.175.
27. *Ibid.,* p.181.
28. VMH to Queen Mary 8 May 1910, RA QM/PRIV/CC 45/324.

29. Frances Dimond, p.511.
30. Ernie to VMH 29 June 1910, HS Abt. D 24 Nr. 45/1.
31. Greg King, Atlantis Magazine, *Requiem,* pp.104-113.
32. Rec., p.183.
33. *Ibid.,* p.184.

Chapter 10

1. Rec., p.186.
2. VMH to Ernie, 26 December 1912, HS Abt. D 24 Nr. 45/1.
3. David Duff, p.294.
4. *Ibid.,* p.295.
5. *Ibid.*
6. Kenneth Rose, p.168.
7. *The Times* of London 27 February 1913.
8. Rec., p.189.
9. Rec., p.188.
10. RA VIC/MAIN/Add A 17/1168.
11. VMH to Princess Louise, Duchess of Argyll, 22 June 1914 RA VIC/MAIN/ Add A 17/1200.
12. Hugo Vickers, p.110.
13. VMH to Ernie, June 1914 HS Abt. D 24 Nr. 45/2.
14. *Ibid.*
15. Marie, p.375.
16. Rec., p.198.
17. *Ibid.,* p.202.
18. *Ibid.,* pp.202-4.
19. *Ibid.,* pp.204.
20. VMH to NK 30 October 1914, BA S 384.
21. *The Times* of London, Letter by Lord Shelborne, 31 October 1914.
22. *The Times* of London, Admiral of the Fleet, Lord John Hay, 31 October 1914.
23. Buxhoeveden, p.198.
24. Prince Louis to NK 20 November 1914 SA MB1/T72.
25. Crown Princess Margarethe of Sweden to Ernie, 24 October 1915, HS Abt. D 24 Nr. 45/2.
26. VMH to NK, Kent House, August 22, 1915, BA S 386.
27. SA MB1/Y10.
28. VMH to NK 13 April 1916 BA S 385.
29. VMH to King George V, 16 April 1916 RA GV/PRIV/ AA 43259.
30. Alix to Nicholas, 8/20 April 1916 Fuhrman, p.445.
31. Prince Louis to Louise 27 May 1916, SA MB1/T90.
32. VMH to Dickie, 26 June 1916 BA S 386.
33. Mountbatten to NK 7 November 1916 SA MB1/A2.
34. Morgan, p.238.

Chapter 11

1. RA PS/GV Q 722/36.
2. VMH to NK 3 January 1917 BA S 387.
3. VMH to NK 9 January 1917 BA S 387.
4. RA GV/PRIV/ GVD/ 1917:15 March.
5. VMH to NK 18 March 1917, BA S 387.
6. VMH to NK 6 April 1917, BA S 387.
7. Prince Louis to Princess Louise 17 May 1917, SA MB1/T90.
8. Brian Connell, p.50.
9. PS/PSO/GV/C/O/1153/III/70.
10. Prince Louis to Lord Stamfordham RA PS/PSO/GV/C/O 1153/III/61.
11. VMH to NK 7 June 1917, BA S 387.
12. Prince Louis to Princess Louise, 6 June 1917 SA MB1/T90.
13. Kerr, p.264.
14. VMH to Thomas Whittemore, 9 August 1918 BA S 368.
15. RA GV/PRIV/ AA 43/286. 10 August 1918.
16. RA GV/PRIV/AA 43/183.
17. Telegram from the D.M.I. to General Poole, Archangel, 9 August 1918 RA PS/GV/PRIV/ M1344A/20.
18. Marie Louise, p.186.
19. *Ibid,* p.186.
20. *Ibid,* p.187.
21. VMH to NK 3 September 1918, BA S 387.
22. RA GV/PRIV/AA 43/183.
23. RA GV/PRIV/AA 43/285.
24. VMH to King George, 22 September 1918 RA GV/PRIV/AA 43/285.
25. VMH to NK 9 November 1918, BA S 387.
26. VMH to NK 6 February 1919, VA S 388.
27. VMH to Alfonso XIII, 22 September 1918 Madrid Archives.
28. *The Times* of London 22 October 1937, 'Grand Duke of Hesse: Bravery in the Face of the Revolutionary Mob' from a Correspondent.
29. *The Times* of London 25 November 1918.
30. Douglas Liversidge, p.102.
31. Coryne Hall, pp. 42, 46,51.
32. VMH to Onor 19 December 1913, HS Abt. D 24 Nr. 35/2.

Chapter 12

1. VMH to Ernie 8 August 1919, HS Abt. D 24 Nr. 35/2.
2. Irène to VMH 14 June 1922 Hemmelmark Archives.
3. VMH to Onor, 22 September 1920 HS Abt. D 24 Nr. 35/2.
4. VMH to NK 13 August 1919 BA S 388.

5. VMH to Ernie 7 October 1919 HS Abt. D 24 Nr. 35/2.
6. Unpublished Diaries of Grand Duke Dmitri Pavlovich Houghton Library, Harvard University: London 30 January 1919.
7. Rose, p.229.
8. VMH to NK 8 January 1920 BA S 388.
9. *Ibid.*
10. Hoover Institute Archives, Collection title: M. Giers, Box Number 39, Folder ID:12.
11. VMH to Ernie, 31 December 1921, HS Abt. D 24 Nr. 35/2.
12. VMH to M. de Giers, 20 September 1920, Hoover Institute.
13. Irène to VMH 1 November 1920, Hemmelmark Archives.
14. Irène to VMH, 22 December 1920 Hemmelmark Archives.
15. *Ibid.*
16. Kerr, p.262.
17. VMH to NK 7 February 1921 BA S 389.
18. Irène to VMH 13 February 1921, Hemmelmark Archives.
19. Irène to VMH 14 February 1921 Hemmelmark Archives.
20. VMH to Ernie 21 February 1921 HS Abt. D 24 Nr. 35/2.
21. *Ibid.*
22. VMH to George Milford Haven, 24 April 1921, SA MB1/Y27.
23. VMH to NK 20 June 1921, BA S 389.
24. The Rt. Honourable Lord Lee of Fareham, First Lord of the Admiralty to Lord Stamfordham 8 August 1921 SA MB1/T39 386.
25. VMH to King George V 15 September 1921 RA GV/PRIV/AA 43/325.
26. *Ibid.*
27. VMH to Queen Mary 15 September 1921 RA QM/PRIV/CC 45/602.
28. VMH to King George V, Fishponds, September 22, 1921, RA GV/ PRIV/ AA 43/326.
29. RA QM/PRIV/CC 45/605.
30. RA GV/AA 43/327.
31. RA GV/PRIV/AA 43/328.
32. Rose, p.303.
33. HS Abt. D 24 Nr. 35/4.
34. VMH to Ernie, 29 November 1921, HS Abt. D 24 Nr. 35/2.
35. VMH to Dickie 15 April 1935, BA S 361.

Chapter 13

1. VMH to NK, 20 February 1922, BA S 389.
2. RA GV/PRIV/AA 43/ 331.
3. VMH to George Milford Haven, 27 March 1922, SA MB1/Y27.
4. VMH to George Milford Haven, 24 April 1922, SA MB1/Y27.
5. Ernie to VMH, Darmstadt, 5 April 1922, HS Abt. D 24 Nr. 35/4.
6. VMH to George Milford Haven, 7 May 1922, SA MB1/Y27.

7. *Ibid.*

8. VMH to NK, 10 September 1922, BA S 389.

9. Robert Golden, *Majesty Magazine*, "Going to the Chapel", Vol. 25, no.7, 29-30.

10. Queen Mary to VMH, 23 June 1922, BA S 347.

11. King George V to VMH, 24 June BA S 347.

12. Robert Golden, email, September 23, 2005.

13. Ernie to VMH, Wolfsgarten, 28 August 1922, HS Abt. D 24 Nr. 35/4.

14. Janet Morgan, p.444.

15. Vickers, p.161-171 for details.

16. VMH to Lord Stamfordham, 4 December 1922, RA PS/PSO/GV/C/M 1823/48.

17. VMH to Lord Stamfordham, 7 December 1922 RA PS/PSO/GV/C/M/ 1823/54.

18. RA QM/PRIV/QMD/1922: 5 November.

19. VMH to Ernie, 26 December 1922 HS Abt. D 24 Nr. 35/2.

20. *Ibid.*

21. *The Times* of London 3 July 1923.

22. Fjellman, p.99.

23. *The Times* of London 3 July 1923.

24. VMH to George V, 26 June 1923, RA GV/PRIV/AA 43/349.

25. Ernie to VMH 30 June 1923 HS Abt. D 24 Nr. 35/4.

26. VMH to Dickie 31 July 1923, SA MB1/Y27.

27. *The Times* of London 10 December 1923.

28. Email The Countess Mountbatten of Burma, CBE to author, 16 September 2004.

29. Ernie to VMH 3 April 1924, HS Abt. D 24 Nr. 35/4.

30. VMH to Georgie, 4 August 1924, SA MB1/Y27.

31. VMH to George V 14 January 1925, RA GV/PRIV/AA 43/ 233.

32. *Ibid.*

33. George V to VMH 15 January 1925 BA S 367.

34. King and Wilson, *see* p.68-69, 141-143, 505.

35. Email Philip Goodman.

36. Ernie to VMH 27 November 1925 HS Abt. D 24 Nr. 35/4.

37. Ernie to VMH 2 December 1928, HS Abt. D 24 Nr. 35/4.

38. *The Times* of London 22 April 1929.

Chapter 14

1. HH Prince Christoph of Hesse-Kassel (1901-1943).

2. VMH to Ernie, 31 January 1930 HS Abt. D 24 Nr. 35/2.

3. VMH to Cecile 13 February 1930, HS Abt. D 24 Nr. 73/6.

4. *The Times* of London, 4 February 1931.

5. HSH Gottfried, 8th Prince of Hohenlohe-Langenburg (1897-1960).

6. HRH Prince Berthold of Baden, Margrave of Baden (1906-1963).

7. VMH to Ernie, HS Abt. D 24 Nr. 35/2.

8. Princesses Louise and Beatrice, the fourth and fifth daughters of Queen Victoria.

9. VMH to Ernie, HS Abt. D 24 Nr. 35/2.

10. VMH to Cecile 31 October 1931 HS Abt. D 24 Nr. 73/6.
11. VMH to Cecile 11 November 1931, HS Abt. D 24 Nr. 73/6.
12. VMH to Dickie, 11 April 1933, BA S 360.
13. Email Lady Mountbatten to author, 16 September 2004.
14. Questions answered by letter, HRH, The Duke of Edinburgh to author, 22 July 2003.
15. Email Lady Mountbatten to author, 31 January 2006.
16. VMH to Dickie, 18 June 1933 BA S 360.
17. VMH to Dickie, 21 June 1934, BA S 361.
18. *The Times* of London, 26 July 1934.
19. VMH to Princess Cecile, 27 May 1933, HS Abt. D 24 Nr. 73/6.
20. VMH to Princess Cecile, 18 October 1933, HS Abt. D 24 73/6.
21. VMH to MB, 13 November 1933, BA S 360.
22. Arturo Beéche, ERHJ, *An Interview...*, Issue X, March-April 1999, p.5. Princess Barbara returned to Germany and stayed with her grandmother Irène, who made Barbara her heir.
23. VMH to George Milford Haven, 3 July 1934, SA MB1/Y27.
24. VMH to Cecile, 29 October 1934, HS Abt. D 24 Nr. 73/6.
25. VMH to Cecile, 5 November 1934, HS Abt. D 24 Nr. 73/6.
26. VMH to Queen Mary RA QM/PRIV/CC 45/957.
27. Ian Vorres, p.192.
28. VMH to Nona, 7 May 1935, BA S 391.
29. VMH to Dickie, 16 June 1935, BA S 361.
30. VMH to Cecile 18 August 1935, HS Abt. D 24 Nr. 73/6.
31. VMH to Cecile, 15 May 1936, HS Abt. D 24 Nr. 73/6.
32. VMH to Prince Philip 17 October 1935, BA S 356.
33. VMH to Prince Philip 13 October 1936, BA S 356.
34. VMH to Prince Philip 28 October 1936, BA S 356.
35. VMH to Ernie 21 December 1936, HS Abt. D 24 Nr. 35/2.
36. VMH to Cecile 9 February 1937 HS Abt. D 24 Nr. 73/6.
37. VMH to Cecile 20 June 1937, HS Abt. D 24 Nr. 73/6.
38. VMH to Ernie 17 July 1937, HS Abt. D 24 36/3D.
39. VMH to Nona 12 September 1937 BA S 392.
40. *The Times* of London 11 October 1937.
41. VMH to Queen Mary RA QM/PRIV/CC45/1111.
42. VMH to Prince Philip 29 October 1937, BA S 356.
43. Morgan, p.259.
44. Queen Mary to VMH 21 November 1937 BA S 368.

Chapter 15

1. VMH to Dickie 27 January 1938 BA S 357.
2. VMH to Prince Philip 7 March 1938, BA S 356.
3. Hough, *Louis and Victoria,* p.360.

4. Email Lady Mountbatten to author, 26 January 2006.
5. Duke of Connaught to VMH 8 April 1938, BA S 368.
6. QM/PRIV/CC45/1149.
7. VMH to NK, 28 August 1938 BA S 392.
8. SA MB 11/1/4.
9. Irène to Princess Louise, Duchess of Argyll, 12 July 1938, RA VIC/ADDA 17/1675.
10. VMH to Princess Louise, 19 July 1938, RA VIC/ADDA 17/1680.
11. VMH to Princess Margaret of Hesse, 22 July 1938.
12. VMH to Prince and Princess Ludwig, 26 September 1938, HS Abt. D 26 Nr. 78/9.
13. Prince Arthur of Connaught (13 January 1883 – 12 September 1938)
14. VMH to Prince Philip 26 November 1938 BA S 356.
15. VMH to Prince Philip 10 December 1938 BA S 356.
16. VMH to Princess Margaret of Hesse 22 July 1938 HS Abt. D 26 Nr. 78/9.
17. VMH to Mountbatten 28 August 1939 BA S 361.
18. VMH to Grand Duchess Xenia 8 September 1939 the Grand Duchess Xenia Archive.
19. VMH to Prince Philip 19 October 1939 BA S 356.
20. VMH to Lady Isabelle Geddes 27 October 1939 HS Abt. D 24 Nr. 103/5.
21. VMH to Lady Isabelle Geddes 28 November 1939, HS Ab. D 24 Nr. 103/5.
22. VMH to Lady Isabelle Geddes 28 August 1944, HS Abt. D 24 Nr. 103/5.
23. VMH to Edwina Mountbatten 9 March 1940 BA S 358.
24. VMH to Queen Mary QM/PRIV/CC45/1206.
25. Hough, *Louis and Victoria,* p.375.
26. VMH to Dickie 20 September 1941 BA S 361.
27. VMH to Lady Isabelle Geddes 11 May 1940 HS Abt. D 24 Nr. 103/5.
28. VMH to Nona 11 May 1940 BA S 392.
29. VMH to Lady Isabelle Geddes 18 June 1940 HS Abt. D 24 Nr. 103/5.
30. VMH to Prince Philip 4 July 1940 BA S 356.
31. Email Lady Mountbatten to author 7 February 2006.
32. VMH to Lady Isabelle Geddes, 22 April 1941 HS Abt. D 24 Nr. 103/5.
33. Queen Mary to Alexander, the Earl of Athlone 17 January 1941 QM/PRIV/CC53/819.
34. VMH to King George VI 2 September 1941 RA GVI/PRIV/ 01/12/1.
35. VMH to Queen Mary 12 June 1942 RA QM/PRIV/CC45/1329.
36. Queen Mary to Alexander, Earl of Athlone 10 June 1942 RA QM/PRIV/CC53/1035.
37. She was born in Bucharest, Romania on 15 November 1852.
38. Questions answered by letter, HRH, The Duke of Edinburgh to author 22 July 2003.
39. *Ibid.*
40. VMH to King George VI 2 September 1941 RA GVI/PRIV/01/12/1.
41. VMH to Nona 10 September 1941 BA S 392.
42. VMH to Mountbatten 28 October 1943 BA S 361 Lady Iris was married and divorced three times.

43. Sophie remarried Prince Georg Wilhelm of Hanover in 1946.
44. Prince Friedrich Wilhelm killed 12/13 September 1916, Prince Maximilian killed 13 October 1914, and Prince Christoph killed 7 October 1943.
45. VMH to Lady Isabelle Geddes 19 June 1944 HS Abt. D 24 103/5.
46. VMH to Nona 19 June 1944 BA S 392.
47. VMH to Nona 30 June 1944 BA S 392.
48. Morgan, p.322.
49. Hough, *Louis and Victoria,* p.383.
50. VMH to Lady Isabelle Geddes 9 April 1945 HS Abt. D 24 Nr. 103/5.
51. VMH to Queen Mary 10 May 1945 RA QM/PRIV/CC45/1415.
52. VMH to Lady Isabelle Geddes 4 September 1945 HS Abt. D 24 Nr. 103/5.
53. VMH to Dickie 31 December 1945 BA S 362.
54. VMH to King George VI 5 July 1946 RA GVI/PRIV 01/12/5.
55. Princess Irène to Queen Mary 18 October 1946 RA QM/PRIV/CC45/1474.

Chapter 16

1. Hough, *Mountbatten...,* p.213.
2. Liversidge, p.124.
3. Perhaps it was just as well. Victoria remarked, "Whoever heard of a nun who smoked and played canasta?" Lady Mountbatten to author, 25 April 2003.
4. Vickers, p.319.
5. VMH to Dickie 4 February 1944 BA S 362.
6. Vickers, p.319.
7. *Ibid.,* p.324.
8. VMH to Queen Mary, 25 November 1947 RA QM/PRIV/CC45/1541.
9. VMH to Queen Mary 17 December 1947 RA QM/PRIV/CC45/1555.
10. ...the family once again dwindled, with the death of Princess Helena Victoria, Aunt Helena's daughter, in March 1948.
11. VMH to Queen Mary 10 October 1948 RA QM/PRIV/CC45/1606.
12. *The Times* of London 15 December 1948.
13. Anthony Holden, pp.54-5.
14. Questions answered by letter, HRH The Duke of Edinburgh to author 22 July 2003.
15. The Earl of Athlone to Queen Mary RA QM/PRIV/CC53/1534.
16. Ziegler, p.191.
17. Vickers, pp.339-40.
18. Ziegler, p.507.
19. *The Times* of London 25 September 1950.
20. Irène to Dickie, 24 September 1950, BA S 354.
21. Lady Irene Carisbrooke to Dickie September 1950, BA S 354.
22. Harold Wernher to Dickie 24 September 1950, BA S 354.
23. Prince Ludwig of Hesse and by Rhine to MB, September 30, 1950, BA S 354.

Bibliography

Archives

Grand Duchess Xenia Archive

Hemmelmarck Archives

Hoover Institute Archives, Collection Title: M. Giers, Box Number 39, Folder ID:12.

Family Archives, Darmstadt OR Hessisches Staatarchiv Darmstadt Section D 22, 24, 26, (Grand Ducal Family Archives).

Royal Archives, Windsor Castle

Royal Archives, Madrid

Southampton Archives, Hartley Library, which also houses Broadlands Archives

Books

Alexander, Grand Duke of Russia, *Once a Grand Duke.* (Farrar & Rinehart: New York, 1932).

Alice, Princess, Countess of Athlone, *For My Grandchildren: Some Reminiscences of Her Royal Highness Princess Alice, Countess of Athlone,* (Evan Brothers Limited: London, 1966).

Almedingen, E.M., *An Unbroken Unity* (The Bodley Head Ltd: London, 1964).

Anolic, Tamar, *The Russian Riddle: Grand Duke Serge Alexandrovich of Russia 1857–1905,* (Eurohistory.com: East Richmond Heights, 2009).

Aronson, Theo, *Grandmama of Europe: The Crowned Descendants of Queen Victoria,* (Cassell & Company: London, 1973, Reprinted by Royalty Digest: Ticehurst, 1998).

Balsan, Consuelo Vanderbilt, *The Glitter & the Gold,* (George Mann: Maidstone, 1973).

Battenberg, Prince Louis of, *Bachelor Recollections of Louis Prince of Battenberg, Marquess of Milford Haven 1854–1884* (written for his wife and children. Unpublished in typed ms. form MB6/M/26: Southampton Archives, Hartley Library).

__________, *Men-of-War Names: Their Meaning and Origin,* (Edward Stanford: London, 1898).

Beéche, Arturo, ed. *The Grand Dukes,* (Eurohistory.com: East Richmond Heights, 2010). *"Few perhaps cherish his memory, but I do."* by Ilana D. Miller.

Beéche, Arturo and Ilana Miller, *Royal Collections IV: The Grand Ducal House of Hesse,* (Eurohistory.com: East Richmond Heights, 2020).

__________, annotated and expanded by, *Recollections: Victoria Marchioness of Milford Haven Formerly Princess Louis of Battenberg,* (Eurohistory.com: East Richmond Heights, 2020).

Benson, E.F., *Queen Victoria's Daughters,* (D. Appleton-Century Company: New York, 1938).

Bothitho, Hector, ed. *Letters of Queen Victoria from the Archives of the House of Brandenburg-Prussia.* Trans. By Pudney, Mrs. J. and Lord Sudley. (Yale University Press: New Haven, 1938).

Buchanan, Meriel, *Ambassador's Daughter.* (Cassell & Company Ltd.: London, 1958).

__________, *Diplomacy in Foreign Courts,* (J. H. Sears & Company Ltd: New York, 1928).

__________, *Queen Victoria's Relations* (Cassell & Co Ltd: London, 1954).

Buckle, George Earle, ed. *Letters of Queen Victoria: A Selection from Her Majesty's Correspondence and Journal Between the Years 1862-1878, Vols.1 and 2,* (Longmans, Green & Company: New York, 1926).

__________, *Letters of Queen Victoria Third Series: A Selection from Her Majesty's Correspondence and Journal Between the Years 1886 and 1901.* In 3 vols., vol. 1 1886-1901. (Longmans, Green & Company: New York, 1931).

__________, *Letters of Queen Victoria Third Series: A Selection from Her Majesty's Correspondence and Journal Between the Years 1886 and 1901.* In 3 vols., vol. 2 1886-1901. (Longmans, Green & Company: New York, 1931).

__________, *Letters of Queen Victoria Third Series: A Selection from Her Majesty's Correspondence and Journal Between the Years 1886 and 1901.* In 3 vols., vol. 3 1886-1901. (Longmans, Green & Company: New York, 1932).

Buxhoeveden, Baroness Sophie, *The Life and Tragedy of Alexandra Feodorovna Empress of Russia,* (Longmans, Green and Co.: London, 1930. Reprinted by Royalty Digest: Ticehurst, 1966).

Chavchavadze, David, *The Grand Dukes,* (Atlantic International Publications: New York, 1990).

Connell, Brian, *Manifest Destiny: A study in five profiles of the rise and influence of the Mountbatten family,* (Cassell and Company, Ltd.: London, 1953).

Cookridge, E.H., *From Battenberg to Mountbatten,* (Arthur Barker Limited: London, 1966).

Corti, Count Egon, trans. Siveveking and Ian F.D. Morrow, *The Downfall of Three Dynasties,* (Books for Libraries Press: Freeport, New York, 1970).

Cyril, HIH the Grand Duke *My Life in Russia's Service – Then and Now* (Royalty Digest Reprint: Ticehurst, 1995).

Dimond, Frances, *Queen Alexandra: Loyalty and Love,* (History and Heritage Publishing: United Kingdom, 2022).

Dmitri Pavlovich, Grand Duke, *Unpublished Diaries of Grand Duke Dmitri Pavlovich* (Houghton Library, Harvard University).

Duff, David, *Hessian Tapestry: The Hesse Family and British Royalty,* (David & Charles: London, 1979).

Eager, M., *Six Years at the Russian Court,* (Charles L. Bowman & Company: New York, 1906).

Epton, Nina, *Victoria and Her Daughters,* (W.W. Norton and Company, Inc.: New York, 1971).

Ernst, Ludwig, Grand Duke of Hesse and by Rhine, *Erinnertes. Aufzeichnungen des letzten Grossherzogs Ernst Ludwig von Hessen und bei Rhein.* (Roether: Darmstadt, 1983).

Fjellman, Margit, *Louise Mountbatten, Queen of Sweden*, (George Allen and Unwin Ltd.: London, 1968).

Fuhrmann, Joseph T., ed., *The Complete Wartime Correspondence of Tsar Nicholas II and the Empress Alexandra: April 1914 – March 1917* (Greenwood Press: Connecticut, 1999).

Fulford, Roger, ed., *Your Dear Letter: Private Correspondence of Queen Victoria and the Crown Princess of Prussia 1865-1871,* (Charles Scribner's Sons: New York, 1971).

Hall, Coryne, *Rasputin's Killer and His Romanov Princess: Prince Felix Youssoupov and the Tsar's Niece Irina,* (Amberley: Stroud, 2023).

Helena, Princess of Great Britain and Ireland, *Alice Grand Duchess of Hesse Princess of Great Britain and Ireland: Biographical Sketch and Letters with Portraits.* (G.P. Putnam's Sons: New York, 1884.

Hibbert, Christopher, ed., *Queen Victoria in Her Letters and Journals,* (Viking: New York, 1985*)*.

Hodgetts, E.A. Brayley, *The Court of Russia in the Nineteenth Century,* (vol.2) (Charles Scribner's Sons: New York, 1908).

Holden, Anthony, *Charles, Prince of Wales,* (Weidenfeld & Nicholson: London, 1979).

Hough, Richard, *Advice to My Granddaughter: Letters from Queen Victoria to Princess Victoria of Hesse,* (Simon and Schuster: New York, 1975).

________, *Louis and Victoria: The First Mountbattens,* (Hutchinson: London, 1974).

________, *Mountbatten: A Biography* (Random House: New York, 1981).

Kerr, Mark, *Prince Louis of Battenberg: Admiral of the Fleet,* (Longmans, Green and Co.: London, 1934).

King, Greg, *The Court of the Last Tsar: Pomp, Power, and Pageantry in the Reign of Nicholas II,* (John Wiley & Sons: New Jersey, 2006).

King, Greg and Penny Wilson, *The Fate of the Romanovs,* (John Wiley & Sons: New Jersey, 2003

Kleinpenning, Petra H.(ed.,trans.,annotator), *Ludwig IV: Grand Duke of Hesse and by Rhine,* (Herstellung un Verlag: BoD-Books on Demand: Norderstedt, Germany, 2023).

Koenig, Marlene A. Eilers, *Queen Victoria's Descendants* (Rosvall Royal Books: Falköping Sweden, 1997).

Liversidge, Douglas, *The Mountbattens: From Battenberg to Windsor,* (Arthur Barker Limited: London, 1978).

Marie, Princess of Erbach-Schönberg (Princess of Battenberg), *Reminiscences,* (George Allen & Unwin Ltd.: London, 1925).

Marie, Queen of Romania, *The Story of My Life* (vol.1) (Cassell and Company, Ltd: London, 1934).

Marie Louise, *My Memories of Six Reigns,* (Evans Brothers Limited: London, 1957).

Marie Pavlovna, Grand Duchess, *Education of a Princess,* (Viking Press: New York, 1931).

Maylunas, Andrei and Sergei Mironenko, *A Lifelong Passion: Nicholas and Alexandra: their own story,* (Doubleday: New York, 1997).

Millar, Lubov, *Grand Duchess Elizabeth of Russia: New Martyr of the Communist Yoke,* (Nikodemos Orthodox Publication Society: New York, 1991.)

Miller, Ilana D., *The Four Graces: Queen Victoria's Hessian Granddaughters,* (Kensington House Books: East Richmond, 2011).

__________, *Reports from America: William Howard Russell and the Civil War,* (Sutton: Stroud, 2001).

Mountbatten of Burma, Earl, *Mountbatten: Eighty Years in Pictures,* (MacMillan & Co.: New York, 1979).

Morgan, Janet, *Edwina Mountbatten: A Life of Her Own,* (Charles Scribner's Sons: New York, 1991).

Noel, Gerard, *Princess Alice: Queen Victoria's Forgotten Daughter*, (Michael Russell: London, 1974)

Packard, Jerrold M., *Victoria's Daughters,* (St Martin's Press: New York, 1998)

Pakula, Hannah, *An Uncommon Woman,* (Simon & Schuster: New York, 1995).

Ponsonby, Arthur, *Henry Ponsonby: Queen Victoria's Private Secretary: His life from his letters,* (The Macmillan Company: London, 1942).

Ponsonby, Frederick, ed. *Letters of the Empress Frederick* (Macmillan and Co., Limited, 1929).

__________, *Recollections of Three Reigns,* (E.P. Dutton and Co., Inc.: New York, 1952).

Ramm, Agatha, ed., *Beloved and Darling Child: Last Letters Between Queen Victoria and Her Eldest Daughter 1886-1901* In completion of the five volumes edited by the later Roger Fulford, (Alan Sutton: Stroud, 1990).

Reid, Michaela, *Ask Sir James: Sir James Reid, Personal Physician to Queen Victoria and Physician-in-Ordinary to Three Monarchs.* (Hodder & Stoughton: London, 1987).

Rohl, John C.G., *Wilhelm II: the Kaiser's Personal Monarchy, 1888-1900* (Cambridge University Press: Cambridge, 2004).

Rose, Kenneth, *King George V,* (PAPERMAC: London, 1984).

Salway, Lance, *Queen Victoria's Grandchildren,* (Signpost Books, Ltd.: Oxford, 1991).

Sullivan, Michael John, *A Fatal Passion: The Story of the Uncrowned Last Empress of Russia,* (Random House: New York, 1997).

The Times of London, *Eminent Persons. Biographies, Reprinted from the Times,* (Macmillan: London, 1892-97).

Van der Kiste, John, and Bee Jordaan. *Dearest Affie...: Alfred, Duke of Edinburgh Queen Victoria's Second Son,* (Alan Sutton: Stroud, 1984).

Vickers, Hugo, *Alice: Princess Andrew of Greece*, (Hamish Hamilton, Ltd.: London, 2000).

Viroubova, Anna, *Memories of the Russian Court,* (The Macmillan Company: New York, 1923).

Vorres, Ian, *The Last Grand Duchess* (Key Porter Books: Canada, 2001).

Warwick, Christopher, *Ella: Princess, Saint & Martyr,* (Wiley: West Sussex, 2006).

William II, Ex-Emperor of Germany *My Early Life,* (George H. Doran Company on Murray Hill: New York, 1926).

Zeepvat, Charlotte, *Prince Leopold: The Untold Story of Queen Victoria's Youngest Son* (Sutton Publishing: Stroud, 1998).

Ziegler, Philip, *Mountbatten,* (Knopf: New York, 1985).

Emails or Letters

Emails from *The Countess Mountbatten of Burma*

Email from *Robert Golden,* 23 September 2005.

Email from *Philip Goodman* on behalf of Sonia Goodman, daughter of Countess Marika Kleinmichel, 1 January 2006.

Questions answered by letter by *Prince Philip, the Duke of Edinburgh.*

Newspapers and Magazines

Atlantis Magazine

Greg King, *The Hessian Royal Family.* Vol.2 No. 2, pp.7-25.

_________, *The Russian Church of St Mary Magdalene in Darmstadt.* Vol. 2 No. 2, pp.60-6.

_________, *Requiem: The Russian Imperial Family's Last Visit to Darmstadt, 1910.* Vol. 2 No.2, 104-113.

European Royal History Journal – (ERHJ)

Beéche, Arturo, *An Interview with Prince Alfred of Prussia,* (Issue X, March/April 1999, pp.3-6).

Miller, Ilana D., *A Family Chapel: The Battenberg Chapel,* (Issue XLIII, February 2005, pp.19-20.)

_________, *The marriage of Prince Louis' parents had been a very romantic affair.* (Issue XXXVIII, pp. 25-8)

_________, *The Other Victoria* (Parts I-III) (Issues X, XI, XII: March-April, May-June, July-August 1999).

Illustrated London News

Majesty Magazine
Golden, Robert "Going to the Chapel", Vol. 25, no.7, 29-30.

Royalty Digest – (RD)
Hall, Coryne, *Royal Malta,* pp.130-4. Vol. VI, no.5, November 1996.
Wynn, Marion, *Eastbourne Remembers Princess Alice Grand Duchess Louis of Hesse,* pp.8-11. Vol. XII, no.1, July 2002.
Zeepvat, Charlotte, *An Ordinary Foreign Princeling...?* pp.194-99. Vol. XIV, no.7, January 2005.
___________, *On Serge and Sainthood,* pp.98-103. Vol. XI, no.4, October 2001.
___________, *Our Ardently Loved Hill: Heiligenberg,* part 1 pp.2-6, part 2 pp.38-42. No. 49, July 1995.

Royalty Digest Quarterly – (RDQ)
Koenig, Marlene A. Eilers, *A Delphinium Wedding: The Marriage of Lord Louis Mountbatten and Edwina Ashley,* pp.1-8, No. 4, 2022.
The Times of London

Websites

Nice and Friendly: A privately made film as a present to Lord and Lady Mountbatten. https://youtu.be/-3K1R5_0qes
Queen Victoria and Family: A film made at Balmoral, 1896 https://youtu.be/kaCzruFqaHQ
UNESCO World Heritage Convention https://whc.unesco.org/en/list/1614/

Index